Analysing Sign Language

Also by Rachel Sutton-Spence

THE LINGUISTICS OF BRITISH SIGN LANGUAGE (*co-author with Bencie Woll*)

Analysing Sign Language Poetry

Rachel Sutton-Spence
With the assistance of
Paddy Ladd and Gillian Rudd

First published 2005 by
PALGRAVE MACMILLAN
Houndmills, Basingstoke, Hampshire RG21 6XS and
175 Fifth Avenue, New York, N.Y. 10010
Companies and representatives throughout the world.

PALGRAVE MACMILLAN is the global academic imprint of the Palgrave Macmillan division of St. Martin's Press, LLC and of Palgrave Macmillan Ltd. Macmillan® is a registered trademark in the United States, United Kingdom and other countries. Palgrave is a registered trademark in the European Union and other countries.

ISBN 0-230-21709-5   ISBN 978-0-230-21709-6

This book is printed on paper suitable for recycling and made from fully managed and sustained forest sources.

A catalogue record for this book is available from the British Library.

Library of Congress Cataloging-in-Publication Data
Sutton-Spence, Rachel.
    Analysing sign language poetry / Rachel Sutton-Spence; with the assistance of Paddy Ladd and Gillian Rudd.
        p. cm.
    Includes bibliographical references and index.
    ISBN 1–4039–3507–6 (cloth)
    1. Sign language. 2. Poetry—History and criticism. 3. Deaf, Writings of the. 4. Deaf authors, I. Ladd, Paddy, 1952– II. Rudd, Gillian. III. Title.
HV2474.S963 2005
419—dc22   2004052319

10 9 8 7 6 5 4 3 2 1
14 13 12 11 10 09 08 07 06 05

Transferred to Digital Printing in 2007

To my parents, **Nick and Sybil Spence**, who gave me my wings and taught me to trust the winds to bear me

Here are my wings;
And there, at the edge of nothing,
wait the winds
to bear my weight.

Dorothy Miles,
The Hang Glider

Contents

Acknowledgements

This book has been written with Paddy Ladd and Gillian Rudd, and it could never have reached publication without great input from Paddy and Jill. Paddy's gentle and protective enthusiasm for the project from the outset was essential, as were his insights into the importance and significance of sign language poetry. His knowledge of whom to ask for help and how to contact them, and his wealth of archive materials, which he has so generously shared, have been incalculably valuable. His passion for sign language poetry (especially Dorothy Miles' work), and our long sessions watching it, made this whole labour of love considerably less laborious and much more lovely. Jill's knowledge of poetry and literary analysis, her rigorous clear thinking and attention to detail, and her ability to get us directly to the point on many occasions have been indispensable. Jill's substantial contributions to the Preface and Chapter 1, and the many suggestions from both Paddy and Jill for improvement throughout the manuscript are especially appreciated. To the both of them I owe an impossible debt of thanks.

In order to comment on sign language poetry in this book, we have drawn heavily on both written translations and recordings of the poems in their original sign languages. We are very grateful to Don Read, to whom Dorothy Miles willed the copyright to her work, for his kind permission for us to use her work and to quote freely from all the translations of her poems and to use other images of Dorothy in her performances. We also thank the BBC for their generous agreement to allow us to use images from performances of Dorothy's poems on *See Hear*! Other valuable recordings of Dorothy's performances of her poems have been generously provided by Paddy Ladd (the performance at the London Deaf Cabaret in 1990) and Susan Rutherford (the performance at the University of California Northridge in August 1980).

We are also grateful to Paul Scott for his kind permission to use his work, and reproduce full translations of *Five Senses* and *Three Queens* and to reproduce images from recordings of performances of these poems. These poems were originally recorded for European Cultural Heritage On-Line (a project funded by the European Union). Chapter 12, the discussion of *Five Senses* and *Three Queens*, is based upon papers also prepared as part of that ECHO project (http://www.let.kun.nl/sign-lang/echo/index.html).

Chapter 12, the discussion of *Trio* is based upon earlier papers that have appeared in: *Journal of Sign Language & Linguistics*, 3(2), 79–100; V. Dively, M. Metzger, S. Taub and A.M. Baer (eds) *Signed Languages: Discoveries from International Research*. Washington, DC: Gallaudet University Press, pp. 231–42; and *Sign Language Studies*, 2(1), 62–83.

Every effort has been made to contact copyright-holders for the work cited in this book, but if any person has been inadvertently overlooked the publishers will be pleased to make the necessary arrangement at the earliest opportunity.

There are many other people who need my thanks for their part in this book. Despite my best attempts to remember everyone, I have certainly forgotten to thank some people. If I have forgotten to thank you publicly here, my gratitude is not lacking – just my organisational skills. I would like to thank the following people here, for all their help, always so willingly given. Don and Marjorie Read, for allowing me access to Dorothy Miles' papers, and for their hospitality and very fine biscuits and apple pies. Doris and Bear, for the use of 2 Pendre Walk where I wrote so much of the book. Bencie Woll, for giving the lecture on sign language poetry that first sparked my interest in it, for being a never-ending source of good ideas, and for nurturing me with such generosity throughout my entire career. Elena Pizzuto, for introducing me to the work of Giuranna and Giuranna, and for providing me with samples of Italian Sign Language (LIS) poetry. Kearsy Cormier and Clark Denmark, for their calm and continual technical help in producing the illustrations and for their help in translation of the ASL poems. Christopher Stone for his last-minute dash with the digital camera and illustrations. Pete Carrs, Dafydd Waters and Onno Crasborn for helping me with digital technology and putting material on the Internet. Jacq Mcfarling, for being so incensed when she saw an unattributed performance of Dorothy Miles' *Language for the Eye* that she finally got the ball rolling and shamed me into writing this. Marion Blondel, for lending me her copy of an impossible-to-get reference. Penny Boyes-Braem for her good ideas and offers of contacts to broaden the scope of this work, even if I was fool enough not to follow them all. Rosemary Wheat, Mike Gulliver, Elvire Roberts, Chris Bojas and many other participants in sign language poetry lectures and seminars I have taught, for all their insights and interest. I am grateful to Jill Lake at Palgrave Macmillan for her enthusiasm for this whole project and her calm support throughout the process of producing this book.

Many people have helped, advised and encouraged me in this project. Despite everyone's best input, there will be mistakes here, and those are mine.

Finally, of course, thanks to Kerry, my Atlas, *sine qua non.*

RACHEL SUTTON-SPENCE

Preface

This book offers a methodology for the analysis of sign language poetry which is based on the detailed exploration of selected signed poems and draws on both the linguistic understanding of sign languages and the techniques of close study of literary texts. As such, this book has two sections. The first part, which is the bulk of the book, deals with ways and means of analysing sign language itself and sign language poetry in particular, and shows how sign language poetry is a distinct form, being poetry composed in sign language, not poetry translated into sign language. Throughout the analysis and discussion, points are demonstrated by using examples drawn from specific signed poems. English translations of these poems may be found in the second part, the Appendix. Readers, especially those unfamiliar with sign language poetry, may prefer to read the poems before embarking on the discussions of it, and may also find it useful to refer to the whole texts at points where the analysis concentrates on selected bits of them.

Sign language poetry varies greatly and it is impossible for a single book to do justice to the full range of poetic compositions and performances made by Deaf poets around the world. We intend that the approach described in this book could be applied fruitfully to the work of any sign language poet, and we do refer to several in this book, including Clayton Valli, Ella Mae Lentz, Wim Emmerik, Rosaria and Giuseppe Giuranna, John Wilson, Philip Green and Paul Scott. However, most of our examples are drawn from the work of Dorothy ('Dot') Miles (1931–1993) whose importance is described in detail in the Afterword by Paddy Ladd. There are many reasons why Dorothy's work is our central resource, not least because, as he shows, she was the founder of signed poetry and a major force behind its development in both America and Britain from the 1960s to the 1990s, and many subsequent poets on both sides of the Atlantic have been influenced directly or indirectly by her work. Dorothy Miles is also a practical choice for this book because she worked in ASL and BSL, and in English, so at least some of our examples will be in languages familiar to most of our readers. In addition, there is a sizeable archive of her poems, both as written texts and (more importantly) as signed performances spread over a 20-year period, which provides a coherent body of work by a single author with which to work. Only a very few of Dorothy Miles' BSL poems are available to general audiences. We hope, then, that our book will add to the signed poetry material in circulation.

This book is aimed at anyone with an interest in sign language, poetry, or both, and includes those who know little about either of them. For this reason, Chapter 1 provides a brief description of the features of sign language that should be understood in order to appreciate how poetry can work in a visual medium. The ideas introduced in this chapter are revisited throughout the book, with examples from sign language poems, and readers may wish to refer back to Chapter 1 where necessary as they go through the book. Chapter 2 is a general introduction to the idea of signed poetry and gives a little background information on Dorothy Miles. Subsequent chapters consider different elements that create poetic effect in sign language, both in form and meaning, and also the important relationship between the text and performance of signed poems. Each element is demonstrated through the extensive use of examples taken from appropriate poems. Having illustrated the various constituent parts of the approach, we move on to show how using all the elements together provides a rich analysis and understanding of two of Dorothy Miles' poems in their entirety: the ASL *The Hang Glider* and BSL *Trio*. Then we offer critical commentaries of two poems composed and performed by Paul Scott, a contemporary British Deaf poet whose sign language poems are informed by (and developed from) Dorothy Miles' approach to poetic construction. The final chapter is an Afterword by Paddy Ladd, which provides a more historically and culturally situated view of Dorothy Miles and her legacy, particularly in regard to poetry. Readers may wish to go directly to the Afterword or follow the exposition of analysis first. The Afterword prepares the ground for the written texts of translations of the poems analysed in the book. While these written poems are included to help a fuller appreciation of the signed works, they also repay study in their own right. Readers may find it useful to read the English translation to get a broad overview of the content of the poem before they read our comments and analyses on the sign version. It is important to bear in mind, however, that these translations are not 'the signed poems written down'. They are translations into a different language, and the poetic elements in the written version and the sign version will often be very different.

A note on the illustrations

Using written English to talk about sign language poetry is not very satisfactory. The constraints of written English make it impossible to capture the visual, spatial and temporal elements of signed poetry. For this reason, the book has a large number of illustrations. The illustrations used here are images taken from video-recordings of performances of signed poems. Some of these, where recordings of the poem were made under ideal 'studio' conditions, especially the images from the BBC's *See Hear!* television programme and those of Paul Scott's poems in Chapter 13, are good quality. However, some of the pictures of Dorothy Miles' performances are not nearly as good. After her sudden death in 1993, there was a plan to collect recordings of her signed poetry performances and preserve them for the Deaf community, perhaps making them commercially available. This plan failed and, to the great detriment of posterity, many of the recordings have been lost. Sometimes the only record of a performance known to us is an amateur video-recording. Dorothy's BSL performance at the London Deaf Cabaret in 1990 and her ASL performance at the University of California Northridge in 1980 have been preserved in two such recordings. In both cases, the recordings were privately made and never intended for publication. The quality and clarity of the images are inferior to those we expect from a professional recording, but the poor quality is greatly outweighed by the impact of being able to see images from Dorothy Miles' own performance.

Finally, readers may wish to look at the performances of the poems. We hope that this book is able to stand alone, without the need for viewing the performances of the poems, but nevertheless, for full enjoyment and appreciation of the poems, they should also be seen in performance, where possible. BSL poems from the 1990 London Deaf Cabaret are available from the Max Planck Institute's ECHO BSL corpus found at www.mpi.nl. Paul Scott's poems *Five Senses* and *Three Queens* and Wim Emmerik's *Hof van Eden* (also called *Tuin van Eden*) are also freely available for viewing at the website referenced on page ix. To our knowledge, at the time of writing, there is very little other sign language poetry available on the Internet. We hope that more of it will become available as digital technology advances.

Other work is available on video or CD. Clayton Valli's poems *The Bridge, Flash, Something not Right, Cow and Rooster* and others, may be found on his video *ASL Poetry*, available from Dawn Sign Press (in NTSC format only). Dorothy Miles' poems *Trio, The Ugly Duckling, The Staircase – An Allegory* and *Christmas Magic* are commercially available (in PAL format only) on the videotape that accompanies the book *The Linguistics of British Sign Language: An Introduction* (1999) by Rachel Sutton-Spence and Bencie Woll (Cambridge University Press and the Council for the Advancement of Communication with Deaf People).

Handshapes and some other conventions

Throughout this book, we will need to refer to the different handshapes used in the signs occurring in signed poetry. Each handshape has a descriptive name, most of them derived from letters of the ASL manual alphabet or counting system, although they are used to refer to the handshapes in any sign language. Three additional symbols accompany some of the names of the letters and numbers. The 'ᵒ' is used to show that the thumb is extended, the 'ˆ' is used where the thumb contacts the pad of any other finger, and the '"' indicates that the fingers are bent at the knuckles. There are many other handshapes that occur in sign languages, but the illustrations here refer to those that arise in our discussion of the poems in the book. For ease of reference, the handshapes we refer to are shown below, with their names.

Following conventions in sign language linguistics, sign glosses will be written in capital letters. To refer to a sign in any given sign language meaning 'cat', we will write CAT. Where more than one English word is needed to give the meaning of a sign, the words will be joined with a hyphen. To refer to a sign that means 'snow on the ground', we will write SNOW-ON-GROUND. BSL signs that are made using fingerspelling from the manual alphabet will be written in lower case, interspersed with hyphens, so to refer to a BSL fingerspelling of the word 'cat' we will write c-a-t. ASL fingerspellings will be written in upper case, interspersed with points, so to refer to an ASL fingerspelling of the word 'cat' we will write .C.A.T. This is in keeping with conventions in other linguistics texts.

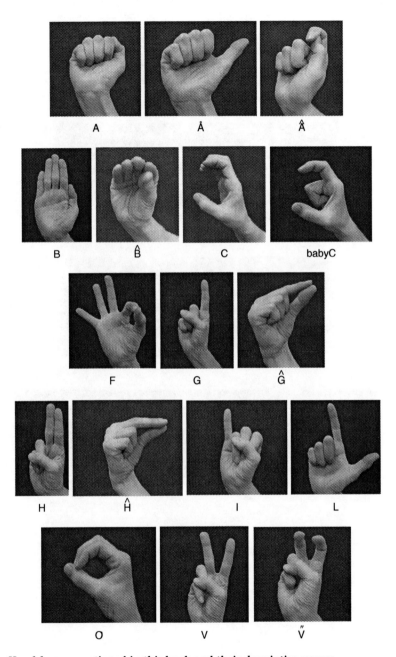

Handshapes mentioned in this book and their descriptive names

xvi

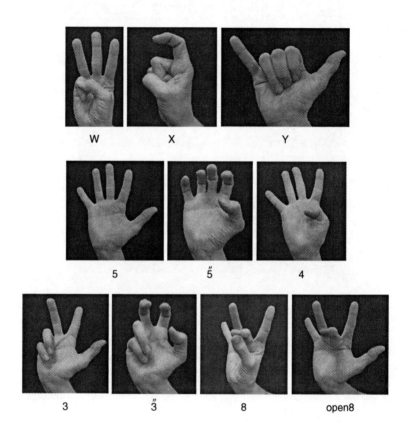

W X Y

5 5″ 4

3 3″ 8 open8

1

Some General Points about Sign Languages

This book is concerned with signed poetry, the highest art form of sign languages. As such, it celebrates and analyses both that art and the language used to express it. Before embarking on a study of sign language poetry, however, it might be useful to review some general and important points about sign languages and about the social issues surrounding the history of sign languages and the Deaf people who use them.[1] These aspects are crucial to this study because sign language poetry has emerged from, and draws upon, the particular social and linguistic heritage of sign languages.

Sign languages are natural, living languages, used by Deaf communities around the world. They are not mere collections of gestures and they are not universal. They are full languages, independent of the spoken languages used by the hearing society surrounding them. Thus, for example, American Sign Language (ASL) and British Sign Language (BSL) are totally different and unrelated, essentially mutually unintelligible languages, despite the fact that hearing people in both countries use the same spoken language, English. It is a commonly held belief that sign languages are simply some form of 'spoken language on the hands' but, in fact, sign language vocabularies and grammars are very different from those of spoken languages. Signers who know one sign language find it hard under normal conversational circumstances to understand the signer of another, as each sign language has a vocabulary and cultural heritage specific to its national Deaf community. In this volume we are primarily concerned with two different sign languages: British Sign Language (BSL) and American Sign Language (ASL). Different national sign languages have different vocabularies but their visual-spatial nature means that many of their other linguistic features are similar enough for a single basic description of their grammar.

Sign languages differ from spoken languages like English in three main ways:

- They are visual-spatial languages (not sound-based),
- They are unwritten (and so do not have any written literary tradition) and
- They are numerically minority languages in comparison to the spoken languages surrounding them, each often having only thousands or tens of thousands of users, with a few, such as ASL, having several hundreds of thousands (although the total number of Deaf sign language users worldwide is in the millions).

Because sign languages are unwritten languages, signers who write a message must currently do it in another language that does have a written register, such as English. Many signers are literate to some extent in the written form of at least one spoken language, but do not write their sign language because it is not a register of that language. This is a common situation for many of the world's minority languages, most of which have no written form, and it has considerable implications for the structure and function of sign languages and for the structure, composition and recording of sign language poetry, just as it does for any 'oral' unwritten language. When someone writes down a signed poem, it is just as much an act of translation of that poem as it would be to sign, for instance, Keats' *Ode to Autumn*.

Figures for sign language users vary depending on how the estimate is made, but a commonly quoted figure for BSL signers is that it is the first or preferred language for nearly 70,000 Deaf people, and for ASL quoted figures vary from 100,000 to 500,000. Sign languages are mainly used by people who are born Deaf or who become Deaf at an early age, although others who have been deafened later may choose to learn sign language and join the Deaf community. The hearing children of signing Deaf parents may also be fluent sign language users. Increasingly in some countries, hearing people who are not members of the Deaf community are learning sign language. These numbers mean an estimated 250,000 people use BSL on a daily basis (figures from the British Deaf Association press statement, 18 March 2003). Paradoxically, this means that there are more hearing people with some knowledge of a sign language than there are Deaf signers, yet despite the larger number of hearing signers, sign languages are still 'owned' by their Deaf communities.

Deaf children are rarely born to Deaf parents and in Britain 90–95 per cent of children born Deaf or who become Deaf in early childhood have hearing parents (although this figure varies around the world). This difference in hearing status between parents and their children means that most Deaf children do not learn sign language from their parents since most hearing parents do not know BSL before their Deaf children are born. In the past, and still in many parts of the world today, hearing parents have been told not to sign to their children in case this prevents them from learning spoken language and socialising with other hearing people. This fundamental misunderstanding of the importance of sign language to a Deaf child's language skills and social well-being has led to the oppression of sign languages in Deaf communities worldwide. Only recently have hearing professionals begun to take notice of Deaf adults who know the importance of having access to their own visual language at an early age.

Deaf communities and their sign languages, as we know them, did not exist until the growth of cities with the industrial revolution. The opening of Deaf schools in the mid-eighteenth century had probably the greatest impact on the development of sign languages and Deaf communities. When children were brought together in residential schools, signing communities were formed and the language developed and expanded. However, although sign languages were used in many European and North American Deaf schools throughout the nineteenth century, there were always educationalists who believed that Deaf children should use spoken language rather than sign language. By the early twentieth century this 'oral method' had become the dominant approach and signing was frequently banned in schools and children punished for its use (see Paddy Ladd's Afterword for a further comment on Oralism and its impact on Deaf people and sign language). In the 1970s, signing in the classroom was reintroduced in some schools. The signing that was permitted was usually a form of sign that was strongly influenced by the grammar of English (Signed English) rather than a fully fledged independent sign language with spatial grammar. But, just when signing became more accepted as an educational language in schools, special schools for Deaf children began to close. Instead, in the name of 'integration', Deaf children were sent to mainstream schools. Today, in Britain, North America and across much of Europe, most Deaf children are educated in the mainstream. Although there may be many educational and social benefits to mainstream education, crucially, and most devastatingly for the Deaf community and the children's cultural and linguistic heritage, mainstreaming has meant that Deaf children have lost access to their community of signers and the linguistic and cultural role model that Deaf schools provided to young Deaf children.

While many countries provide some sort of primary and secondary education for Deaf children, in the field of tertiary education, so far only the United States of America (USA) has provided higher education for Deaf adults at a university entirely dedicated to Deaf students. Gallaudet University in Washington DC was founded as Gallaudet College in 1864, and has been a world focus for Deaf intellectual achievement and sign language use.

Within the Deaf community at large, sign language has always been accepted and highly valued. National Deaf Associations have worked with sporting bodies and political organisations to promote sign language, Deaf culture and the Deaf community. In the 1970s, politically active members of the British Deaf community, concerned by the dominance of hearing people over their lives and the banning of sign language and Deaf teachers in schools, formed the National Union of the Deaf to fight for the acceptance of BSL within the wider society. Other countries experienced similar political revivals between the 1960s and the 1980s. One major success for such organisations was the introduction of sign language on television. Sign language broadcasts in Europe and North America especially have had a major impact on the status, use and public awareness of sign languages.

The structure of sign languages

Sign languages are fundamentally different from spoken languages because of their different modalities, as spoken languages are sound-based and sign languages are based on visually perceived signs. One of the most striking aspects of sign language is the richness of its visual aspect, which allows for a degree of subtlety that comes into its own in sign poetry. Although not all signs have a close tie to the visual forms of their referents, many signs are visually motivated to some degree. Nonetheless it is crucial to remember that such signs are distinctive language units, not gestures.

The formation of signs

For many years, it was commonly believed that signs were merely gestures, each one being an unsystematic, unanalysable whole. This was compared unfavourably to words in spoken languages, which could be described as being made up of 'phonemes' – small, meaningless units of a language. Bill Stokoe (1960) realised that signs in sign languages are also made up of phonemes, but the visual form of the languages means that the phonemes are different from those in spoken languages.

Stokoe described the three parameters of signs as handshape, movement and location, each one being the equivalent of a phoneme in spoken language. Most sign linguists now accept that there are more manual parameters, including orientation of the hand, and that non-manual features, such as facial expression or mouth pattern, may also be considered to be phonemes. Within each sign language there is a range of permissible handshapes. As with spoken languages, each sign language allows some handshapes not seen in other languages, and does not allow some handshapes that are seen in other languages. The hand-shape of the sign will be made at a certain location, such as the temple, cheek or chest, or may be articulated simply in 'neutral space' – the area directly in front of the signer. Signs may be one-handed or two-handed, and one-handed signs may contact the body or simply be articulated in neutral space, while the hands in two-handed signs may contact each other or the body or simply be made in neutral space. Sign languages have clear rules specifying permitted location of the hands. For example, in BSL and ASL, there are no signs in the vocabulary located on the inside of the upper arm. A description of the sign must also mention the movement made by the hand or hands articulating the sign. As with location and handshape, there is a limited set of permissible movements for a sign.

Any sign can be described by its specific handshape, location, move-ment and orientation (and in some cases by a specific non-manual element, such as a head-nod or a particular facial expression). Crucially for sign languages, it is important to understand that these parameters are articulated simultaneously. It is impossible to articulate a handshape without also selecting its orientation and some location and without some specified movement (even if that movement is 'null' or a simple 'hold').

Some handshapes are more common than others. 'Unmarked' handshapes are the most motorically simple and are the most commonly occurring in signs. 'Marked' handshapes involve more com-plex arrangements of the fingers and occur in fewer signs. The point of contact between the two hands may also be marked, so that, for example, the dominant hand in a two-handed sign is more likely to con-tact the palm or the side of the non-dominant hand than its back (see below, p. 10, and see Fig. 6.3 for an example of a sign that uses the palm of the non-dominant hand and Fig. 3.8 for signs using the back of the non-dominant hand).

Understanding these basic principles of sign formation is essential for understanding sign language poetry. When poets select signs for aesthetic and poetic effect, they will choose them according to patterns of handshape, location, movement and orientation. When they push back the boundaries of the language, they may select handshapes, locations or movements that are not normally permitted within the language. We will repeatedly refer to these elements of signs in our analysis of signed poetry.

Visually motivated signs

Although sign languages have systems which build up signs out of limited sets of elements, the signs themselves often reflect the visual form of the object, action or state being referred to (the 'referent'). One sign meaning CAT in BSL is made at the cheeks, with a movement sketching out the whiskers of a cat, and a similar sign is used in ASL. Although some signs appear to have no visual motivation (for example, the signs WHO and SISTER could not be guessed at by anyone who did not know ASL or BSL) most signs share some visual form with whatever they refer to, as they may reflect the shape, size or movement of the referent.

Because the vocabulary of sign languages contains many signs that appear to reflect the visual form of the referent, we might expect that the sign for a particular object would be the same across different sign languages. However, different sign languages may focus on different aspects of the same object, so that a sign can be visually motivated but the particular aspect that is represented is arbitrary. For instance, a BSL sign meaning TEA can be seen as a reflection of the way we might hold and drink from a tea-cup, while an ASL sign TEA is derived from the action of dipping a teabag in a cup. The sign COFFEE differs, depending on whether we focus on drinking it or grinding it: BSL focuses on the drinking and ASL focuses on the grinding. Cultural differences are also important so that, although both the British and the Brazilian signs COFFEE focus on the act of drinking the coffee, the signs are different because the size of the coffee cups are very different in the two cultures, with British cups being very much larger than the Brazilian ones.

There is a parallel example of this situation in spoken languages. Although spoken languages cannot incorporate the visual form into speech, they can use the sounds made by certain referents in their words, using onomatopoeia. Most words that describe a sound in English are onomatopoeic to some extent (e.g. 'whisper', 'crash' and 'squeak'), yet despite this, onomatopoeic words for the same idea vary between languages. For example, the Dutch 'fluisteren', the Portuguese 'sussurrar' and the English 'whisper' all refer to the same action but are different, even though all three words are onomatopoeic, using soft, whispering speech sounds.

Some signs are more visually motivated than others, and are motivated in different ways. Mark Mandel (1977) suggested a classification of the way in which signs reflect the visual form of the referent, dividing them into those that show the real action or object and those that represent an action or object by the shape and movement of the hands. Some referents can be pointed to because they are there. Parts of the body are pointed to for their meaning, for example, NOSE, EYES and more abstractly MIND (indicating the head, where the mind is). Pointing may seem unsophisticated to people who are used to the arbitrary words of a spoken language, but it is the most logical choice for a visual language. The signs to show certain actions involve signers using their body to perform the action that is being referred to, for example COUGH or STROKE, which are strongly visually motivated but still conventionally stylised. There are also actions that are carried out with the handshapes showing how the object is held as part of the action, or the related object (e.g. BROOM or SWEEP). In other visually motivated signs, the hands draw the shape or form of the object, leaving an imaginary trace of the shape of the referent. For example, in the sign DINNER-PLATE an index finger sketches a round outline over an open palm; for the sign WALL one flat hand rises from the edge of the other, marking out the area of the wall. Alternatively, the hands may become the entire referent. The signer no longer draws the outline but creates the object with the hands (e.g. AEROPLANE and TREE).

The extensive use of visual motivation in signs permits a great deal of 'productivity', so that new signs can be created, and understood, with considerable ease. Within our discussion of sign poetry we will make a distinction between established (sometimes called 'frozen') signs, which are part of the recognised vocabulary of the language, and productive signs, which are not part of the fixed vocabulary, but have been created *ad hoc*, for the purposes of the utterance. Although these productive signs (which may also sometimes be termed 'neologisms') are not uncommon in everyday signing, they are an especially important part of sign poetry.

Fingerspelling and manual alphabets

Most signs have no relation to the spoken language, but the written form of spoken languages can be represented in sign languages through fingerspelling. Fingerspelling is the representation of the spelling of words through the use of letters from the manual alphabet. In manual alphabets, each letter has a handshape or hand-configuration corresponding to the written alphabet (although there are no capital letters in manual alphabets). Different sign languages use different manual alphabets, and although most manual alphabets, including the ASL alphabet, are one-handed (i.e. the letters are formed using finger-configurations on one hand), several two-handed alphabets (where hand-arrangements of both hands form the letters) are used around the world, including in BSL. The extent to which fingerspelling is used varies among different sign languages, but in all national sign languages that use a manual alphabet, fingerspelling is only a minor part of the language and is mainly used for words borrowed from the spoken language.

Sign languages that have one-handed manual alphabets may use letters from these alphabets as part of their sign-formation processes. Signs that are visually motivated in their location and movement may nevertheless have their handshape determined by the initial letter of the corresponding word from the spoken language. For example, the two hands can describe a circular path, encompassing a small area that is visually motivated by the idea of a 'group', and different handshapes can be imposed upon this basic sign movement: for FAMILY, the sign has the 'F' handshape from the manual alphabet; for TEAM, the hands have the 'T' handshape; for GROUP, they have the 'G' handshape; for SOCIETY they use the 'S' handshape, and so on. These 'initialised signs' are fairly common in ASL, and many of them are now established signs within the ASL lexicon, despite their origins. Initialised signs have very little parallel in BSL, where the two-handed manual alphabet does not permit this sort of initialisation.

Some manual letter handshapes are coincidentally the same as handshapes that occur naturally in sign languages. For example, the 'B' handshape is used in many signs that show a flat surface (such as in DOOR, FLOOR and WALL) and have no relationship to any word beginning with the letter B. Similarly, the 'F' handshape is not only used for the letter F but also occurs in signs that refer to grasping small objects (such as a pin or a piece of paper) and occurs in ASL signs like SEW, TEA and VOTE, where there is no link to the letter 'F', but the handshape represents holding a needle, or the edge of a teabag or the ballot-paper. The 'ABC games' that are often described as being a part of American Deaf Culture (see Chapter 3) exploit the coincidental relationship between visually motivated handshapes and manual letters. In these games, the signer creates stories in ASL using signs whose handshapes match the letters in the manual alphabet. In a well-known example, the first sign uses the 'A' handshape, the next uses the 'B', then the 'C', then the 'D' and so on, so the sequence is KNOCK-ON-DOOR (using the 'A' handshape), DOOR-OPENS (using a 'B' handshape),

LOOK-FOR-PERSON-WHO-KNOCKED (using a 'C' handshape), and continues through to a handshape that is used in the manual letter 'Z'. This playful device can be used by sign poets, and in Chapter 3 we will see how the ASL poet Clayton Valli used patterns of handshapes in his poems.

Use of space in sign languages

One often-overlooked but nevertheless remarkable difference between sound-based and visual languages is the option for the latter to use space. Written forms of language can make deliberate use of their two dimensions (e.g. the place or size of a word on the page); sign languages necessarily use all three dimensions. Signs can be placed in different areas simply by placing the hands there. Placing and moving signs in the space around the signer are central to sign language grammar.

There are two different ways of using signing space. In the first, signs are placed in a layout that represents things as they really are. As we will see in the poem *The Staircase*, the signs are placed and moved in the signing space to represent exactly the movement and location of people advancing through a forest and climbing a staircase. The second use of space is less literal and more metaphorical. We will see in the poem *Five Senses* that pleasant-tasting food is signed to one side, and unpleasant food on the other. This placing of the two types of food is just to allow the signer to refer to them distinctly.

In order to use space to its maximum effect, sign languages make use of 'proforms'. These are used in place of signs that for various reasons (such as being made at a location fixed to the body or being two-handed) cannot be placed in, or moved through, signing space to show grammatical meaning. Proforms are much less specific than the signs they stand for (usually just showing the general shape of the referent) and take their identity from the context in which they are used, but they can move freely in signing space. For example, the signs MAN and WOMAN, in both ASL and BSL, are located on the body, so if we wish to show that the man approached the woman, we cannot show this by moving the sign MAN towards the sign WOMAN. Instead sign languages use proforms. In this case, one index finger, referring to the man, moves towards the other index finger, referring to the woman. Proforms are thus an essential part of the spatial grammar of sign languages, and because they tend to be one-handed and can be placed and moved anywhere in space, they are frequently recruited to create patterns within sign language poems.

Simultaneous signs

Both spoken and signed languages can articulate their words one at a time but only signed languages can produce two (or more) words simultaneously because they use two hands and the head, face and mouth for linguistic meaning. This simultaneous use of both hands also allows the signer to show the relative locations of two things. Different objects may be shown at the same time in different places but in the same field of view. Sign languages can also show two events happening relative to each other, by showing the two events on two different hands, or one event on the hands and one on the face. If we think about someone who opened the door while smoking a cigarette, English uses a construction such as 'while' or 'as' to show the two events happened simultaneously but sign languages can show opening the door with one hand at the same time as signing holding a cigarette with the other.

Most signers have a 'dominant' and a 'non-dominant' hand when they sign (right-handers usually sign with a dominant right hand and left-handers with a dominant left). One-handed signs are normally made with the dominant hand, and in two-handed signs where one hand is active and the other hand operates as a base-hand location for the active hand, the dominant hand is normally the active hand. In the simultaneous signs described above, the non-dominant hand is more likely to move first and then be stationary while the dominant hand moves. In both two-handed signs and simultaneous signs, the dominant hand may have a much larger variety of handshapes, while the non-dominant hand is more likely to use only a few of the more unmarked, physically simple handshapes. In sign language poetry, the poet may deliberately upset all these expectations to create poetic effect, reversing dominance of the hands, or calling upon the non-dominant hand to act like the dominant hand.

Mouth patterns

Sign languages can use the mouth as well as the hands to articulate meaning. Research in many different sign languages has shown that there are two main types of mouth patterns in sign languages, termed 'mouthings' and 'mouth gestures'. Mouthings are the mouth patterns derived from spoken languages, so that in many cases, the signer appears to be mouthing the corresponding spoken word. For example, while signing DOG on the hands, the mouth will carry the mouth pattern of the English word 'dog'. The existence of mouthings in sign languages is an outcome of the many years of close contact between signed and spoken languages, and has arisen especially from the educational methods for Deaf children. Where the Oral education system has obliged Deaf children to speak, it should not be surprising that spoken language mouth patterns have become a part of the sign language. Not all sign languages use mouthings to the same extent, however. For example, BSL and Sign Language of the Netherlands (SLN or NGT) use mouthings extensively, but ASL and Irish Sign Language (ISL) have traditionally used far fewer mouthings (Boyes-Braem and Sutton-Spence, 2001). Mouth gestures are the mouth patterns that have no link to the spoken language, and include, for example, pursed lips to indicate something very small, or air escaping through vibrating lips to indicate a steady movement.

Mouthings and mouth gestures have quite clearly defined roles in sign languages. Mouthings are especially used with the signs that establish what the signer is talking about in sign language (and tend to occur with the established, frozen signs that already exist in the vocabulary), whereas mouth gestures are more commonly used with signs that are part of the elaboration upon these established signs (and are often seen in productive signs that have been created *ad hoc*). Mouthings tend to occur with noun signs, while mouth gestures are more common with verbs. The differences between mouthings and mouth gestures are summarised in Table 1.1.

There are occasions in BSL when the mouthing is derived from an English word that is different from the meaning of the sign on the hand. For example, the signer may sign JUMPER on the hands and use the mouthing 'red' to produce a phrase meaning 'red jumper'. Alternatively, the mouthing of one sign may be extended over two signs so that the signer could sign DEAF HIM (meaning 'He's deaf') while using the mouthing 'deaf' to cover both signs. These mismatches of mouthings to signs are fairly common in BSL (and many other sign languages, see Boyes-Braem and Sutton-Spence, 2001), but they are always within the language rules of BSL. Poets can exploit this mismatch of mouthings and manual signs as part of their language creativity.

Table 1.1 Different roles of mouthings and mouth gestures

Mouthings	*Mouth gestures*
Derived from spoken words	Not related to spoken words
Common with established vocabulary	Common with productive signs
Used especially to establish	Used especially to elaborate
More common with noun signs	More common with verb signs
More common in BSL than in ASL	Equally common in ASL and BSL

Although mouthings are derived from words in spoken languages, they have been borrowed into sign languages as part of the signs. In everyday signing the manual signs control the use of mouthings. We might think that it should be possible to sign and speak at the same time, because signed languages are made on the hands and spoken languages are made on the mouth. However, it is not possible to speak grammatical English and sign grammatical BSL (or ASL) at the same time because of the grammatical differences between English and the sign languages. If signers allow the grammar of the spoken language used through their use of mouthings to dominate their signs, this interferes with the production of grammatical, visually motivated, spatial sign language. We will consider the effect of mouthings on sign poetry during our investigation of 'blended' poetry.

Throughout this book's exploration of sign poetry it will be important to bear all the above elements of sign language in mind.

2
What is Sign Language Poetry?

The idea of sign language poetry may seem unlikely to many people unfamiliar with sign language. Indeed, even members of Deaf communities using sign language have believed in the past that such a thing is impossible. This belief may be the result of the close association of poetry with sound and the rejection of sign languages as full languages by Oralists. However, as we work out the parameters of sign language poetry throughout this book, we will see that sound is not a prerequisite for poetry.

It is almost impossible to define poetry without assuming that the reader already has some idea what it is. Given this, the question that arises is how we know that something is a poem, and the most useful answer is that the text itself signals that it is. In this book we will be looking in detail at what those signals are, where sign language poetry shares them with spoken language poetry (drawing most comparisons with English) and where sign language invents its own signals. To do this we will draw freely on the various tools for analysis already available within the relevant areas of linguistic textual analysis, literary criticism, sign linguistics and Deaf studies.

Many of the poems that we will analyse here to illustrate points of sign language poetry were composed by Dorothy ('Dot') Miles. Dorothy Miles was a literary student, an actress, a creative poet (in English, as well as in ASL and BSL) and an active member of the Deaf community. Her education, her involvement in the political climate of the time and her love of language, written and signed, led her to try to make others (Deaf and hearing) aware of the potential of sign language as a creative medium. This made her the foremost sign poet of her time, and she is credited with being the person who founded modern sign language poetry and gave it its identity. It is fitting that the majority of our examples are drawn from her work.

Sign language poetry is the 'ultimate' form of aesthetic signing, in which the form of language used is as important as – or even more important than – the message. Like so much poetry in any language, sign language poetry is a means of expressing ideas unusually succinctly, through means of heightened 'art' language. In an interview on the BBC television programme *See Hear!* (in 1983) Dorothy Miles explained this relatively new idea of sign language poetry to the Deaf audience, saying, '[It's] a way of putting meaning very briefly so people will see it and feel very strongly'.

Geoffrey Leech (1969) gives a clear account of a way to identify poetic language, using linguistic principles. Much of Leech's work builds on the ideas of linguists working in Prague in the 1950s. He explains that poetic language deviates from – and even violates the norms of – everyday language. This deviation creates 'foregrounding'. The language norms (and other norms of social expectation) are challenged by the poem so that the deviation stands out (or comes to the foreground) from the background of normal language. In other words, we notice poetic language because it is odd. The foregrounding serves to increase the significance of the poem. As poetry is 'an aesthetically purposeful distortion of standard language' (Freeman, 1970: p. 7), the language in poems deliberately distorts the rules of standard language in a creative way, in order for the language to be noticed. Poets may use the established possibilities of the language in a creative way, or they may go beyond these established possibilities and create new possibilities that are not in the language at all (or at least, not yet). The poets' linguistic creativity leads to some sort of literary effect, where it adds significance in some way to the poem.

Written poetry can be identified by its layout on the page: it looks like poetry because the layout is different from that of prose. Spoken poetry (and sign language poetry) can be recognised by the style of declamation if people adopt a certain way of speaking (or signing) when they recite poetry. Generally, rhythm, heightened language, metaphor and repetition of various elements are all devices used to maximise the significance of the poem. The language devices in sign language poetry are rather different from the rhymes and meter that are familiar to most hearing audiences, and repetition of elements of signs and creation of new signs are important features of most sign language poems. However, the idea of maximising the message through specially heightened language is the same in poetry in all languages, whether signed or spoken.

Poetry is a cultural construction. Different societies have different cultural traditions that dictate the features of poetry and we should not assume that any definition of English language poetry would necessarily also apply to British Sign Language or American Sign Language poetry.[1] Poets usually grow up within their own cultural traditions and heritage of poetry, and will be influenced by them, whether they conform to these traditions or try to break from them. However, Deaf communities have not usually maintained a poetic tradition – within our definition of poetry – although they have often had very strong storytelling traditions. Storytelling uses an artistic form of language but the sign language storytelling traditions did not develop into poetry until very recently (and many signed poems still have strong narrative features). Most people would agree that American Sign Language poetry only began in the 1960s and a poetic *tradition* in ASL or BSL only dates from the 1980s or 1990s.

Because poetry is a social construction, a community's poetry may also change as the community changes. Poetry is a matter of fashion as well as an elevated art form. Its style alters with time and social group, just as fashions in clothes and music change. Some poems rhyme and some do not. Some have clear rhythms and others are composed in 'free verse' with no clear meter. Some are epics of tens of thousands of lines and others are short lyric poems (one of the shortest perhaps being the poem *Fleas*. In its entirety, it runs, 'Adam 'ad 'em'). Some are concerned with great metaphysical matters and some are light-hearted frivolities (although perhaps *Fleas* comes into both categories). Even though sign poetry has only existed for a short time, we will see in this book that its features have changed as the understanding of sign language and sign language poetry has changed, and as Deaf communities have changed. Today, there are Deaf artists around the world who compose and perform their sign language poetry and have very different styles. For example, Wim Emmerik (Sign Language of the Netherlands), Rosaria and Giuseppe Giuranna (Italian Sign Language), Patrick Graybill, Ella Mae Lentz and Clayton Valli (ASL), and Jerry Hanafin, Paul Scott and John Wilson (BSL) have all been recognised in their communities as poets, yet their poetry has different styles and they create their aesthetic effect using different techniques.

The distinction between prose and poetry is artificial. Even in our Western heritage – where we do make a distinction – it is clear that it is only a relative one. We can easily find pieces of prose with poetic features, and poetry that seems more like prose (Matterson and Jones, 2000). Brianne Brown (2001) has quoted the ASL artist Ben Bahan as saying that he watches an ASL performance of something called a 'poem' and thinks it looks like a story, and watches a 'story' and sees poetry within it. Clayton Valli (1993) has highlighted some distinctions between prose and poetry in ASL, in which he uses words such as 'less' and 'more', 'tend' and 'often' in his points. Heidi Rose (1992) has also observed that some ASL poets perceive one difference between stories and poetry to be the degree to which the poem has become 'frozen', with 'each sign and phrase set, while stories will adapt to new audiences and change with each performance' (p. 13).

The question of performance of sign language poetry is also important. In the sense that sign languages are unwritten languages (see Chapter 1), any sign language utterance, including poetry, must be 'performed' in order to exist, because a performance is simply a communicative event. However, there is a narrower definition of performance that may be relevant to sign language poetry, which is that the event is marked in some special way to be a 'display' for the audience. When sign language poetry is performed, the presentation is framed as a special display to signal to the audience that this is a poetic performance. We will explore the relationship between sign poems and their performance in more depth in Chapter 9.

In some unpublished notes from June 1990, Dorothy Miles summed up the situation in sign language, with reference to what she termed 'Art Sign':

> Art sign can perhaps be defined as sign that has been planned to create the best effect. However, storytellers, speech-makers, preachers and so on often produce spontaneous art sign in different ways. Story-tellers and preachers may for example use more classifiers and roleshift; speech-makers may effectively prefer placement, emphasis and repetition. Certain individuals are known for making everyone laugh with their play on signs or vivid role shifts. These examples suggest that every fluent user of BSL is a potential poet.

Although we might be working towards a rough idea of *what* sign language poetry is, we also need to ask what it is for.

What is sign language poetry for?

Poetry is not essential for communication, and basic communication can occur perfectly well without it. Indeed, what we call sign language poetry does not appear to have existed before the late 1960s, so we should ask why it exists now. In some unpublished notes from the early 1990s (undated), Dorothy Miles wrote about sign language poetry: 'Aim: To change the world.' It might seem a grand aim, but maybe in its implications that is what sign language poetry can be for.

One reason that sign language poetry exists is because there are at least a few people who compose and perform it. Without them, there would be none. Although sign language poetry has its roots in the Deaf community, it has not emerged as a community-driven force. Instead, it has come from very few, often well-educated, individuals of varied social, educational and language backgrounds within the community (as art forms often do in any society). The poetry they have composed survives – or is lost – due to a range of unpredictable events.[2] Without these few individuals, there would be no sign language poetry. Clayton Valli saw the need to 'introduce ASL poetry to the Deaf Community' (1993: p. 11), with the clear implication that poetry was not yet a community event. There is no evidence of original sign language poetry before Dorothy Miles began working with sign poetry in the 1960s. There were signed 'chants' and sign language games, signed translations of songs and signed translations of English poems but apparently no original, single-authored sign language poetry as we see it today.[3] There was nothing linguistic preventing its development, but the social traditions simply did not include it. This was partly, Alec Ormsby (1995) has argued, because ASL was in a social relationship with English that prevented the development of sign language poetry.

For a long time, Deaf people were surrounded by the notion strongly advocated by Oralism that English was the language to be used for high status situations and that 'deaf signing' was inferior and only fit for social conversation. Poetry was seen as a variety of language that should be conducted in English, because of its status. Ormsby (1995) remarks, 'No poetic register existed in ASL because poetic register was socially inconceivable, and as long as it remained socially inconceivable, it was linguistically pre-empted' (p. 119). However, social changes in the 1960s and 1970s, especially the emergence of 'Deaf Pride' and the increasing recognition of ASL as a language, fully independent of English, allowed a poetic register to become conceivable.

Sign language poetry, as we know it today, can be seen as a phenomenon made possible by the videotape. Heidi Rose (1992) has divided ASL literature into the eras of 'pre-videotape' and 'post-videotape' because of the importance of videotape to the preservation and distribution of sign language compositions. In the pre-videotape period, Deaf folklore and ASL oral traditions were transmitted 'orally', but the post-videotape period has allowed for the development of single-authored works composed in sign language and preserved on videotape. She claims that,

'The video form of preservation parallels the invention of the printing press' (p. iii). It can be argued that sign language poetry, with its rich complexity demanding constant review for full appreciation could only begin with the development of a medium that permitted such reviewing and repeated study. Rose credits Dorothy Miles' 1976 film, *Gestures* with being 'one of the first recorded examples of *original authored* sign language poetry' (p. 42, original emphasis).

Sign language poetry also exists today because influential Deaf and hearing people noticed it and helped validate and publicise it. Alec Ormsby (1995) has suggested that the true extent of ASL poetry has been exaggerated and phrases like 'the poetic tradition of sign languages' or 'the poetry of the Deaf Community' are misleading. Many Deaf people are still not interested in sign language poetry and have a general negative attitude to poetry. Even though Dorothy Miles made great strides in the development and variety of her own poetry, members of the Deaf community in Britain were slow at adopting her ideas. In unpublished notes for a class that she gave in 1990, she wrote:

> poetry is associated in the Deaf person's mind with English, and this discourages the BSL user from attempting it; original signed poetry is rarely taught or encouraged; and few people know how to analyse it and/or teach it. In addition, BSL poetry requires the poet to be a performer of his/her personal work.

However, emphasising the importance of sign language poetry helps to establish its credibility and (in Ormsby's words, 1995: p. 165) 'hastens its advance'. When respected academics gave their support to sign language poetry, and training was given in the analysis and appreciation of the poems, the art form gained credibility. Edward Klima and Ursula Bellugi's (1979) linguistic analysis of the art sign performed by Dorothy and Lou Fant (a hearing person with Deaf parents) helped to create the 'tradition', as the idea moved into key educational establishments in the USA.

Another reason for sign language poetry is because people enjoy it. Poetry is a game or a linguistic luxury, and its purpose can just be enjoyment – to appeal to the senses and the emotions. Poetry can be to language what sweets are to nutrition: a treat. Humans are naturally playful animals and we play with language, simply because we can and because it is fun. Poetry in any language can be enjoyable – or, at least, intensely satisfying – to hear or see, and to compose. A hedonist would be happy to accept that the primary purpose of poetry is pleasure, or the stimulation of emotions, and would argue that the language form of poetry is its own end and should just be enjoyed, treasured or marvelled at for its own sake. In the introduction to her 'Animal Poems' in *Gestures*, Dorothy noted that 'for complete *enjoyment* of [*The Cat*] it should be seen in sign language as well as read' (1976: p. 22, emphasis added). She wanted people to enjoy her work. There is no great metaphysical meaning to be had from *The Cat* (p. 240), and there is no hidden meaning. It is simply a pleasurable romp in sign language and it makes us smile.

Sign language poetry also shows hearing people the beauty and complexity of sign language and teaches them to respect Deaf culture, proving to them that sign language poetry is possible. No one would express surprise that the English, Arabic or Inuit languages have poetry, yet when most hearing people learn that sign poetry exists, their reaction is one of surprise. These people have probably given little thought to sign language or the possibility of sign language poetry but, nevertheless, their immediate thought is that it would not be possible. Several of Dorothy Miles' early ASL poems were motivated by this desire to inform hearing people about ASL and its potential for aesthetic use. In the introduction to one of her earliest signed poems *The Gesture*, published in the *Gestures* anthology, she wrote:

> I wanted to write English poetry to demonstrate the beauty in sign language. Back then [1968] not many hearing people knew Ameslan,[4] but many of them used gestures, so I thought that if I showed them that gestures could replace words or phrases they would understand sign language a little better. That's why I wrote ... *The Gesture*. (1976: p. 9)

She also explained in a television interview for *Deaf Focus* in 1976 that her poem *Language for the Eye* (p. 243) 'was really written for hearing children to show them some of the fun things you can do with sign language'. Of the body of her poetic work, Dorothy listed several poems as being those that provide an 'Introduction to Sign Language Poetry'. They are as much to introduce Deaf people to the poetry as they were to introduce hearing people to sign language, and we can see them as 'demonstration pieces', showing sign language (in this case, ASL) at its best. Her 'Introductory' poems that we will consider in this book included her *Seasons* haikus (1976: p. 245), *Language for the Eye* (1975: p. 243), *The Cat* (1976: p. 240), and *Our Dumb Friends* (1976: p. 244).

Clayton Valli (1993) remarked on the irony that hearing people frequently appear to know more about signed poetry than Deaf people do.

The paradox that outsiders know more about the principles behind the highest language art-form of a community than the members themselves do is balanced by the fact that only a member of the community can compose and perform and really understand all the cultural implications of the poetry. Analysis and critical appreciation are still new concepts to most members of the Deaf world (although this is slowly changing), but creating sign language poetry and appreciating it as part of a cultural identity is still an inside job.

The Deaf American anthropologist Tom Humphries has warned, 'We need to do more than just explain ourselves to the other [i.e. hearing people] in our art and literature' (2002: p. 3), and sign language poetry also enables Deaf people to realise themselves through their creativity. Poetry can empower both the poet and the audience. In our society, which values the rights of the individual, we should not be surprised that one claim for the purpose of poetry is that it benefits the poet. It allows poets to express their emotions and to understand themselves and their world a little more. Indeed, from her unpublished notes, it is clear that Dorothy Miles strongly believed that one aim for sign language poetry is to satisfy 'the need for self-identity through creative work', and she listed some of her more personal poems under the heading 'My Point of View'. These include *Sinai* (1981: p. 245) and *The Hang Glider* (1975: p. 242), which we will consider in more depth later. Each of these poems contains images that expressed her feelings – some very powerful – and showed how she dealt with the world she knew. Although they are not expressly 'Deaf' poems and deafness is not mentioned in any of them, they are all from the perspective of a Deaf person. Anyone, Deaf or not, should be able to relate to and learn from the experiences in these poems, but they might be especially empowering for a Deaf audience. Clayton Valli (1993) wrote, 'Empowerment is highly needed in Deaf people, to increase in strength and assertiveness and to create pride in themselves' (p. 143). Part of Valli's work was to take sign language poetry to Deaf children in schools to empower them, but empowerment through sign poetry is possible for the whole adult Deaf community, too.

Deaf poets in the past have written about deafness to explain their experience to hearing people and these 'experiences' (as Alec Ormsby (1995) has observed, and we will discuss more in Chapter 7) have often focused on ideas of loss and suffering. However, many sign language poems have been empowering for being about 'difference' not 'deficiency'. The poems Dorothy Miles listed as 'Poems of Difference' that we will look at here are *The Ugly Duckling* (1988: p. 249), *Elephants Dancing*

(1970: p. 242), *To a Deaf Child* (1976: p. 247), *Total Communication* (1976: p. 248), *Walking Down the Street* (1990: p. 251), and *Unsound Views* (1985: p. 250). Such poems empower the Deaf community by writing about deafness and sign language in a positive way. They are optimistic and show Deaf people as people in control of their own destiny. They do not deny problems faced by Deaf people. Indeed, arguably some of the best sign poems are the ones that identify the role that hearing people have played in oppressing Deaf people. They are angry poems, but they are often also wickedly funny, and show the strength of Deaf people living in a hearing world.

Some sign poems are best described as being of 'Deaf Pride'. These include *The Staircase* (p. 246) and *The BDA is ...* (p. 240), celebratory and inspirational poems that we will look at in some detail later (especially in Chapters 7 and 10). They praise the achievements of community members and affirm their continuing strength as a Deaf Nation. Paul Scott's *Three Queens* (p. 253) is another poem that comes from a strong sense of Deaf Pride. For a community that has been denigrated too often by outsiders, this sort of poetry is truly empowering.

Perhaps most importantly, sign language poetry also empowers Deaf people by focusing on the beauty and potential of sign language. It encourages signers to play with their language and to take the language to its limits and see what it can do. Many of Clayton Valli's ASL poems that we will consider (including *Flash* and *The Bridge*), and Wim Emmerik's SLN poems (including *Garden of Eden*) are notable for the elegant language they use. Paul Scott's *Five Senses* (p. 252) and Dorothy Miles' *Trio* (p. 249) are BSL poems where the beauty and potential of sign language are shown very clearly. For a people who have been told for too long that their language is inferior to spoken language, this elevation of sign language allows them to take pride in their language and their identity.

As Dorothy Miles said, sign poetry can change the world.

Dorothy Miles' contribution to sign language poetry

Dorothy Miles was the key figure in modern sign poetry, and although we will refer to the work of several other sign poets in this book, much of our analysis will be based on her poems. For this reason, we will take some time here to outline her contribution to the art form.

She was born hearing into a hearing family living in north Wales, and became Deaf in 1939 at the age of eight and a half from cerebrospinal meningitis, by which time she had acquired English as her mother tongue. From 1946 to 1950, she attended Mary Hare Grammar School (Britain's only grammar school for Deaf children) where sign language was strongly discouraged in favour of English. Dorothy's early experience as a hearing child and the prevailing attitude against sign language as being inferior to English meant that, although she learned and knew BSL like other Deaf children, she had to use it clandestinely and she did not identify as a sign language user when she left school. When she was at Gallaudet College (now University) in Washington, DC, where she studied English literature, from 1957 to 1961, she learned American Sign Language. Gallaudet College had its own traditions of 'chants' and language games, including ABC stories and number stories (see Chapters 1 and 3). Such language games were passed down through successive generations of students. Some of the traditional 'games' contained language elements that she later used in her sign language poems. These chants and other communal language performances used repetition of signs, careful placement and balance of signs, changes of speed and size of signs, creation of new and visual signs, and role-shift, all of which we will later see to be important elements of sign poetry. However, they were not recognised as containing elevated poetic language in any formal way and they were part of Deaf student culture and Deaf club culture, rather than single-authored original art forms of the language created through poetic principles.

Despite Dorothy's familiarity with this 'art' language, she did not yet view it as poetry of an equivalence with English. It was only when she saw the way that the National Theatre of the Deaf (NTD), which she joined as an actress in 1967, were experimenting with sign language, treating it as a language that could be analysed like any spoken language, that she began to consider ASL as a language for her poetry. She was encouraged to translate some of her English work into ASL. Translation from English poetry into ASL was not radical in itself, and there was already a tradition of sign translations of English poems and of signing hymns within church services for Deaf people. The way she approached her translations, however, was novel, as she drew on her in-depth knowledge of English poetic features and sign language folklore, recognising the poetic principles that would create good sign language translations of English poems. It was also at this time that she began composing original sign language poetry according to these similar elevated poetic principles, transferring the English rules by which poems are composed and judged to sign language. This idea – so obviously a possibility to us now with hindsight – was a radical departure from anything that anyone had done before. In the television interview for *Deaf Focus* in 1976 she explained, ' I am trying ... to find ways to use sign language according to the principles of spoken poetry. For example, instead of rhymes like "cat" and "hat", I might use signs like WRONG and WHY, with the same final handshape' (in this case, the 'Y' handshape).

As a consequence of this thinking, most sign language poems today are essentially 'lyric poems' – short poems, densely packed with images and often of considerable linguistic complexity. These lyric poems suit sign language and Deaf culture, so there is no reason to reject the genre, and they are blended with folklore traditions from sign languages, with features such as personation, anthropomorphisation, and the ABC, one-handshape and number games of the sign language traditions (see Chapters 3 and 9 for more detailed discussion of these).

Knowing English and English poetry and being a fluent ASL user with experience of using sign language as an aesthetic art form from her time as an actress at NTD, Dorothy was thus in a unique position to develop a clear understanding of sign poetry principles. We can argue that she was the right person in the right place at the right time for a revolution in poetry. Non-signing poets were never going to produce sign language poetry – not even deaf poets. Skilled signers knowing nothing about poetry composition were unlikely to produce sign language poetry, either. A Deaf poet skilled in English poetry composition and skilled in a sign language was the ideal person to bring poetry to ASL.

The translation of existing English poems into sign language was a useful first step in the development of sign poetry. Signers were able to play with elements of sign languages that could bring out the aesthetic element, but they were still safe within the respectability conferred upon them by the status of the English poem. As Alec Ormsby has put it:

> This period of translation served, I think, as a sort of intermediate phase, during which signers used English texts to explore the poetic possibilities of ASL to test the acceptability of finished poems in sign. Poetic translation was both a proving ground for the legitimacy of poems in a language deemed substrate, as well as a process that, as it occurred, began to define for ASL a poetic register. (1995: pp. 122–3)

Translation of written poetry into sign language, as we have seen, was popular in the years before Dorothy started her own original compositions and it still continues alongside original composition. A great difference between the translations and the original compositions, however, was that the signer devising the translation was working with the ideas and emotions of someone else, usually hearing poets. When signers compose their own poem in sign language, they are not only free to use the language they find most comfortable, but can also express their own ideas and emotions. The 'half-way-house' style that Dorothy developed, of writing poems that worked in English and ASL simultaneously, was the next crucial step in sign poetry. At last she could express her own ideas and emotions in ASL, even if they were also expressed in English. It is possible, as Alec Ormsby has suggested, that the signed poems in her *Gestures* collection needed the poetic prestige of English in order to be taken seriously by a world that still doubted the ability of ASL to create poetry at all.

After her return to England in 1977, Dorothy translated some of her ASL poems into British Sign Language and, as she settled into the British Deaf community, she began to compose BSL poetry without reference to English. Freed from the constraints of needing to accommodate two languages, her BSL poetry rose to new heights and some of her finest sign language poems, such as *Trio*, are from these later years. Once sign language poetry had received recognition in its own right there was less need to rely so heavily on English. This approach to sign poetry has now become widespread, so that there are now many sign poets who create sign language poetry with little or no reference to spoken languages.

Now that we have reviewed some of the general features of sign language poetry, and placed it within its historical context, we can start the process of analysing sign poems. We have seen that a poem may be enjoyed for the sensory experience and perhaps for the intellectual challenge it presents. In order to enjoy the experience to the utmost, it is useful to appreciate how a poem fits together, and to do that, it can be helpful to work out how to take it to pieces. The following chapters will offer some ideas on the ways we might 'take apart' signed poetry in order to see how the parts work together to create the language art form described in this chapter.

3
Repetition in Sign Language Poetry

Repetition is a key feature of sign language poetry. Within the text of a poem in either signed or spoken language, elements (such as words or parts of words) can be repeated to create patterns that stand out as being unusual, so bringing the language of the poem into the foreground. Repetition creates an aesthetic effect, as the patterns make a poem sound or look elegant or entertaining and we admire the poet's skill in achieving a poem within the strict discipline of certain repetitive patterns. Additionally, the repetition can highlight unusual relationships between words and ideas, creating further significance in the poem. Many of the repetitive effects we consider in this chapter are part of what Klima and Bellugi (1979) termed 'internal poetic structure', which is the structure of a poem that is created by a particular choice of signs. The repetitive effects of similar elements (particularly words or phrases) in poetry can be termed 'parallelism'.

Repetitive effects between signs do not need to be limited to repetition of the same element. We saw in Chapter 1 that each sign is made up of four main parameters – handshape, location, movement and orientation – and certain parameters might be altered systematically within a poem to create a pattern. For example, signs might employ a series of handshapes with increasing or decreasing numbers of fingers open from the fist. Alternatively, signs could be placed in successively ascending or descending locations on the body or they could steadily move from one side of the signing space to the other.

Repetition of handshape

Study of almost any sign language poem will reveal repeated handshape patterns in signs. Sometimes these are simply for visual effect – they are elegant, pleasing or fun. In many cases the handshapes have more important roles to play in the poem. They can link ideas, or bring out further connotations behind signs in the poem, often drawing on the emotional effects commonly associated with particular handshapes. In general, the '5' and 'B' handshapes, being open, are symbolically more 'positive' in connotation than closed handshapes, such as 'A' or 'Å'.[1] Handshapes that are bent at the knuckles, such as '5̈' or 'V̈' are associated with more tension and are 'harsher' than other non-claw handshapes, which are more relaxed and 'softer'. The 'G', 'V', 'I' and 'Y' handshapes are 'sharp', while 'A' and 'O' handshapes are not. 'G' and 'I' are more uni-dimensional, while the 'B' and '5' handshapes have more substance, and 'A', 'O' and 'C' handshapes are the most solid. (For handshapes, please refer to the illustrations on pp. xv-xvi.) Any of these distinctions can be used symbolically in sign language poetry, as the following consideration of some of Dorothy Miles' compositions will show.

In Dorothy's *Seasons* ASL haiku quartet (p. 245), *Winter* uses the signs HARD ICE SOFT WHITE-SNOW-FALL ('hard ice, / soft snow'). HARD uses the clawed 'V̈' handshape and ICE uses the clawed '5̈' handshape. These signs are contrasted (in this poem of contrasts) with SOFT, which uses a more relaxed 'B̂' handshape and SNOW-FALL, which uses the gentle, fluttering open '5' handshape (Fig. 3.1). In this way, the shapes and internal movements of the signs echo and reinforce the lyrical meaning of the short poem.

Exaltation (p. 242) is a poem about a moment of pure bliss, and the handshapes of the signs in the ASL poem lend themselves to the atmosphere. There are 40 occurrences of signs with either a 'B' or a '5' handshape and only 25 other signs have other handshapes. The key ideas in the poem all use these 'open' handshapes – TREE, SKY, BREEZE, REACH-UP, PEACE, HEAVEN, LIGHT, TOUCH and GOD. When used together, the overall impact of the poem is very positive (Fig. 3.2).

In contrast, the ASL poem *Total Communication* (p. 248) is concerned with a lover's attempts to reconcile problems of communication between herself and her lover. Much of this meaning is carried by the use of space and location of signs (which we discuss below) but it is also shown in selected handshapes which are similar and yet different in subtle ways – just as mismatched lovers are. The poem is dominated by signs using the 'sharp' handshapes 'V', 'I', 'Y', the 'open 8' and 'G'. These give the poem a sharp, 'on-edge' feel, symbolising the frustrations and tensions expressed by the poem. The connotations carried by signs using the 'Y' handshape are also important in *Total Communication*. The 'Y' handshape is closely associated with a sign meaning 'Yes', which is

HARD ICE SOFT SNOW-FALLS

Fig. 3.1

SKY REACH-UP PEACE TOUCH

Fig. 3.2

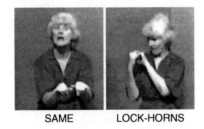

SAME LOCK-HORNS

Fig. 3.3

FEEL EXCITEMENT FIRE

Fig. 3.4

the positive outcome hoped for in the poem. The deliberate pun on the English words 'I', 'Eye' and 'Aye' is carried over into the ASL signs so that the 'Y' handshape links to the word 'Aye'. The sense of conflict is carried by using the same 'Y' handshape for the signs YES and SAME, and in the creative sign LOCK-HORNS, showing two creatures locking horns and fighting (Fig. 3.3).

Dorothy's two BSL Christmas poems *Christmas Magic* and *Christmas List* are filled with repetitions of handshapes in different signs. In *Christmas Magic* (p. 241), of the 99 signs that may be glossed in the poem, 35 have the '5' handshape and a further 23 have the 'B' handshape, while signs with 'A' or 'Å' handshapes account for another 22. This means that over three-quarters of the poem is expressed in handshapes that carry a positive mode, contributing to the joyful effect of the whole. *Christmas Magic* takes a theme of magic, sparkling and excitement. It emphasises this through repetitive use of the '5' and 'B' handshapes. These hand-shapes have general connotations of openness and giving, both ideas we strongly link to Christmas. In many cases, the fingers in the signs wiggle or flutter to add extra 'sparkle'. Some of the signs are 'established' signs (signs that are known, fixed items of vocabulary) that Dorothy selected for effect. Signs such as FEEL, EXCITEMENT, MAGIC, FIRE, TREE and GLITTERING are all recognised vocabulary items where the 'open 8', '5̈' and '5' handshapes add significance, even to signs that would not have connotations associated with magic in any other ways (Fig. 3.4).

There are also a great many specially created neologisms in *Christmas Magic*. (A neologism is a newly created sign that is not a part of the standard vocabulary of the language but which the poet has created as part of the poem. We will consider neologisms in more depth in Chapter 5.) All the following signs are complex and highly creative signs, all made with the '5' handshape, and all related to the excitement of a child's Christmas: MAGIC-FLIES-OVERHEAD, EXCITEMENT-BUBBLING-UP, MAGIC-EXPLODES, MAGIC-SHIVERS-UP-ARMS, FEEL-BUMPS-DOWN-STOCKING, MAGIC-FOLLOWS-ME-DOWNSTAIRS and THROW-MAGIC-DUST (Fig. 3.5).

Another handshape theme is the closed fist. There are many established vocabulary signs in this poem using either an 'A' or an 'Å' handshape. These include COLD, REMEMBER, BLACK, GOOD, RUN and STILL-THERE. Creative signs in the poem with the same handshape include PERSON-SIT-UP, HOLD-BED-CLOTHES-AND-SIT-UP, PUSH-BACK-BED-CLOTHES, GOOD-THROUGH-TIME and SANTA'S-SACK (Fig. 3.6). In the line translated in English as 'I know at last, it's Christmas Day', a sequence of signs with the 'A' or 'Å' handshape makes an aesthetically smooth

| MAGIC-FLIES OVERHEAD | MAGIC-SHIVERS-UP-ARMS | FEEL-BUMPS-DOWN-STOCKING | MAGIC-FOLLOWS-ME-DOWNSTAIRS |

Fig. 3.5

| STILL-THERE | GOOD-THROUGH-TIME | SANTA'S-SACK |

Fig. 3.6

| KNOW | AT-LAST | CHRISTMAS |

Fig. 3.7

flow of signs. Additionally, each sign adds to connotations of things related to Christmas that are positive and good. CLENCHED-FISTS of excitement (excitement = good) change to KNOW (knowledge = good, and Å = good), to AT-LAST (= achievement = good, and Å = good), to CHRISTMAS, the central topic of the poem (Fig. 3.7).

In *Christmas List* (p. 240) we see a different use of repetitive handshapes. In common with many of Dorothy's poems, *Christmas List* is divided into three main sections. In the first section, she takes us back to her childhood Christmas and how the children asked for presents. The use of handshapes in the second section is worth analysing in depth, as it is here that the poem describes how they played with their presents as children. Interestingly, the playing element is completely absent in the English version of the poem, which instead lists the different presents whose names fit an aural rhyme scheme.

The English lines of the signed poem run:

> We of course, were children, so we asked for funny pets,
> And cake and lots of chocolate, and candy cigarettes,
> And cannons and tin soldiers, and cut-out dolls and swords,
> And games like Snakes and Ladders, and games you play with words.

In the version of this poem reproduced in *Bright Memory*, the first line of the verse ends: ' ... so we asked for drums and balls'. The English version that Dorothy made to accompany the BSL poem fits better into the 'aabbccdd' rhyming scheme that the English poem shifts into for this section.[2] It also allows for much more poetic potential for the equivalent BSL signs, and it is the sign version that really exploits the imaginative world of this poem.

The use of PET and CAKE allows repetition of handshape arrangements. Both signs are made with the dominant hand contacting the back of the non-dominant hand (which has the 'B' handshape). In PET, the dominant hand has a 'B' handshape, and in CAKE it has a '5̈' handshape. The back of the non-dominant hand is an unusual, 'marked' location for BSL signs, so two signs with this location occurring so close together make a powerful repetitive impression. They also have strong formational connotations with the sign she uses for CHRISTMAS in this poem. It is also made with the dominant hand contacting the back of a non-dominant hand with a 'B' handshape. The dominant hand in CHRISTMAS changes from a 'B' to an 'A' handshape, echoing both PET and CAKE (as the '5̈' is a 'solid' handshape in a similar way to an 'A' handshape) (Fig. 3.8).

PET   CAKE

Fig. 3.8

FUNNY   LOTS   CHOCOLATE

CANNONS   TIN   CANDY

Fig. 3.9

STAND-UP-DOLL   STAB-DOLL-WITH-
                  SWORD

Fig. 3.10

The 'L', 'baby C' and 'X' handshapes are all 'marked', unusual hand-shapes and are similar in form. The 'L' has the index finger and thumb extended and not bent at the knuckles, the 'baby C' also has the index finger and thumb extended but they are bent at the knuckles. The 'X' handshape has only the index finger extended, but this is bent at the knuckles. The signs FUNNY, LOTS, CHOCOLATE, CANNONS, FIRE-CANNONS, TIN and CANDY use these three similar, unusual hand-shapes, creating an elegant effect of similarity in the signs used in these lines (Fig. 3.9).

The two signs STAND-UP-DOLL and STAB-DOLL-WTH-SWORD are also related by sharing similar handshapes. The sign DOLL is made with 'B' hands, but the sign used for the shape and position of the paper doll as the character stands it up uses the 'Â' handshape. The sign that occurs when the narrator takes on the role of the character in the poem (in a common sign language device termed 'role shift') and folds her arms and looks with satisfaction at the paper doll uses 'A' handshapes. This then links nicely with SWORD, also made with an 'A' handshape on the dominant hand (representing holding the sword), and another 'A' hand-shape on the non-dominant hand (representing the scabbard from which the sword is drawn) before the dominant hand signs STAB-DOLL-WITH-SWORD, again with an 'A' handshape. At first, we might think that the dolls and the swords are merely items on a list and unrelated in the children's play. However, STAND-UP-DOLL and STAB-DOLL-WITH-SWORD are signed at the same location in signing space and their shared handshapes link them further. When Dorothy role-shifts to show the child using the sword, the sword thrust is made with an 'A' hand-shape at exactly the location of the paper doll, giving a lovely image of the sibling rivalry at Christmas (Fig. 3.10).

The snakes and ladders game is particularly dominated by the 'V̈' handshape. Although this is a relatively unusual, marked handshape, Dorothy uses it here with comic effect by drawing together the snake with movement up and down ladders. The handshape is seen in the vocabulary item SNAKE and also in the sign representing human legs as the person slides down a snake and climbs a ladder. It is also used in the sign representing the snake rearing up to stare the child in the eyes.

The 'baby C' handshape that dominates the section of the word-game leads to larger, more open handshapes of what the adults actually gave the children ('The adults gave us shoes and clothes – perhaps a golden chain'). The sign ADULTS uses two 'B' hands, palms down. It is followed by GIVE-US, which uses two 'B' hands, palms up. The subsequent signs SHOE, CLOTHES and GOLDEN use either '5' or 'B' handshapes and

33

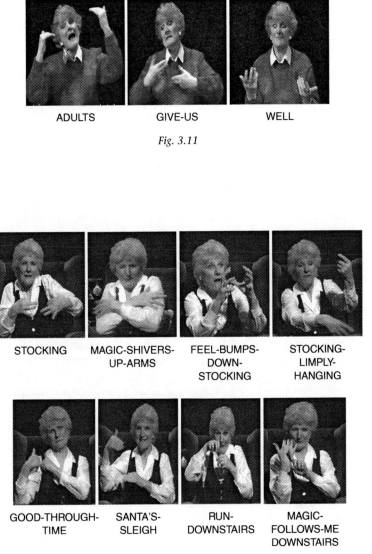

ADULTS   GIVE-US   WELL

Fig. 3.11

STOCKING   MAGIC-SHIVERS-   FEEL-BUMPS-   STOCKING-
              UP-ARMS   DOWN-   LIMPLY-
                               STOCKING   HANGING

GOOD-THROUGH- SANTA'S-   RUN-   MAGIC-
TIME   SLEIGH   DOWNSTAIRS   FOLLOWS-ME
                                         DOWNSTAIRS

Fig. 3.12

CHAIN uses the predominantly open 'F' handshape. Although the sign PERHAPS uses a 'Y' handshape, each of the three gifts is preceded by a sign made with two '5' hands, glossed as WELL, meaning something like 'perhaps' and this enables the poem to retain the 'open' pattern of signs in this section (Fig. 3.11).

Variation and repetition

Although these repeated handshapes described in these poems are an important part of repetitive patterning in sign language poetry, we also need to consider poems that use 'varying patterns' of handshapes. In ASL especially, there is a long tradition in the Deaf community of language games using numbers and letters of the manual alphabet. (We should note, however, that not every Deaf community shares this tradition, and it is not so widespread in BSL traditions, perhaps in part because BSL uses a two-handed manual alphabet.) The aim of the games is to produce a meaningful story using signs that share the handshape of sequences of numbers or letters. We saw in Chapter 1 that signs may coincidentally share the same handshape as a manual letter. In a similar way, signs might coincidentally share the same handshape with a sign numeral. (In some cases the handshape in ASL numerals may be the same as – or very similar to – letter handshapes, as well as visually motivated handshapes. The handshape in the ASL numeral sign SIX is similar to the 'W' handshape, TWO is made with the 'V' handshape and ONE with the 'G' handshape.) In the numbers games, sign sequences are created in which the signs use handshapes that are coincidentally the same as sequences of numerals. In a simple pattern, for example, the first sign must have the 'G' handshape (that is, ONE) the next the 'V' (that is, TWO), then '3', then '4', '5', 'W' (SIX), '7', '8' and so on. So the sequence creates signs that have handshapes that 'count' but also tell some story that is quite unrelated to numbers.

Clayton Valli's short ASL poem *The Bridge* uses signs that follow the handshape sequence of numbers. In *The Bridge*, a distant boat approaches a bridge, the bridge opens, and the boat passes through while people watch it. The bridge then closes and the boat sails into the distance. The signs in this poem are not related to numerals at all, but the pattern of their handshapes follows the sequence: 6, 5, 4, 3, 2, 1, 2, 3, 4, 5, 6, 5, 4, 3, 2, 1.

The poem may be roughly glossed as follows, with the number corresponding to each handshape given in brackets after each sign:

WATER (6)
WATER-ALL-AROUND (5)

BOAT-BOBS-THROUGH-WAVES (4)
BOAT-CL-BOBS-THROUGH-WAVES (3)
SEE (2)
FAR-AWAY-BRIDGE-WITH-PLATFORMS-CLOSED (1)
ORNATE-SHAPED-BRIDGE (2)
ORNATE-BRIDGE-STRUCTURE (3)
BRIDGE-OPENS (4)
BOAT-BOBS-THROUGH-WAVES (5)
FLAG-ON-MAST (6)
MANY-PEOPLE-LOOK-DOWN-TO-BOAT (5)
MANY-PEOPLE-LOOK-UP-FROM-BOAT (5)
BRIDGE-CLOSES (4)
BOAT-CL-BOBS-THROUGH-WAVES (3)
SEE (2)
FAR-AWAY-BRIDGE-WITH-PLATFORMS-CLOSED-RECEDES-INTO-
DISTANCE (1)

(The 'CL' in this gloss with the '3' handshapes refers to a classifier hand-shape in a sign. Classifiers show the class to which the language assigns some referents. A boat is seen in ASL as belonging to a class of 'vehicles' and when the sign BOAT has been used, the classifier sign that shows how the boat moves uses a 'vehicle' '3' handshape.) The falling, rising and falling pattern of the numbers reflects the bobbing movement of the boat on the water as it approaches and recedes, and the numbers go up and down, as the bridge goes up and down. The poem is signed with little emotion, but with a marked, steady rhythm, suggesting that the boat's passage is part of a natural ordered sequence of events, like numbers.

Like the 'numbers' games, the traditional ASL 'ABC' letters games play with the handshapes of signs, but this time in relation to the manual alphabet (see Chapter 1). The game might be a straightforward attempt to work through the alphabet while still creating a meaningful utterance or, alternatively, the handshapes of the signs used in a meaningful ASL utterance can spell out a given English word. When this is done skilfully, the subject matter is also related to the word spelled out. Whether or not all examples of this genre should be considered poetry (and Heidi Rose (1992) makes the claim that these games are usually more properly classed as folkloric language games, having originated well before sign language poetry and the age of the videotape); some are, and several of Clayton Valli's poems use this device.

Valli's poem *Flash* uses signs with handshapes that occur in manual letters. Taken in order, the handshapes of the signs spell the word 'flash' several times, both forward and in reverse, although, just as the signs are not related to numerals in *The Bridge*, the signs in *Flash* are not initialised or related to fingerspelling (see Chapter 1). The poem is concerned with a challenge to run a race, where the central character is outclassed by faster runners. The overall pattern of the handshapes in the whole poem is: HSALFFLASHHSALFFLASHHSALF. The first three sign sequences of the poem may be roughly glossed as follows, and the handshape of each sign is given in brackets:

TWO-PEOPLE (H) CAN (S) HOW (A) RUN (L) NOTHING (F)
CATCH-SIGHT (F) ZOOM-OFF (L) DISAPPEAR-INTO-DISTANCE (A)
GONE (transition across sign space) (S) BUMP-INTO-TWO-PEOPLE (H)
TWO-PEOPLE-CLOSE-UP (H) OH-NO! (S) NOT (A) ME (L) WOW-
SKILL-CAN-DO! (F).

In these three sequences, the handshapes of the signs spell the word 'flash' successively, first in reverse, then forward, then in reverse again. And, as the whole poem is about speed and running, the handshapes in the poem's signs are directly related to the content of the poem.

In *Flash*, the signs are not initialised, but in another of Valli's poems, *Something Not Right*, almost all of the signs are initialised. The poem describes how the tendency to prescribe medical cures for deafness and insistence on speech acquisition for Deaf children have failed the very Deaf children they were supposed to help. Meanwhile, the letters forming the initialisation handshapes of each sign spell out 'Deaf education fails':

DOCTOR EVALUATE AGGRESSIVE FIDDLE-WITH-EAR-TO-FIX-IT (not an initialised sign, but using an 'F' handshape)
ELEMENTARY-SCHOOL DISCRIMINATION USE CONCEPT ABSTRACT THEORY IDEAS OPINIONS NO
FAMILY AGGRESSIVE ISOLATED BIG-EGO (not an initialised sign but using an 'L' handshape) SOCIETY

This is a particularly pointed use of initialised signs and handshapes normally reserved for representing English, as English and the manual alphabet are major tools of educators of Deaf children. To use it here to attack that education is a witty, subversive act.

Repetition of movement

Movement of signs includes both any internal movement of the fingers in the handshape (such as wiggling or fluttering) and the path movement (and speed of movement) of the hand. Path movement of a sign has two main functions in sign languages. It can be a part of the sign's essential make-up because each sign must have a movement parameter, even if that movement element happens to be 'no movement' or 'hold'. Using several signs that share the same basic, formational movement in the same poem creates some sort of poetic movement pattern. Alternatively, the movement could be something additional to the basic form of the sign and be a part of the grammatical meaning. We will consider this sort of grammatical movement later, in our discussion of grammatical repetition. Both these types of movement can contribute to the overall rhythm of the poem, where signs with fast, slow, smooth or sharp movements may be selected to contrast or create patterns of regularity. We will discuss the rhythm of signing below.

The movement path in several key signs in *Christmas Magic* (p. 241) follows a curving 'J' shape through space. This allows the signs to have general connotations with the idea of a Christmas stocking which has a 'J' shape in reality and whose sign is made with a 'J'-shaped movement. These signs include the established sign STOCKING itself and also the productive neologisms MAGIC-SHIVERS-UP-ARMS, FEEL-BUMPS-DOWN-STOCKING, STOCKING-LIMPLY-HANGING, GOOD-THROUGH-TIME, SANTA'S-SLEIGH, RUN-DOWNSTAIRS and MAGIC-FOLLOWS-ME-DOWNSTAIRS. This repeated movement path is not as immediately obvious as the fluttering, wriggling internal movement in the handshapes that we considered above in our discussion of repeated handshapes. Nevertheless, it is a little piece of poetic fun, and perhaps all the more fun for its subtlety (Fig. 3.12).

In the celebratory BSL poem about the British Deaf Association, *The BDA is …* (p. 240) there is a noticeable use of outward movement of the signs. In the final verse and the chorus, 13 of the 29 signs (45 per cent) move forward, echoing the dominant theme of progress (forward = progress = good). There is also a theme of the inclusion of all Deaf people within the BDA, and this is shown by circular movements in 14 of the signs (48 per cent), either by twisting circular wrist-movements or circular movements of the arms. Several signs, including the final sign EQUALITY combine a circular movement with a forward movement.

The English version of the final verse and the chorus of *The BDA is …* may be seen in the Appendix (p. 240). The gloss of the BSL version runs as follows (circular movements are marked with a '$_c$' and forward movements are marked with an '$_f$'):

NINETEEN NINETY WE$_{cf}$ INCREASE$_f$ STRONG$_f$
PRINCESS$_f$ -d-i- TOP SHE CAN'T$_{cf}$ GO$_f$ WRONG

WE-ALL$_c$ MOVE-FORWARD/CONTINUE$_f$ WORK$_c$ WILL$_c$ SEE$_f$ FULL-
COMPLETE$_{cf}$
ALL$_{cf}$ DEAF OUT-OF-SHELL$_f$
-b-d-a- WHO$_c$ YOU-ALL$_c$ ME$_c$
TOGETHER$_c$ I$_c$ FIGHT$_f$ ACHIEVE$_c$ EQUALITY$_{cf}$

Repeated speed and timing of movements are used carefully in the
Seasons haiku verses (p. 245) to set the mood for the seasons. The fast,
trilling, sharp movements in several signs in *Spring* symbolising the
excitement of new growth are contrasted with the much slower
movements in the signs in *Summer*, a time of still heat. In *Autumn*, the
movements start slow and measured, before becoming fast and then
coming to a sudden halt with the hold of the final sign, just as the calm
of early autumn gives way to wild autumn winds before the first cold
snap of ice. In *Winter*, a poem of contrasts as we have already seen, the
movements of the signs are contrasting. They are initially sharp and
staccato, with brittle movements in the early signs, especially BARE and
BARE-TREE. The slow, tense, jerky movement of BARE-TREE contrasts
with the last time that the sign TREE was seen in the quartet – in *Spring*.
Then the movement was rapid, but loose and fluttering. In the four
signs HARD ICE SOFT SNOWFALL, the signs HARD and ICE made with
fast, tense movements, before the next, strongly contrasting signs SOFT
SNOWFALL, are made with much softer, more relaxed movements.

Repetition of location

Although spoken words must occur linearly, sign language poems can
exploit the possibility that signs may be placed in space to create visually aesthetic patterns and contrasts, just as they might in visual arts
such as painting (Bauman, 2003). Signs may be articulated in different
areas of space – some high and some low, for example, or left and right –
or they may connect smoothly in different parts of space, creating flowing
patterns across space. As with the movement of the sign, the location of
a sign's articulation may be determined by the citation form (or basic
'dictionary' form) of the sign because each sign must have its location
parameter (see Chapter 1). Alternatively, the larger structure of the language may dictate the location to show the larger visual layout of the
whole utterance. We saw in Chapter 1 that these discourse factors deter-
mine where we place things in space so that we can refer to them and
understand the relationship between the signs and their referents in our
signing space. If we talk about trees and flowers, we might place signs

relating to the trees on the left of the signing space and signs relating to the flowers on the right of the signing space. Signs that are located in the general 'neutral space' in front of the body in their citation form can be meaningfully placed in areas of space relevant to the trees and flowers.

We saw earlier that handshapes can carry different connotations, but we can also see that the location of a sign has connotations. Signs contacting the body can be seen as more 'personal' than signs that do not contact the body or move away from the body. Signs located higher in space will carry connotations of things that are more 'positive' than signs located lower in space. This is a general metaphor in many cultures that associates 'up' with 'good' and 'down' with 'bad'. Signs lower down in space can also be associated with youth and signs higher up can be associated with greater maturity (because children tend to be shorter than adults). There are also general connotations linked to individual sign languages where signs of general shared meaning are made at a certain location. Many signs associated with mental processes are made at the forehead and temple regions, in both ASL and BSL. Many signs associated with emotions are made at the chest. There is also a general association of 'head = thought' for many signs, although some mental process signs are not made at the head (such as PLAN and DECIDE in BSL) and there are signs unrelated to mental processes that are made at the head (such as BAPTISE and SHEEP in BSL). Just as with handshapes, again, there are two options for obtrusively regular locations to occur poetically: repetitive use of the same location, and patterns of systematically varying locations.

Exaltation (p. 242) uses the high area of signing space. Once again there is an important connotation behind the use of space as high = happy = good. Some of the signs are naturally 'high' signs. The first sign of the poem, operating almost as a prologue, is LOOK-UPWARD and the main body of the poem starts with the signs THINK and REMEMBER. All these signs are made at eye-height or higher. Shortly after this, there is a sequence of signs NOTICE NOTICE-TREE TREE AGAINST-TREE SKY/HEAVEN ('That sudden glimpse of trees against the sky'). All these signs are made with the hands in a high area of space (Fig. 3.13). The trees are 'newly dressed / In summer's green' and the signs for this line are NEW CLOTHES SUMMER GREEN GREEN-ON-TREES. Of these established signs, only SUMMER is articulated at any height (across the forehead) but the final sign here is a newly created neologistic sign GREEN-ON-TREES, which allows the poem to place the sign GREEN high up at tree-height. In a similar way, the sign HIGH is placed high at tree-height, creating a sign better glossed as HIGH-AT-TREES. The same device of using the sign

40

NOTICE   NOTICE-TREE   TREE   AGAINST-TREE

Fig. 3.13

GREEN-ON-TREES   HIGH-AT-TREES   HIGH-TREE   BLUE-SKY

Fig. 3.14

GLIMMERING-LIGHTS   APPLAUD

Fig. 3.15

TREE as a location for signs that would not normally be located at this height is also used for TREE and TOUCH. Both these established signs are altered to form neologisms that can be glossed as HIGH-TREE and TOUCH-TREE. BLUE is also articulated high up in the same area as SKY, creating the neologism BLUE-SKY (Fig. 3.14).

Clayton Valli's *Deaf World* uses signs located at different heights throughout the poem. All the signs are located in the right-hand side of the signing space but at first they are located at waist-height, then signs are made in a plane slightly higher, then the plane is raised again, until finally the signs are made at head-height. The use of space here is not just for aesthetics but reflects how a Deaf person's confidence grows (moves up, and becomes more 'positive') as he or she physically grows.

Dorothy Miles' BSL poem *The Staircase* (p. 246) also makes use of patterns of space. Like *Deaf World*, it uses the general metaphor of increasing height with improvement of a situation. At first, when the people are wandering, lost in the forest, the signs are made low down at waist height, with the connotation that low = bad. Their goal is placed at the top of the staircase, high in signing space, with the connotation that high = good. As the people embark on their journey towards their goal they move higher and so do the signs depicting this rise.

Another connotation of location used in this poem is the metaphorical idea that forward is better than back. Front = good; behind = bad. The characters, and the signs representing them, are moving forwards towards the staircase (= good) until they reach the staircase which could lead them on to great things. When they reject the staircase out of fear of the risks, they turn and the signs move backwards (= bad). There are interesting signs when the hero encourages them up the stairs. The character is facing forward (= good) and the signs involved (such as COME-ON! and HELP-PERSON-UP) move from behind (= bad) to the front (= good).

The repeated location of two very similar signs is also relevant here. The lights that the people see glimmering at the top of the stairs are signed using two '5' handshapes facing the signer and extended to the top of signing space (they are so high in the recording we have, that the hands are outside the camera shot). When the travellers are awarded their certificates, the hero applauds them. The sign APPLAUD uses the same location as the sign for the lights glimmering and the same handshape, but with a slightly different movement. The unusual location of these two signs links them, and in both cases it brings out the connotation of high = good (Fig. 3.15).

Repetition and 'rhyme'

We have seen that when signs containing the same handshape, location or movement are repeatedly selected in a sign language poem, this repetition becomes noticeable and it creates poetic effect. This repetition might loosely be called 'rhyme', but the distinctions of rhyme, assonance, alliteration, consonance and others that are made in spoken language poetry are not directly applicable to signed poetry. These distinctions in spoken poetry only arise because of the sequential nature of spoken words, and in sign languages the parameters such as handshape, location and movement tend to occur simultaneously.

Choosing words with the same sound patterns is a central poetic device in many poetic traditions. Sound patterns in poetry will make use of repetitive parallelisms at any stage during a word (see Table 3.1 below). These sound patterns all depend upon the fundamental fact that words are pronounced and written in sequence. It might seem superfluous to point out that we say the start of a word then we say the next part, and the next, until we get to the end of it. However, only spoken languages need to produce the parts of words in temporal sequences: sign languages do not need to.

As a convenient way of considering the six different forms of repetition occurring within English words in poetry, we can see that each is a different pattern of repetition of a basic pattern of the consonant-vowel-consonant arrangement that is common in English words. In three cases, only one of the three parts is repeated in both words and in the other three, two of the three parts are repeated in both words. Thus the 'rhymes' (rhyme, reverse rhyme and pararhyme) have more parts in common than do alliteration, assonance and consonance. Table 3.1 illustrates this. (The consonant or vowel element that is the same in both words is highlighted. Note, that 'consonant' can also be taken to mean 'consonant cluster' here.)

Table 3.1   Poetic repetitive patterns of vowels and consonants in English

Alliteration	**d**eaf/**d**ome	**C**VC
Assonance	gr**ee**t/l**ea**n	C**V**C
Consonance	stee**l**/pear**l**	CV**C**
Reverse rhyme	**bre**ad/**bre**ak	**CV**C
Pararhyme	**sh**i**ne**/**sh**u**n**	**C**V**C**
Rhyme	p**at**/m**at**	C**VC**

Although the sequences of English consonants and vowels do not compare with the simultaneous sign parameters, it would be possible to construct the same logical set of distinctions in sign languages, using the four simultaneous parameters of handshape, movement, location and orientation (H, M, L and O).[3] There are four ways that two signs can share only one of the parameters (the shared parameters here are in bold type): **H**MLO, H**M**LO, HM**L**O and HML**O**. There are six ways that two signs can share two parameters but not the other two parameters: **HM**LO, **H**M**L**O, **H**ML**O**, H**ML**O, H**M**L**O**, HM**LO**. Finally, there are four more ways that two signs can share three parameters so that only one parameter will be different: H**MLO**, **H**M**LO**, **HM**L**O**, **HML**O. In Table 3.2 we can see what this would look like for three parameters – excluding the occasionally problematic parameter of orientation. We could make a table showing all 14 variations, but these six should suffice to make our point.

Using the similar approach to the one taken for spoken languages, we could say that the signs sharing two of the three parameters are more like 'rhymes' and the signs sharing only one parameter are more like alliteration, consonance and assonance. Unfortunately, that is as far as our analogy can go between the two language modalities. Firstly there is no way to assign the terms derived from sequential similarities to these simultaneous similarities. Secondly we have a three-part scale of closeness (one parameter shared, two parameters shared or three parameters shared) and the English scheme has only two.[4] Only when conventions emerge for terms for these six variables (or 14 if anyone cared to attempt a system that included orientation) can we make a more systematic naming system. Until then, we will simply refer here to any repetition of one parameter or more as a 'rhyme', as a convenient shorthand.

The repetition of handshape, location and movement that occurs in signed poems is not always regular or predictable. In traditional English poetry, the repetitive effects of rhyme typically occur at the end of each

Table 3.2 Shared parameters in signs

What is shared by two signs	*BSL examples*	*ASL examples*
Handshape Location Movement	TREE WIND	COFFEE WORK
Handshape **Location** Movement	KNOW CONSIDER	MOTHER TRUE
Handshape Location **Movement**	WANT WOMAN	CORRECT SIT
Handshape Location Movement	THINK CRAZY	TRUE RED
Handshape **Location Movement**	THINK KNOW	CANDY APPLE
Handshape Location **Movement**	READY DEER	LUCKY SMART

line (although line-internal rhymes also feature in English poetry), but there is no strong evidence for the regular occurrence of rhymes at the end of lines in most sign language poems. This is partly because the idea of a 'line' in signed poetry is very problematic in poems composed and performed in an unwritten medium. Clayton Valli (1993) made an early attempt to define line-endings in signed poetry, suggesting that line division could be identified by repetition of elements such as handshape, path movement or non-manual features (such as eye-gaze). Where there is repetition (Valli suggested), this could be seen as a 'line-terminator'. However, to say that this means that rhymes in sign language poetry occur at the end of lines is a circular argument because lines are defined as occurring where there is a rhyme. Marion Blondel and Chris Miller (2001) have questioned this approach and have suggested instead that lines in sign language poetry have some regular internal cohesive pattern (what they call a 'unifying internal motif': p. 29) and that line breaks occur when there is a shift to a new or contrasting pattern. The pattern may be of rhythm, syntax, orientation of the body, hand dominance, handshape, location or movement, or even be of a semantic nature. Line-termination may be seen when one or several of these features change at an 'anchor point' in the poem (2001: p. 37), but this approach allows for repetition of elements (creating rhymes) to occur anywhere in the poem, not just at the end of lines.

Repetition of timing – rhythm

The idea underlying 'rhythm' is the concept of a regular beat, such as the tick of a clock or the beat of a heart. When we consider poetic rhythm in English poetry, we look at it according to the rhythm of the language and the metrics of the verse tradition, and the relationship between the two. We should note, though, that there are no metrical verse traditions in sign language poetry yet. Poets are still developing different methods of using the stress and timing of the language within sign language poetry. Nevertheless, rhythm still plays an important part in signed poetry.

In English poetry, much of the idea of meter comes from the fact that different words have different stresses on the sequence of their different syllables. However, in sign language poetry it is more rewarding to think about the duration of signs (and especially of their movement) and their repetition in relation to rhythm. Carol Padden and Tom Humphries (1988), in their description of the rhythmic chants seen in the folklore of Gallaudet students and other members of the American Deaf community show how one dominating pattern of repetition was 'one, two, one-two-three'. An example they give from a film made in the 1930s is:

> Boat, Boat, BoatBoatBoat
> Drink, Drink, DrinkDrinkDrink
> Fun, Fun, FunFunFun
> Enjoy, Enjoy, EnjoyEnjoyEnjoy

The Gallaudet University football chant or 'fight song' also shows this pattern, starting with:

> Hail to our mighty bisons!
> Snort, Snort, SnortSnortSnort

and continuing in much the same vein. We will see below, in the description of *The Cowboy*, how this repetition of signs serves to build a rhythm in the poem.

Rhythm in sign language poetry can be described in terms of the changes that occur within signs or in the transition between signs ('movements') and periods of no change ('holds'). Clayton Valli (1993), describing his own poems, wrote about the ways in which the rhythm of signed poetry may be created, and focused upon the movements or changes that occur within and between signs. Within a general idea that he termed 'stress', he singled out four categories of movements and holds that can be manipulated to create poetic rhythm:

1. Hold emphasis (long pause, subtle pause, strong stop)
2. Movement emphasis (long, short, alternating, repeated movement)
3. Movement size (enlarged movement path, shortened movement, reduced movement path, accelerating movement)
4. Movement duration (regular, slow or fast).

Blondel and Miller (2001) also consider the patterns of changes and movements in relation to rhythm. We will see later in discussion of performance of poetry how some of these elements are used as part of the recitation of the poem to create rhythm. However, for now we can consider repetitive elements in the text that lead to a noticeable rhythm in sign language poetry. Although not all sign language poems have a steady 'metronome beat', some do, and several of Clayton Valli's poems, such as *The Bridge*, *Cow & Rooster* and *Flash* contain signs that are timed to be of the same length to produce an obtrusively regular rhythm. This regular rhythm is aesthetically entertaining and serves to highlight the repetitive patterns of other elements, such as handshape or orientation of the hands. In these poems, the signs are also repeated a given number of times. For example, in *Cow & Rooster*, many of the signs are repeated three times each (creating the dominant overall pattern of the poem), with the third repetition ending in a longer hold (Valli, 1993).

Repetition of signs

Patterns within poems can be repeated at many levels, not only at the 'sub-word' or 'sub-sign' phonological level described above. A particular phrase could be repeated, or perhaps a single word (or sign) is used deliberately several times. Alternatively, the repetition could be of similar grammatical structures within a poem so that although the words (or signs) vary, they repeat the same grammatical pattern. At the largest level, whole structures of a certain pattern can be repeated. This is the repetition that leads to what we would normally term a stanza or a verse.

Repetition of individual signs

Repeating words might seem paradoxical in a language art-form where as much meaning as possible is squeezed into as few words as possible. However, repeating words in poetry adds extra significance to the meaning carried in the words alone. The effect of repeating the word is to bring into the foreground the sounds or parameters that make the words as well as the meaning of the words. Repetition is also an important part of building up rhythm in a poem. This repetition of words in English poetry is particularly obtrusive because English does not ordinarily repeat words. Using an ordinary word with extraordinary frequency in poetry will create an effect of obtrusive regularity. We can see this effect in Shakespeare's *Othello*, when in Act III, scene iii, Othello says:

> Farewell the tranquil mind! Farewell content!
> Farewell the plumed troop and the big wars
> That make ambition virtue! O, farewell!

Unlike everyday English, however, everyday non-poetic sign language has a general tradition of repeating signs. Sign languages, like many unwritten languages, may say the same thing in several ways (as we will see in our discussion of neologisms) and they may also simply say the same words (or sign the same signs) more than once (see Branson and Miller, 1998). Examples taken from some everyday conversational BSL include:

IT THEY-WATCH-IT IT. THEY ENJOY THEY WATCH-IT ENJOY IT
('They enjoyed watching it'),

THEY WORK WRITE MUST FINISH MUST THEY
('They must finish their written work')

The amount of repetition that occurs in everyday signing means that, in some ways, the general *lack* of repetition of signs in signed poetry is obtrusive. The tightness of construction and succinct expression that we see in many signed poems means that many things are *not* repeated in poetry that might be repeated in normal signing. This is particularly true when the signed poems are working in parallel with English versions of the poem, as occurred in some of Dorothy Miles' work.

The importance of repetition of signs in popular sign language art-signing can be seen in the ASL poem-story *Cowboy*. The version reproduced here was posted on the Internet in 1993 by Jean Boutcher, who explained that it was passed on manually by students at Gallaudet College, where she learnt it in 1948. It uses considerable repetition in order to create a strong rhythm and build up a powerful visual image of the cowboy's riding. The opening lines run as follows (words to the left and right of the central column represent signs that are made to the left and right of signing space):

	Cowboy	
	galloping	
	galloping	
	galloping	
	galloping	
	galloping	
mountain		mountain
mountain		mountain
mountain		mountain
	galloping	
	galloping	
	galloping	
	galloping	
gun-slapping-hip		gun-slapping-hip
gun-slapping-hip		gun-slapping-hip
gun-slapping-hip		gun-slapping-hip
	galloping	
	galloping	
tree-tree-tree-tree		tree-tree-tree-tree
	galloping	
	galloping	
tree-tree-tree-tree		tree-tree-tree-tree

```
                        galloping
                        galloping
    tree-tree-tree                          tree-tree-tree
                        galloping
                        galloping
    sand-sand                               sand-sand
```

Dorothy Miles' poems were built upon the blending of the two traditions of sign language art-sign and English poetry, so it is not surprising that her poems use repeated signs and sign phrases. Repetition can highlight a particular poetic image created through a newly coined productive sign (or neologism). The poetic neologism is presented once, then explained or elaborated upon, and then is repeated to allow the audience to enjoy it further. In the haiku *Spring* (p. 245), the neologism BREEZE-CARESS-TREE is repeated in the sequence BREEZE BREEZE-CARESS-TREE FLUTTERING-TREE BREEZE-CARESS-TREE ('breeze, / among singing trees') (see Fig. 5.6). In *Autumn* the neologism WHIRLING-LEAVES occurs twice in the sequence WHIRLING-LEAVES WIND WHIRLING-LEAVES ('Scattered leaves, a-whirl / in playful winds'). (See Chapter 10 for a more detailed discussion of signed haikus.) In *Exaltation* (p. 242), the neologism MOVE-SKY-ASIDE is repeated in IF LIKE TRY MOVE-SKY-ASIDE BLUE-IN-THE-SKY MOVE-SKY-ASIDE ('As if they sought to part the veil of blue'). In *The Ugly Duckling* (p. 249), the beautiful neologism that describes the duckling bending his neck down and seeing his reflection is used twice in the sequence BUT WHEN HE BEND-NECK-DOWN-TOWARDS-REFLECTION-OF-NECK-BENDING-UP SEE HIMSELF BEND-NECK-DOWN-TOWARDS-REFLECTION-OF-NECK-BENDING-UP   ('But when he bows and sees himself'). This neologism is such a treat that it occurs again in the final line of the poem WHEN BEND-NECK-DOWN-TOWARDS-REFLECTION-OF-NECK-BENDING-UP SEE SWAN ('And bowing, see a swan') (see Fig. 4.7).

Repeating the same sign in two different areas of signing space is a useful device to create balance and symmetry in the poem. We will consider the use of symmetry in poetry in more depth in the next chapter, but for now we will focus on the importance of repetition. In *The Staircase* (p. 246), the same sign is often articulated on the left- and the right-hand sides. There is important symbolism behind this, because much of this poem is about unity. Keeping both sides of signing space balanced shows the unity of the group climbing the staircase to reach their goal. As the people are introduced, walking through the forest, the signs ONE-PERSON, TWO-PEOPLE and MANY-PEOPLE are repeated on each hand.

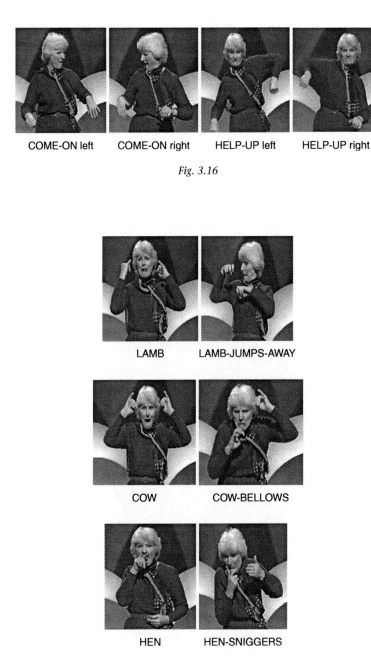

COME-ON left   COME-ON right   HELP-UP left   HELP-UP right

Fig. 3.16

LAMB   LAMB-JUMPS-AWAY

COW   COW-BELLOWS

HEN   HEN-SNIGGERS

Fig. 3.17

Later, the hero of the poem encourages his companions to climb the staircase with him. Once he is on the first step, he signs COME-ON! to the left-hand side of signing space and the next sign may be glossed as HELP-UP (a person) (Fig. 3.16). This is then repeated to the other side of signing space, creating symmetry in the poem. The next sign PERSON-CLIMBS-ONTO-STEP is then made to the left and also to the right.

Repeating a word serves to underline the message carried by or behind the word. This is often the case where strong emotions are concerned and is clearly the purpose behind Othello's repetition of 'farewell'. Geoffrey Leech (1969) sums this point up well when he comments that it 'may further suggest a suppressed intensity of feeling – an inspired feeling, as it were, for which there is no outlet but a repeated hammering at the confining walls of language' (p. 79). In *The Staircase* (p. 246), the wanderers at the foot of the staircase wonder about the possible dangers ahead. Each danger is prefaced with MAYBE DON'T-KNOW in order to increase the tension of expectation in the audience. After three of these possibilities are considered, the climax of this section is reached, as they turn to go. Repetition serves the same purpose when the hero helps them up the stairs. The repetition of signs such as ALL-OK, COME-ON! and HELP-UP occurs at increasingly higher steps. This shows that they all achieved their goal together, but repeating the signs shows that it was only achieved slowly through gradual steps.

Christmas List (p. 240) uses repetition at increasing speed, too, to create the climax before a resolution. When the children play snakes and ladders, the signs run CLIMB-LADDER ELBOW-PARTNER-left ELBOW-PARTNER-right CLIMB-LADDER ELBOW-PARTNER-left ELBOW-PART-NER-right, before the final sign RUN-UP-LADDER. When the children play word-games, the signs placing and moving the words from left to right are repeated at increasing speed before the climax of placing the words correctly and scratching the head, bemused. The repetition of the signs MINE, YOURS and OURS eventually blend into the sign PUNCH-UP and the climax of this frenzied repetition of flying fists is resolved into THROUGH-TIME AT-LAST CHRISTMAS HAPPEN AGAIN ('Till Christmas came again').

Repetition of grammatical structures

The repetition of grammatical structures is another common way of creating poetic effect. As with the repetition of single words and signs, the repetition of grammatical sequences raises our expectation of a climax of the sequence. This effect of repetition has developed from rhetoric or public speaking and is common in persuasive writing and speaking. In Act III Scene i of Shakespeare's *Merchant of Venice*, Shylock famously asks: 'If you prick us, do we not bleed? If you tickle us, do we not laugh? If you poison us, do we not die? And if you wrong us, shall we not seek revenge?'

In *The Ugly Duckling* (p. 249), the duckling does not know why the other animals in the farmyard are behaving oddly. The threefold repetition of structures is visible in the lines that in English run as:

> Lambs leap from him, cows low at him,
> Hens, staring beady-eyed,
> Snigger behind their wings.

The signs in one of the performances of this poem[5] may be glossed as follows (signs that are not manual, but all information comes from the facial expression and eyes, are in brackets):

LAMB
LAMB-STAND
(lamb-looks-in-horror)
LAMB-JUMPS-AWAY
COW
(cow-throws-back-head)
COW-BELLOWS
HE WHY HE
BIRD [i.e. hens] THEY LOOK
GROUP-OF-BIRDS
LOOK BEADY-EYE LOOK
HAND-OVER-MOUTH-IN-SHOCK
SNIGGER-BEHIND-RAISED-WING

In this section, the three animals are each introduced by name (in bold type in the gloss), then they are briefly described in some way and then they react to the duckling (Fig. 3.17). At the end of this section, the action returns to the duckling as he waddles his way quickly down to the pond.

In *The Staircase* (p. 246) there is also repetition of grammatical structures, as the people wander, lost in the forest. In English translation, this part runs as:

> . . . A figure creeps forward, peering ahead,
> Then comes another and another.
> They draw together in uncertainty, then in a line, they advance.

The BSL may be glossed as:

ONE-PERSON-MOVES-FORWARD ONE-PERSON-MOVES-FORWARD
TWO-PEOPLE-MOVE-FORWARD TWO-PEOPLE-MOVE-FORWARD
EIGHT-PEOPLE-MOVE-FORWARD
MANY-PEOPLE-MOVE-FORWARD

In this section, the repeated forward movement of the signs, each with increasing numbers of fingers, reaches its climax as the maximum number of fingers are open and the signs come to a sudden stop as the wanderers come to a wall. Later, as they stand at the foot of the staircase they wonder what dangers may lie ahead and again there is a pattern of threefold repetition of signs. In the English translation, the lines run:

> Perhaps the one who climbs will face a lion's claws.
> Or sink into the ground.
> Or meet a giant with a sword and lose his head.

The BSL lines may be glossed as:

PERHAPS DON'T-KNOW
CLIMB-UP
THERE HAVE THERE
LION
LION-STALK
LION'S-PAW-STRIKES
WHO-KNOWS OR
PERHAPS DON'T-KNOW
CLIMB-UP
SINK-INTO-GROUND
GROUND-RISES-ABOVE-HEAD
PERHAPS DON'T-KNOW PERHAPS
CLIMB-UP
THERE
GIANT
GIANT-STRETCHES
DRAW-SWORD STRIKE-WITH-SWORD
HEAD
HEAD-OFF
HEAD-HITS-GROUND
HEAD-ROLLS-AWAY

In this section, the signs PERHAPS and CLIMB-UP are repeated each time to set up the new possible danger. Using the same pattern as we saw in *The Ugly Duckling*, each danger is named before there are two more complex, productive signs that add more descriptive information and show what could befall the people as the lion attacks, the swamp engulfs and the giant draws his sword. The section concerning the giant contains a further sub-section, which continues the same grammatical pattern of naming the head and then showing what could happen to it when the giant strikes.

Stanzas in sign language poetry

At the largest level of repetition in a poem, the repetition can be of a certain number of lines or of a particular rhyming pattern (e.g., a poem may contain three eight-line stanzas, each with a rhyming pattern of ababcdcd). Songs that have several verses, each interspersed by a chorus or a refrain, are showing this sort of repetition. On the whole, stanzas are easy to identify in written poetry because there is a gap on the page between each one. In unwritten poetry, the 'gap' might be signalled in other ways, including a pause or a change in posture or a change in loudness or speed. Signed poems can mark stanzas with pauses and also with changes in posture and facial expression.

The refrain is one way to use repetitive effects to divide stanzas. We see this in Philip Green's powerful and painful – but ultimately liberating – BSL poem *No Regrets*, which tells of a Deaf man's experience of AIDS. Each stanza describes a different element of his experience of the disease, including problems of communicating with the hearing medical staff and the effects of the drugs used to treat him, but the refrain that separates the stanzas (identical each time it occurs) describes the effects of the three illnesses that he suffers from – KS (Karposi's sarcoma), CMV (cytomegalovirus) and PCP (pneumocystis carinii pneumonia). Repetition of exactly the same signs in the description of KS, CMV and PCP in the refrain allows the poet to remind the audience that whatever else might be happening in the rest of the poem, the reality of the three 'acronym' diseases is constantly there.

Dorothy Miles' poem *The BDA is …* has several verses with a refrain at the end of each one, and is a rare example of a poem by Dorothy that was for collaborative inclusion with an audience. As refrains are particularly common in collaborative poetry, where the audience actively participates in the poem, we should not be surprised to see a refrain here. Collaborative performance was not unusual in the art sign traditions before the development of signed language poetry traditions and still occurs in sign language chants.

Most sign language poems do not use refrains to divide them into stanzas, though. The stanzas are far more likely to be distinguished by repeated signs or phrases, which introduce the new theme of the new stanza. In *The Ugly Duckling* (p. 249), the stanzas are marked by the repetition of the phrase POOR BIRD at the start of each one, as well as by the clearly different themes. This same device is used in *To a Deaf Child* (p. 247), where the phrase WORD WORD-IN-HAND is used at the start of each of the three stanzas. *Language for the Eye* (p. 243) marks its stanzas by repeating phrases of a similar grammatical pattern at the end of each of its two stanzas – WORD BECOME PICTURE IN THIS LANGUAGE FOR EYE and WORD BECOME ACTION IN THIS LANGUAGE FROM HEART.

In other sign language poems the stanzas are only identified by their changing themes. The signed haiku quartet of the *Seasons* (p. 245), for example, is clearly divided into four stanzas by the separate season theme of each one. (In the performance record that we have of the *Seasons* quartet, the four haiku verses are performed separately, with several other poems between each haiku. This is further evidence that the overall poem *Seasons* can be split at those boundaries.) *Christmas Magic* (p. 241) has three stanzas – the first setting the scene for the poet's Christmas memories, the second describing what she did as a child, and the third bringing us back to the present time. This pattern of theme-changing is also seen in *Christmas List* (p. 240), where the first stanza describes how the children asked for their presents, the second stanza describes the presents they asked for and the ones they got, and the final stanza comes back to the present day to consider the presents the poet would ask for now. This threefold division of poems is very common, and threefold repetition of many elements in sign language poems is a common feature.

Having considered what might be termed the 'internal structure' of the poem, created by the choice of signs in the poem, we will now turn to an area that is often considered to be part of the 'external structure' of sign language poetry. This feature of sign language poetry (described by Klima and Bellugi, 1979) looks at the overall layout of the selected signs in a poem within the signing space and is concerned in part with the spatial device of symmetry.

4
Symmetry and Balance

Symmetry is the idea that something has an equal and opposite counterpart. Increased use of symmetrical signing and signing balanced in opposing areas of space is another way that unusual language regularity brings the language to the foreground in a sign language poem. In any sign language, some signs use a single hand in their citation form and other signs use two hands in their citation form, Additionally, some of the two-handed signs are symmetrical (each hand having the same handshape and movement and being articulated in symmetrically opposing locations) and some not symmetrical (especially where the two hands have different handshapes). Everyday signing uses a random mixture of one-handed and two-handed signs, symmetrical or not, but poets can deliberately select a sequence consisting entirely of two-handed signs, or even articulate two one-handed signs at the same time, to create an aesthetic effect. It is also possible for the poet to select only one-handed signs. In sign language poetry, sequences of one-handed signs are especially notable and meaningful precisely because most poems attempt to create balance and symmetry through the use of two hands. All of this allows the sign language poem to make use of symmetry and balance. The Italian Sign Language linguists Tommaso Russo and Elena Pizzuto worked with the Deaf poet Rosaria Giuranna to compare the proportion of two-handed symmetrical signs used in sign language poetry and non-poetic language used in lectures. In their data, they found that 20 per cent of signs in the lectures were two-handed symmetrical signs, compared to 50 per cent of the signs in the poems, confirming that symmetry is indeed a significant feature of poetic sign language.

Symmetry appeals to our collective cultural consciousness, especially vertical (left–right) symmetry. Research has shown that people find symmetric faces more attractive than less symmetric faces, and it is generally understood that wherever human beings find asymmetry, they try to make it more symmetric, in order to produce something more orderly and comfortable and bring it closer to 'perfection'. It should be no surprise, then, that the random asymmetry that we might find in everyday signing should be minimised in sign language poetry, creating linguistic balance and harmony.

There are many sorts of symmetry but we will consider the three most relevant to sign language poetry: vertical, horizontal and front–back. Vertical symmetry is left–right symmetry. This symmetry is seen in human bodies, if we imagine a line down the middle, where the left-hand side of our bodies looks remarkably like the right-hand side, with the axis of symmetry running vertically down the middle of the body. Chris McManus (2002) has pointed out that, 'Because the world is full of vertical symmetries – not only the face, but also the arms and legs in people, the bodies of many other animals, and flowers and trees – it is hardly surprising that we are good at recognising vertical symmetry quickly, efficiently and automatically' (p. 352). (Vertical symmetry may be seen in the signs in Fig. 4.1.) Horizontal symmetry is much less common in nature and it occurs when the top half of a shape has an equal and opposite counterpart in the bottom half. If the horizontal axis were drawn at our waist we would find that the human top half looks nothing like the human bottom half, but when we see something reflected in water, we are seeing horizontal symmetry in action. (Horizontal symmetry may be seen in the signs in Fig. 4.2 and in the first sign in Fig. 12.1.) There is also front–back symmetry, but that, too, is not common in nature, and is not seen in our bodies – we do not look the same from the front and the back. (Front–back symmetry may be seen in the signs in Fig. 4.15.)

To appreciate the importance of symmetry in sign language poetry, we need to make a brief diversion into the ways that languages deal with symmetry. In order for symmetry to function, a person first needs to understand concepts such as left and right, top and bottom and front and back. Vertical symmetry, where the person needs to know about 'left' and 'right', presents a real problem for spoken languages. All spoken languages that have ever been documented have had words to *refer* to left and right, yet no spoken language can *describe* left and right because sound in speech is heard in a continuous stream that gives no physical clue to left and right. Despite this, speakers have learned to talk about their left and their right because they were *shown* it. As soon as we have been shown what is left and right, we can use spoken language to talk about it. Of all the world's languages, only sign languages can directly describe and refer to left and right because they show symbols

WINTER   CONTRAST   STRONG

Fig. 4.1

HARD   TALK

Fig. 4.2

SPRING   SUNSHINE   RIPPLED-WATER

Fig. 4.3

LIGHT   BUT   DARK

SKY   READY   CAT'S-WHISKERS

Fig. 4.4

in three dimensions to talk about the concepts. The unique ability of sign languages to show left and right, and to show symmetry itself while describing, is barely noticed in everyday language, yet the potential that this holds for sign language poetry is enormous.

Because our culture sees a strong relationship between symmetry and perfection (as we see, e.g., in classical architecture), we might expect poetry to use symmetry to create beauty and some sort of 'language perfection'. Written poetry may attempt to create some sort of symmetry as it can exist in two dimensions. However, apart from some written poems, especially the highly visual 'concrete' poems (which we will discuss in more depth in Chapter 7), symmetry is a short – and ultimately blind – alley in written and spoken poetry because spoken language has no inherent symmetry. In signed poetry, however, symmetry can become a priority. Although vertical (left–right) symmetry is the most common symmetrical device in signed poetry, front-to-back, horizontal (top–bottom) and diagonal symmetry also occur in signed poems.

There are different ways of creating symmetries in signed poetry. Firstly, the signs chosen may be two-handed signs, in which the handshapes, locations and movements of the two hands are mirror-images of each other. These signs may be established signs or newly created neologisms. Examples of established signs like this include (in both ASL and BSL) WINTER, CONTRAST and STRONG. These examples are all taken from Dorothy Miles' poems where symmetry is deliberately created, but these two-handed symmetrical signs are already common in everyday sign language vocabularies (Fig. 4.1).

We should note that two-handed signs are most commonly symmetrical across the vertical axis. The examples listed above are vertically symmetrical, with the hands being left–right mirror images of each other. There are signs that are symmetrical about the horizontal (top–bottom) axis – for example, the ASL signs HARD and MAKE, and the BSL signs DAMAGE, TALK and WORK (all used in Dorothy's poems) – but there are far fewer of them. There are even fewer established signs that are front–back symmetrical. This is simply because our bodies – and importantly the hands and arms needed to produce signs – are arranged symmetrically about the vertical axis. This physical arrangement of our bodies is also the reason why poetic neologisms using single two-handed signs across the horizontal axis are especially notable (Fig. 4.2).

Another way of creating symmetry in sign languages is to place signs in opposing areas of space. Klima and Bellugi (1979) described this use of signs as being part of the 'external structure' of a signed poem. This symmetry may be simultaneous, placing two one-handed signs simultaneously in symmetrically opposing areas, or it may be sequential, so the poem may place signs in one area and place the next signs in the symmetrically opposite area. Simultaneous creations of symmetry with two one-handed signs are not very common, even in signed poetry, and the sequential creation of symmetry by placing signs in one area and then in an opposing area is far more common. This latter sort of symmetry occurs in the haiku *Seasons* quartet (p. 245). In *Spring*, the first signs, SPRING and SUNSHINE, are made at the top left of signing space and the final signs FLUTTERING-ON-FLAT-SURFACE ON DANCE ON WATER RIPPLED-WATER ('to dance on rippled water') are made at the bottom right of signing space (Fig. 4.3).

A certain balance can be maintained in signed poems even when one of the hands is not actively involved in signing anything new. One hand (usually the non-dominant hand, but not always) holds the final part of the sign while the other hand (usually the dominant hand, but again not always) articulates a new sign. This maintenance of a sign on the non-dominant hand while the dominant hand signs something new is not exceptional in everyday signing. It is a way to create units of meaning that are more closely related than signs that are articulated in simple sequences. However, it is used far more often in poetry, allowing the poet to keep both hands in the poetic frame and maintain the balanced use of space, even if the signs are not symmetrical. On top of this aesthetic discipline of keeping balance, maintaining the presence of the non-dominant hand can increase the effectiveness of the visual images that are being created. This retention of the non-dominant hand is extremely common and can be seen in almost any sign language poem.

Vertical symmetry

The most common use of symmetry in poetry occurs across the vertical axis, making a left–right balance in space. Looking at Dorothy Miles' poem *The Cat* (performed in both BSL and ASL), we can see the extent of use of two-handed signs to create left–right symmetry. The ASL poem may be glossed with 49 signs, of which only 11 are one-handed. The BSL version of this poem may also be glossed with 49 signs, of which only 10 are one-handed. The BSL poem is helped by the fact that the BSL sign DOG used here is a symmetrical two-handed sign. The sign BUT in BSL is normally one-handed but in this poem for one of the instances of BUT the non-dominant hand takes on the same handshape as the dominant hand, to maintain the balance of the signs.

The Cat (p. 240) is also interesting in our discussion of symmetry because it contains some signs that are not just vertically symmetrical but also cross the axis of symmetry. There are relatively few signs in the vocabulary that are made with the hands crossing over the central vertical axis, so the selection of several of these for the poem is very noticeable. The signs LIGHT and DARK (or NIGHT) are used when describing the cat's eyes ('in the light / her eyes wink and blink / but at night / they open as wide as the sky') and both these signs use both hands which cross the vertical axis in symmetrical opposition. The ASL sign BUT also uses two 'G' hands crossed over. In the ASL poem, the sign READY is made with the two hands, each with an 'R' handshape, crossed over in a similar, marked way. These signs set the precedent within the poem by crossing the hands, and the productive signs follow the same pattern. The sign SKY does not necessarily cross over the vertical axis of symmetry, but here the hands do start crossed over before they spread apart to sketch out the width of the sky. In both the BSL and ASL poems there is also a productive sign that essentially means CAT'S-WHISKERS. The established sign WHISKERS is a two-handed symmetrical sign, made by sketching out the length of each whisker, using an 'F' handshape at the cheeks (or '5' for BSL), but the hands do not cross the axis of symmetry. In the productive sign CAT'S-WHISKERS the hands both have the '5' handshape (each finger representing a whisker) and they do cross over the axis of symmetry at the chin (Fig. 4.4).

On top of this careful symmetry, there is further retention of both hands so that, even when a one-handed sign is articulated on the dominant hand, the non-dominant hand is still maintained in some way. In the BSL version of *The Cat*, the signs HE, WINK, BUT, WHEN, SOFT and COME-BY are all one-handed. However, as we can see in the glosses below, the poem creates the impression of two-handed balance by holding the lingering elements of the previous two-handed sign on the non-dominant hand during articulation of the one-handed sign before both hands make the next two-handed sign. (In this gloss, the meaning of the two hands is shown on separate lines. The 'nd' stands for 'non-dominant', 'd' stands for 'dominant', and the line after 'nd' shows that the non-dominant hand is still holding the form from the previous two-handed sign.)

d CAT HE WITH ...
nd CAT___ WITH [Fig. 4.5]

d CLAWS-OUT WHEN DOG COME-BY ...
nd CLAWS-OUT _____ DOG _____ [Fig. 4.6]

Proform signs (see Chapter 1) that are used to represent the actions of numbers of individuals can also be used to create symmetry. If there is an even number of individuals, half of them can be shown on each hand. This occurs in *The Staircase*, creating symmetry in the opening lines as the people wander, lost, through the forest. The English lines run:

> A dark forest. A figure creeps forward, peering ahead,
> Then comes another and another.
> They draw together in uncertainty, then in a line,
> They advance.

This may be glossed in BSL as follows (subscripts $_{c, L}$ and $_R$ refer to centre, left and right for the locations of the signs):

$FOREST_R\ DARK_C$
$PEOPLE_C\ HAVE_C$
ONE-PERSON-MOVES-FORWARD$_R$ ONE-PERSON-MOVES-FORWARD$_L$
TWO-PEOPLE-MOVE-FORWARD$_R$ TWO-PEOPLE-MOVE-FORWARD$_L$
EIGHT-PEOPLE-(2x4)-MOVE-FORWARD$_C$
MANY-PEOPLE-(2x5)-MOVE-FORWARD$_C$

We can see here that the signs are placed symmetrically across the central vertical axis. As the numbers in the group grow, there is initially some asymmetry as one of the handshapes changes to reflect the increased number, but symmetry is restored each time as the numbers shown on each hand balance out. This pattern of asymmetry followed by symmetry occurs again in the poem when the hero helps the group up the stairs. People are encouraged up the step on one side of space and then on the other so that both sides are balanced again. This maintenance of symmetry despite occasional shifts to asymmetry is an important part of the poem, which uses 'unity in change' as a central theme.

A slightly different way of using space to create vertical symmetry in signed poetry is to move the entire body to the left and right while signing. This is the device that Dorothy uses so effectively in *Walking Down the Street*. The poem contains two characters (one hearing and one Deaf) and one is placed on the left of signing space and the other is placed on the right. They address each other across the central vertical axis of symmetry (this may be seen in Fig. 9.5, as we discuss this poem in more depth in Chapter 9). Normally we would expect a signer to show this relationship by placing the hands whose signs represent the

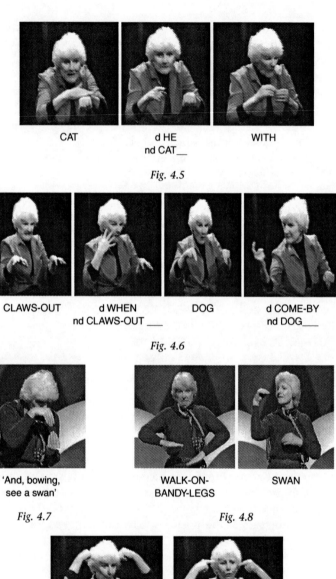

CAT d HE WITH
nd CAT___

Fig. 4.5

CLAWS-OUT d WHEN DOG d COME-BY
nd CLAWS-OUT ___ nd DOG___

Fig. 4.6

'And, bowing, WALK-ON- SWAN
see a swan' BANDY-LEGS

Fig. 4.7 *Fig. 4.8*

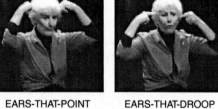

EARS-THAT-POINT EARS-THAT-DROOP

Fig. 4.9

characters to the left or right of the body, but this poem places the *entire body* to the left or right of the central axis. Making such a gross shift across the axis serves to intensify the effect of the symmetry, emphasising how similar the two women are, and also how different they are – indeed, perhaps they are opposites.

Horizontal symmetry

Horizontal symmetry (top–bottom symmetry) may be created by using symmetrical signs or by symmetrical use of signing space. This type of symmetry is used in Dorothy's poem *The Ugly Duckling* (p. 249), through images reflected in water. The idea of reflection could equally as well be portrayed in an English-language poem with words that imply 'reflection', but only a sign language poem can directly *show* reflection by using the horizontal axis of symmetry. In this poem, horizontal symmetry occurs as the non-dominant hand is placed to produce a reflection of the sign on the dominant hand, showing the duckling's head as it bends towards the water. The English translation of the final line runs, 'And bowing, see a swan.' The English gives little direct clue to the symmetry created in the final sign – the best it can do is to imply that there is a reflection to be seen in the water. In the symmetrical sign in the BSL poem, the arm of the dominant hand represents the duckling's neck, and the hand itself represents his head. The axis of symmetry here is at the fingertips, as the non-dominant hand and arm reflect the dominant hand exactly underneath it (Fig. 4.7).

Further examples of symmetry about the horizontal axis can be seen in two signs that differ only in their orientation about this axis. In *The Ugly Duckling*, the sign WALK-ON-BANDY-LEGS is almost exactly the horizontal inverse of the sign SWAN (Fig. 4.8). In Dorothy's BSL poem *Our Dumb Friends* (p. 244), the signs EARS-THAT-POINT and EARS-THAT-DROOP are identical in handshape, start-location and movement but the first sign moves upwards and the second sign moves downwards, making them mirror images of each other (Fig. 4.9).

The ASL haiku *Winter* (p. 245) uses both the vertical and horizontal axes of symmetry, to show ideas of contrast and difference. It uses two main methods of creating symmetry – two-handed symmetrical signs and placement of signs in opposite areas of the signing space. The sign WINTER is a two-handed sign, symmetrical across the vertical axis, as is the sign CONTRAST. The one-handed signs BLACK and WHITE are made on separate hands: BLACK on the dominant hand, which is then held to the far side of the dominant side's signing space and WHITE on the non-dominant hand, which is then held on the far side of the non-dominant side's signing space (Fig. 4.10). The reference to a bare tree is placed carefully on one side of the vertical axis, and the tips of the fingers emphasise the height of the tree. This is followed by reference to the covered ground, which is placed low down on the other side of the axis to emphasise the contrast in elevation. The contrasts here are thus shown across both the horizontal and the vertical axes. In the final few signs HARD ICE; SOFT WHITE-SNOW-FALLS; SNOW-ON-GROUND; BIRTH IN DEATH ('hard ice, / soft snow; birth in death') we see the horizontal axis again in signs that contrast through the orientation of the palms, as they shift repeatedly between facing up and facing down. The sequence is: sideways (HARD), down (ICE), up (SOFT), sideways (WHITE) down (SNOW-FALLS), down (SNOW-ON-GROUND), up (BIRTH) down (IN) and, finally, both up and down (DEATH) (Fig. 4.11).

In the first line of the haiku *Summer* ('Green depths and green heights'), DEPTHS is signed using two hands in the lower part of signing space. At the end of the sign, the non-dominant hand remains in place, while the dominant hand articulates GREEN and HEIGHTS in the upper part of signing space. Retaining the non-dominant hand has three important poetic uses here: it keeps both hands in use so the poem remains balanced; it allows the two hands to create simultaneous signs across the horizontal axis of symmetry; and it allows the poem to show the clear contrast between the depths and the heights. Retaining the non-dominant hand after a two-handed sign while a sign is made on the dominant hand occurs three times in this haiku, so that after the initial one-handed sign GREEN, both hands are present throughout the rest of the poem (Fig. 4.12).

The same use of the non-dominant hand occurs in *Spring*, so that after the initial one-handed sign SUNSHINE, the non-dominant hand is always present, and in *Winter*, where both hands are present throughout. Given that *Autumn* is already entirely two-handed, this tactic of retaining the non-dominant hand makes the entire haiku quartet (barring two initial signs) a balanced, two-handed enterprise. This is no mean feat, and permanent presence of the second hand is extremely obtrusive. It also makes for lovely poetry.

Front–back symmetry

In Dorothy's poem *Language for the Eye* (performed in both BSL and ASL) (p. 243), proforms on each hand allow the poem to use symmetry in the front–back plane. The English lines in the second stanza run 'and people meet and part'. In the ASL and BSL poems, two one-person proforms

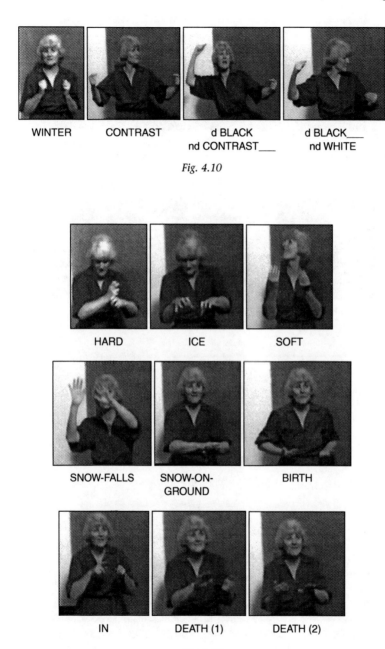

WINTER CONTRAST d BLACK
nd CONTRAST___

d BLACK___
nd WHITE

Fig. 4.10

HARD ICE SOFT

SNOW-FALLS SNOW-ON-
GROUND

BIRTH

IN DEATH (1) DEATH (2)

Fig. 4.11

DEPTHS	d GREEN nd __DEPTHS	d HEIGHTS nd __DEPTHS

Fig. 4.12

PEOPLE-MEET	PERSON- LEAVES	PERSON- RETURNS	PEOPLE-SIDE- BY-SIDE

Fig. 4.13

COMMUNICATE

Fig. 4.14

SAY-YES-TO- EACH-OTHER	LOOK-PAST- EACH-OTHER	SEND-MESSAGES- TO-EACH- OTHER'S-MINDS	SAY-YES-TO EACH-OTHER'S- MINDS

Fig. 4.15

are used, one on each hand, symmetrical across the central vertical axis to show the two people. The right-hand sign moves leftward towards the axis and the left-hand sign moves rightward towards the axis until the hands meet at the central axis point to make the sign glossed as MEET. However, the sign PART is not the reverse of this movement, as we might expect. Instead, one proform moves away from the body and one moves towards the body, along a different axis of symmetry. At the end of the poem, there are two extra signs that have no equivalent in the English poem: PERSON-RETURNS-TO-PERSON-WAITING and TWO-PEOPLE-SIDE-BY-SIDE (looking forward). In these signs, the proforms that had parted along the new front–back axis come together again and the two people are reunited, with the proforms returning to the original vertical axis to stand symmetrically side-by-side (Fig. 4.13).

Another poem that makes great use of the front–back symmetry is Dorothy's ASL poem *Total Communication* (p. 248). This poem refers to the attempt of lovers to communicate. Although the lovers could be side-by-side, here the frustrated lover is addressing her partner face-to-face and, so, across the front–back axis of symmetry. This is driven symbolically by the signed idea of communication. For Deaf people, communication is most comfortable when signers face each other straight on; watching someone signing from the side is much less satisfactory. The sign COMMUNICATE is a two-handed symmetrical sign, with the hands arranged around the vertical axis, but – importantly – the movement of the two hands is across the front-to-back axis (Fig. 4.14).

As this poem is about the desire for ideal communication, the most appropriate symbolic axis of symmetry is front-to-back. For physical comfort, many of the signs are not placed exactly front to back (our joints do not work best at these angles) but the general impression is of reference to the space in front of the signer, rather than to the side. Also, in the initial part of the poem, when communication is not going well, the signs are less face-on. As the poem reaches its successful climax with the achievement of full communication, the signs are more face-on.

There are pairs of signs in this poem which are essentially front–back mirror images of each other, including LEARN and EXPERIENCE, YOU and I, and YOUR and MY, and are important signs for this pattern of symmetry. The sign REVERSE (meaning something like 'over to you') turns around this axis and the very creative neologisms MY-LIFE-TRANSFERRED-TO-YOU and NOTHING-THERE are made with a twist around the front–back axis. The simultaneous symmetrical signs that work across this axis here are important for the poem, because they highlight the opposition in a poetically obtrusive way as they show the reciprocal nature of attempts to communicate. This is seen with signs such as:

> SEE-EACH-OTHER, LOCK-HORNS-AND-STRUGGLE (see Fig. 3.3), SAY-YES-TO-EACH-OTHER, LOOK-PAST-EACH-OTHER, SEND-MESSAGES-TO-EACH-OTHER'S-MINDS and
> SAY-YES-TO-EACH-OTHER'S-MINDS (Fig. 4.15)

This review of symmetry and balance in poetry has shown how poets can use several devices to create symmetry. Existing, established symmetrical signs can be selected, or new signs may be created and used to present symmetrical signs in space. This creation of new signs is not only for the purpose of symmetry, and we will now look in detail at the poetic use of creative signs.

5
Neologisms

Neologism – the creation of new words – can be used for poetic effect in many ways, bringing the language to the foreground because the poet has produced a form that is not already a part of the language. The creative use of sign language to produce new signs has also been called poetic 'wit', and is related to the way that signers can produce strong visual imagery by creative treatment of the visual form of the signs.

Words are familiar and predictable and we scarcely notice them in everyday language, except for the overall message that groups of them convey. New words, however, make us sit up and take notice. Newly created words in a poem are unfamiliar, and so unpredictable that we have to think carefully about them and why the poet made them in that way. The poet wants the audience to focus on the language in the poem, and using a new word is a good way to get it noticed. Although all speakers or signers use their knowledge of the formational rules of the language to create occasional new words when necessary, the poet's creativity has been to apply word-making rules with unusual frequency, to create words that no one else has thought to create, perhaps with a new meaning that no one has thought of. There are, essentially, two different ways of making new words: making up the word from existing elements in the language, or borrowing a word from another language. Both these strategies occur in sign language poetry.

Visually motivated neologisms

Poets in the English language make up new words in their poems. The Irish writer James Joyce was a great creator of neologisms, and his works such as *Finnegans Wake* are full of them. His words are often made by blending elements of other words in new ways. Neologisms such as *museyroom* and *grasshoper* have recognisable elements in them ('muse', 'room', 'grass' and 'hope') but the reader's task is to work out, based on the sounds of the words, what the new word might mean. For example, the museyroom could be a room in a museum where a person can take time to muse on the exhibits. Another famous example of neologistic creativity occurs in Lewis Carroll's poem *Jabberwocky* (which has also been performed in ASL). The poem's opening lines run as follows:

> 'Twas brillig, and the slithy toves
> Did gyre and gymble in the wabe:
> All mimsy were the borogroves
> And the mome wraths outgrabe.

Unlike Joyce's new words, these do not have recognisable basic meaning elements, but they are all, nevertheless, believable words in English. They obey the word-formation rules of the language and they clearly use English grammar, such as adding an -s to make a plural. It's not fully clear what *toves* and *borogroves* are (although we know that they must be 'things' because these words behave like nouns) nor exactly what *slithy* and *mimsy* mean (even though from the context we can guess that they are adjectives). But we do have a feeling from the sounds of the words that slithy toves were more sinister than the more friendly-sounding mimsy borogroves.

Creating new signs is an important part of signed poetry. Poets can modify an existing sign in order to make it fit the scheme of the poem (equivalent to Joyce's *museyroom*), or they can produce totally new signs (more like *borogroves*). However, sign neologisms are frequently much clearer in their meaning than the words in *Finnegans Wake* or *Jabberwocky*. This is because sign languages are generally far more productive than spoken languages in everyday use. They can afford to be because the signs' visual motivation gives them meaning that signers can immediately understand in the context. Russo, Giuranna and Pizzuto (2001), working with Italian Sign Language (LIS), compared the proportion of signs showing 'dynamic iconicity' (which are essentially what we are terming neologisms here) in non-poetic lectures and in poems. They found that the productive, 'dynamically iconic' neologisms did occur reasonably frequently in a normal, non-poetic lecture – accounting for 13 per cent of the signs. However, they found that these signs occurred in 53 per cent of all the signs in the LIS poetry that they analysed.

We will consider the signs made by modifying an existing sign first. In the ASL poem *Exaltation* (p. 242), the sign BLUE is placed high above the head and swept across the signing space to mean BLUE-SKY. The citation form of the ASL sign BLUE is made at shoulder-height and does not move through signing space. The sign in *Exaltation* is still basically the sign BLUE, but it has been altered to give it additional meaning. This new sign breaks the normal formational rules in order to place the idea of 'blueness' across the whole of the wide sky. It also allows it to 'rhyme' with the earlier signs GREEN and HIGH, which have already been placed in the same area of signing space in the poem (and, in fact, placing GREEN and HIGH in this location is also unusual). This poem also uses a neologism that might be glossed as NOTICE-TREE. The ASL sign NOTICE is usually made in neutral space, and is directed towards the area of the thing that is being noticed. Normally, to sign the idea of noticing a tree, a signer would first sign TREE and then direct the sign NOTICE towards that location. In the neologism, however, the 'X' handshape of the sign NOTICE is articulated against the sign TREE. Instead of two signs, NOTICE TREE, the creative sign becomes a single sign NOTICE-TREE (Fig. 5.1).

In *Total Communication* (p. 248), the sign EXPERIENCE is made at head-height, in order to show that the experience is a mental experience, rather than any physical or practical one. Again, this change of location of an existing sign to create a slightly different variant makes good poetic sense. The sign SAY-YES-TO-EACH-OTHER'S-MINDS in this poem is also made above the head. Normally the sign SAY-YES-TO-EACH-OTHER is placed lower down at chin- or chest-level, but raising it well above head-level shows that this nodding comes specifically from understanding each other's thoughts (see Fig. 4.15). In Dorothy's BSL poem *Christmas Magic* (p. 241), the sign GOOD has an unusual movement away from the body, meaning 'being good through a period of time' (see Fig. 3.6). This modification of the sign not only gives the original sign a new, extra meaning but also allows it to 'rhyme' with other signs that have a similar movement in the poem such as STOCKING, SANTA'S-SLEIGH and RUN-DOWNSTAIRS (see Fig. 3.12). In the haiku *Winter* (p. 245), the sign TREE has been modified to give it a slightly different handshape, which adds extra meaning. The idea to be conveyed is one of a 'bare tree'. In the ASL poem, Dorothy first signs BARE, which is made by the dominant hand with an 'open 8' handshape moving across the back of the non-dominant hand. This dominant hand is then placed with the orientation, movement and location of the sign TREE but the 'open 8' handshape is retained, rather than the '5' handshape that is usual in the sign TREE. Making the sign TREE with the handshape that was used to make the sign BARE has created the new sign BARE-TREE (Fig. 5.2).

NOTICE-TREE

Fig. 5.1

BARE　　　　　BARE-TREE

Fig. 5.2

REACH-UP　　　TOUCH　　　SKY

PART-BLUE-SKY　LIGHT-SHINE-
　　　　　　　　FROM-SKY

Fig. 5.3

LIGHTS-GLIMMERING

Fig. 5.4

Sometimes, making new signs involves bending the rules of the language. In *Exaltation* (p. 242), many of the signs are placed much higher than we would expect, drawing our attention to the greater metaphorical meaning they carry in this poem. The signs that are placed high up are all related to the way that the trees on the skyline appear to be reaching up to heaven. In order to reflect the unusual idea that the trees can actually touch the sky, the signs REACH-UP TOUCH SKY, PART-BLUE-SKY and LIGHT-SHINE-FROM-SKY (or from HEAVEN) are all made far higher than would normally be expected (Fig. 5.3).

In *The Staircase* (p. 246), several signs are made outside the signing space. In this poem, the characters come across an enormous staircase, the top of which is barely visible. This is signed by placing the top of the stairs – and the glimmering lights at the top – well outside the accepted upper limit of the signing space. When Dorothy performs this poem, she needs to stretch to make the signs. This deviant use of space adds extra significance to the ideas of a tall staircase and distant lights. This is meaningful at a fairly literal level – signs far outside normal signing space must represent something very far away indeed. However, there is also a metaphorical meaning to this deviant use of space. We know that the staircase is being used to represent a series of apparently insurmountable hurdles to members of the British Deaf community who wanted a university education in the mid-1980s, and the lights are the tantalising glimpse of the apparently unattainable rewards. Placing these signs so far away intensifies the feelings of awe at the challenge and the longing for the rewards (Fig. 5.4).

The location of many signs in *The BDA is* ... (p. 240) is also deviant. This obtrusively irregular use of space is due to the performance element of the poem and the importance of the live audience. The poem was performed to a very large audience, creating signs that were irregularly and obtrusively large. Their movements were much bigger than would occur in conversational signing, and because of this their location was unusually far from the signer. Internal movements of signs such as WORK and CAN'T were much larger than normal. The signs FIGHT, WELL (meaning 'done well') and TOGETHER were located unusually far in the front of the signing space (Fig. 5.5). Another clear example of a change in size and location of the signs to encompass the audience is seen in the final chorus: 'The BDA is you and me'. Here, 'BDA' was fingerspelled b-d-a. Normally BSL fingerspelling is made at the midriff, close to the body, with the two hands close to each other. However, in this performance, the letters were spelled out with the arms fully outstretched towards the audience (Fig. 5.5). Dorothy then leaned far

WELL   TOGETHER

'The BDA' (using letters -b-, -d- and -a-)

Fig. 5.5

TREE-CARESSED-   TREE-CARESSED-   TREE-CARESSED-
BY-FIRELIGHT   BY-BREEZE   BY-BREEZE
(Christmas Magic)   (Exaltation)   (Spring)

Fig. 5.6

forward to create the sign YOU that was as wide as possible, in order to include as many people in the audience as possible. Even ME was made with a very large movement towards the chest. The end result of this large signing was to involve the poem's audience directly in the poem. In all these examples above, we can see that the poet has tinkered with an original sign to produce a new form of the old sign. The original signs are still recognisable in their new forms but some extra meaning has been added for a poetic reason. However, it is also possible to create entirely new signs through the productive process, and these are far more common in sign language poetry.

We saw in Chapter 1 that signs can be divided into two broad groups: 'frozen' (or 'established') and 'productive'. Frozen signs are conventionalised signs that are established and recognised as items within the language's vocabulary. Productive signs (also known as 'classifier signs') can be used at any time to create entirely new signs, using what Sarah Taub (2001) has called 'a set of iconic building blocks for the description of physical objects, movements and locations' (p. 34). She goes on to explain that each productive sign:

> contains a handshape that identifies some class of entities, plus movements, locations and orientations that may further describe the entity's appearance or else its path or location in space. Signers can freely create new signs from this set to describe a huge variety of different situations. (p. 34)

In explaining the difference between frozen and productive signs, she says:

> Frozen signs tend to represent a whole category, rather than a specific referent. ... [Productive signs] are *less* specific than frozen signs in that they identify larger classes of referents (e.g. *long, thin objects* rather than *pens* or *logs*), but *more* specific in that they show what an individual of that type is doing in a particular situation. (p. 35, original emphasis)

Sarah Taub's explanation of frozen and productive signs is part of her general description of sign languages in everyday use. All signers use productive signing in many language styles for many functions, but Clayton Valli (1993) has highlighted the special use of productivity in signed poetry. Firstly (as we will see later in discussion of ambiguity) in everyday language a frozen sign usually identifies the referent before the productive sign is used, but in poetry the productive sign can be used without any identifying frozen sign. Secondly, in everyday signing, invented signs need to be 'approved' by the signing community through regular use, while in poetry the poet can invent the signs and not rely on community approval before using them. We should note that the poet's inventions are usually considerably more creative than those in everyday signing, and the poet will often create the sign so that it has specific formational characteristics that add to the language patterns in the poem. Although these signs may 'bend' the rules a little for the sake of the poem, they are all governed by the rules of the language. In sign poetry there is no room for gesture or pantomime; new signs may be new, but they are still signs.

Productive signs may describe the appearance of objects that have been identified using frozen signs, or they may show the way the people acted on those objects or reacted to the objects or events. This is an important element of sign language and can be summarised by the phrases 'Establish then Elaborate' or 'Tell then Show'. Frozen signs are used for establishing and telling. The art in sign language poems comes from the creation of productive signs to do the elaborating and showing in a novel way.

One of Dorothy's neologisms occurs, with very little variation, in at least three different poems. This creative sign basically means TREE-CARESSED-BY-(SOMETHING) and is made with the non-dominant hand signing the frozen, established sign TREE and the dominant hand in a '5' handshape gently fluttering and stroking the 'tree'. It is a beautiful and highly visual sign, and well worth recycling in several poems. In *Christmas Magic* it means TREE-CARESSED-BY-FIRELIGHT, and in the context of both *Spring* and *Exaltation*, the sign means TREE-CARESSED-BY-BREEZE (Fig. 5.6).

Creation of these new signs is such an important part of signed poetry that almost any poem will contain examples of neologisms, but we will limit ourselves to three of Dorothy Miles' poems: *Christmas List* (BSL), *Our Dumb Friends* (ASL and BSL) and *Ugly Duckling* (BSL). In *Christmas List* (p. 240), the children's choice of 'Useless Presents' in the poem is told with a combination of frozen and productive signs. The frozen signs tell us what they chose, and productive signs – created with the poet's skills – tell us more about them. We are already familiar with the version of the poem (the English subtitles accompanying a televised BSL performance) whose lines relate most closely to the frozen signs in the poem, and run as follows:

We, of course were children, so we asked for silly pets
All kinds of cake and chocolates and candy cigarettes
And cannon, and tin soldiers, and cut-out dolls, and swords.
And games like Snakes and Ladders, and games you play with words.

These lines may be seen in the gloss below (signs in parenthesis are entirely non-manual), where we can see that the productive signs have no simple equivalence in the English translation. The productive signs are set in bold type in this gloss (and several of them may be seen in Figs. 5.7 and 5.8):

BUT WE OF-COURSE WELL CHILDREN
I ASK FOR WELL FUNNY PET
AND CAKE AND LOTS CHOCOLATE CANDY CIGARETTE
CIGARETTE-FLOPPING
EAT-CIGARETTE-AND-LICK-FINGER-WITH-SATISFACTION
CANNONS AND TIN SOLDIER
ROW-OF-SOLDIERS
SHOOT-CANNONS
ROW-OF-SOLDIERS-FALL
(look-on-in-delight)
AND CUT-OUT DOLL
STAND-UP-DOLL FOLD-HANDS-LOOKING-PLEASED-AT-DOLL
AND SWORD
STAB-DOLL-WITH-SWORD
AND GAME LIKE SNAKE LADDER
SNAKE-FANGS
PLAYER-SLITHER-DOWN-SNAKE SNAKE-STARE-IN-FACE
CLIMB-LADDER
ELBOW-PEOPLE-TO-LEFT-AND-RIGHT
CLIMB-LADDER
ELBOW-PEOPLE-TO-LEFT-AND-RIGHT
RUN-UP-LADDER
AND GAME YOU PLAY WITH WORD
PLACE-WORD-TO-RIGHT PLACE-WORD-TO-CENTRE
(look-questioningly)
MOVE-WORD-TO-LEFT
(shake-head)
MOVE-WORDS-AROUND-RAPIDLY-IN-SEVERAL-DIRECTIONS
SCRATCH-HEAD

In this gloss, we see clearly how the productive signs are used to flesh out the experience of the children's presents. Not only do we know what they had (thanks to the frozen signs) but we also have a very clear visual image of what they did with their presents (thanks to the productive signs). This imagery is an essential feature of sign language poetry,

CIGARETTE-FLOPPING   ROW-OF-SOLDIERS   STAND-UP-DOLL

SNAKE-STARE-   PLACE-WORD-   PLACE-WORD-   SCRATCH-HEAD
IN-FACE   TO-RIGHT   TO-CENTRE

Fig. 5.7

CLIMB-LADDER   RUN-UP-LADDER

Fig. 5.8

celebrating the richness of the creative potential in the language and inviting the audience to share in the experience of the poem.

Beyond the strength of the imagery, however, are other elements that can be used for poetic effect. The productive signs can create changes in scale in the poem because they allow the signer to take on the character through role-shift and also to show the actions of the character through the role of narrator by using proforms. This shift in scale is seen here in the productive signs CLIMB-LADDER (role-shift) and RUN-UP-LADDER (proform). The sign RUN-UP-LADDER also uses the 'V' handshape that echoes the handshape used in all the signs referring to the snake's activities, creating a sub-sign repetition or 'rhyme' (Fig. 5.8).

In *Our Dumb Friends* (p. 244) the productive signs focus less on how objects move or what people do with the objects, and more on what things look like. In this poem there are basic frozen signs that name parts of the dog, such as EAR and TAIL, and the skill in this poem comes from the creation and use of productive signs that describe what these parts look like. The English lines were written to match the visual richness of the signs that can describe the dogs' appearances, and require some English neologisms (such as 'thumb-thumb-thumpy'). The BSL and ASL versions of this poem are similar in this section, and can be glossed using the same words. In this poem, productive signing is a vehicle for testing and displaying the extent and boundaries of a sign language. The productive signs do more than show an entertaining range of dogs' features: they use a variety of sign-formation processes to show the versatility and richness of the language, while also producing clear visual images of the dogs. The productive signs are set in bold type in this gloss of part of the BSL version (the signs describing some of the ears can be seen in Fig. 5.9 and signs describing the tails can be seen in Fig. 5.10):

EARS
EARS-THAT-POINT
EARS
EARS-THAT-DROOP
FLOPPY-EARS
PRICKLY-EARS
EARS LIKE SCOOP
EARS-LIKE-A-SCOOP
AND TAIL
WOW
MANY-DIFFERENT-ONES
TAIL-SHORT-AND-STUMPY [measured against a thumb extended from fist as an 'Å' handshape]

80

EARS-THAT-POINT   EARS-THAT-DROOP

FLOPPY-EARS   PRICKLY- EARS   EARS-LIKE-A-SCOOP

Fig. 5.9

TAIL-SHORT-   TAIL-TEENY-   TAIL-THICK-
AND-STUMPY   WEENY   AND-BUMPY

TAIL-LONG-HAIRED   LONG-TAIL-   TAIL-CURVED-   TAIL-FINGER-
                    SWEEPS   AND-BUSHY   SLENDER

Fig. 5.10

SHORT-AND-STUMPY-TAIL-WAGS [using the 'Å' handshape to wag]
TAIL-TEENY-WEENY [measured against the little finger extended from the fist as an 'I' handshape]
TEENY-WEENY-TAIL-WAGS [using the 'I' handshape to wag]
TAIL-THICK-AND-BUMPY [made by sketching the thickness of the tail]
TAIL-THUMPS [made using the fist as an 'A' handshape to thump]
TAIL-LONG-HAIRED [made sketching along the length of the arm]
STROKE-LONG-HAIR-OF-TAIL
LONG-HAIRED-TAIL-SWEEPS [made using the arm as a tail]
SWEEP-FLOOR
SHORT-BRUSHY-HAIR
TAIL-CURVED-AND-BUSHY [made using a 'B' handshape and the extent of the forearm]
TAIL-FINGER-SLENDER [measured against the index finger extended from the fist as a 'G' handshape]

Importantly, from the perspective of language play in signed poetry, many of the productive signs here use contrasting orientations and handshapes within the signs. The signs showing the pointing ears and the drooping ears are mirror-images of each other in the horizontal plane. (We saw in our discussion of symmetry in Chapter 4 that these symmetries across the horizontal plane are not easily created.) The description of the tails uses all the maximally contrasting handshapes in sign languages. The 'Å' handshape is the opposite of the 'I' handshape (the former using the thumb extended from the fist and the latter using the little finger extending from the fist). The thumping tail uses the completely closed fist of the 'A' handshape and this is contrasted by stroking the long hair of the tail using the completely open '5' handshape. The largest sign articulator (the whole arm) is used to sweep the floor, then a smaller articulation unit (the forearm and 'B' handshape) is used for the curling tail, before finally showing the smallest unit (the index finger in the 'G' handshape) for the finger-slender tail.

In *The Ugly Duckling* (p. 249), the productive signing allows the poem to explore representations of the wide range of actions and appearances of different animals, most particularly of the duckling himself. The words in the English translation of this poem are more familiar than the neologistic descriptive words used in *Our Dumb Friends*. The signs in the BSL poem, however, are mostly productive items. (In the gloss below

the productive signs are set in bold type and entirely non-manual signs
are in parentheses.)

THERE POOR-THING BIRD
THERE WHEN FIRST HE
**PRESS-BACK-OF-HEAD-AGAINST-FLAT-SURFACE-OF-EGG-
SHELL**
CRACK-ON-TOP-OF-SHELL
SHELL-CRACKS-OPEN
LEGS-CLIMB-UP-AND-OUT-OF-SHELL
(looks-pleased-with-self)
POP-EYES
WIDE-BEAK
GREY **FUR-ON-CHEST**
BANDY-LEGS
LEGS
THIN-BANDY-LEGS
WALK-NERVOUSLY-ON-BANDY-LEGS

In this section, we can see that the poem uses several different signs to
make what is essentially the same point. As the duckling hatches, we see
his head pushing against the shell and also the effect that this has on the
shell, until the crack leads to the shell cracking open entirely. In the English
poem, we only see this from the view of the duckling's actions, but in the
BSL poem, we see it from the views of both the action and the reaction. We
also see several ways to describe the duckling's legs. Not only do we have
the frozen sign LEGS, but we also have different productive signs to show
us what the legs look like. There is a sign showing the outline shape of the
legs, a sign showing the 'G' handshape proform of the thin legs, and also
a sign in role-shift, showing the duckling walking, in which the forearms
bent at the elbows represent the bandy legs. This multiple 'faceting' of an
idea is common in BSL and is a feature of the language that the poet can
use to celebrate the richness of the visual imagery available (Fig. 5.11).

Again, however, the productive signs do more than allow the poet to
create multiple compelling visual images. They also allow the poem to
create patterns. In this case, the sign for the bandy legs that is made with
the forearms has a later echo in the signs SWAN-BENDS-NECK and
SWAN-GLIDES. As we also saw in Chapter 4, with the dogs' ears in *Our
Dumb Friends*, they also allow signs to contrast through symmetry about
the horizontal plane, and WALK-ON-BANDY-LEGS has the forearm
pointing down, while SWAN-GLIDES has it pointing up.

OUTLINE-OF-BANDY-LEGS   THIN-BANDY-LEGS   WALK-NERVOUSLY-ON-BANDY-LEGS

Fig. 5.11

CAT-PEERS-OUT-BEHIND-WALL

Fig. 5.12

Letter -y- from s-p-y   Changing letter -y-   CAT'S-EARS/AERIALS

Fig. 5.13

I (using letter .l. handshape)

Fig. 5.14

Productive signs are neologisms that come from the heart of visual languages – creating visual images from the raw material of a visual language is the bedrock of the form and meaning relations in sign languages. Signers take great pride in their language's potential to create new signs and in their skills in realising this potential. The other way of creating new signs in sign languages is almost the polar opposite of this – borrowing signs from non-visual, spoken and written languages such as English. The origin of these loan signs should mean that they could not create visual images and so we might expect such words to have no place in sign language poetry, where the creation of strong visual imagery is of paramount importance. Yet we will see that English can, nevertheless, play a part in sign language poetry.

Fingerspellings

As we saw in Chapter 1, fingerspelling is one way of creating new signs in BSL and ASL, by borrowing words from English. In fingerspelling, the individual letters of a word are spelled out using letters from the manual alphabet. Although many sign languages use fingerspelling, we should be clear that fingerspelling is only a supplement to visually motivated signs. The fingerspelled word used in BSL or ASL is not a neologism in English because it already exists in English, but it is a 'new' sign in that sign language. While signed poetry focuses on the unique elements of sign such as space and visual motivation, and may bend or even break the rules of the language for poetic reasons, fingerspellings break the formational rules of signed languages in a much more serious way. They are formationally very different from signs in ASL or BSL, usually having more than two changes of handshape in a single sign, so they can interrupt the rhythm of signs and be jarring in a smooth flow of visually motivated signs. The starting point of sign language poetry is the visual beauty of sign language, and influences from spoken language, such as fingerspelling, are usually deliberately rejected. However, poets not only break the established rules of everyday language, but they can also go further and break the established rules of poetic language and using fingerspelling is an example of this. Poets do not normally break rules solely in a spirit of anarchy, though, so where fingerspelling occurs there is a poetic reason for it.

In *The Cat* (p. 240), we are told that the cat's whiskers make it a perfect spy. The final line in the English poem ends with the word 'spy'. The ASL poem uses the fingerspelled word .S.P.Y. – a device that breaks the conventions of sign language poetry. However, the handshape of the manual letter .Y. creates great poetic potential. It has the thumb and the little finger extended, while the remaining fingers are closed into the fist, so it can be used to represent the shape of the cat's head and its ears. Fingerspelling conventions in ASL dictate that the word should be spelled at shoulder-height, but in *The Cat* the letters are spelled lower down, and behind a 'wall' signed by the non-dominant hand. Thus the letter .Y. peeks out from behind the wall, spying as the cat, before slipping behind the wall again (Fig. 5.12).

The BSL poem *The Cat* has problems with fingerspelling s-p-y. The BSL manual alphabet is different from the ASL alphabet. It is two-handed (compared to the one-handed ASL alphabet) and the forms of each letter are different, so the spelling of s-p-y does not produce the potential pun of .S.P.Y. The British letter -y- looks nothing like a cat's head and the non-dominant hand is needed as part of the letter -y- so it cannot be used to sign the 'wall'. Nevertheless, using the fingerspelling is important because the joke of the poem relies on this final word/sign. The BSL letter -y- has the non-dominant hand as a 'B' handshape with the thumb out from the fingers. The dominant hand may be a 'G' handshape, but can also have an 'L' handshape. The index finger of the dominant hand touches the back of the non-dominant hand at the base of the gap between the thumb and index finger. This can create two 'open triangles' – one on each hand – as the thumb and index finger creates a 'V' shape. Cats' ears are triangular. When Dorothy has fingerspelled s-p-y, she has two 'open triangle' handshapes in the final letter, which she then inverts, raises to the top of her head and plants as two cat ears. These ears then move in several directions, as an aerial for a spy's radio receiver (Fig. 5.13).

In both these poems Dorothy shows how much fun a poet can have in playing with fingerspelling. The original form comes from the sound-based English and is alien to sign language, yet she takes the letters and creates visual puns with them in both BSL and ASL. At other times, she uses signs derived from fingerspelling for poetic reasons. There are two ASL signs meaning the first person singular 'I'. One, described by Martin Sternberg (1990) as 'the natural sign', uses the index finger of a 'G' hand-shape pointing to the chest (and this is also the BSL sign 'I'). The other is an 'initialised sign' and uses the manual letter handshape .I. (a closed fist with only the little finger extended) against the chest. Poetic conventions in sign language would require a sign poet to use the for-mer pronoun, and in nearly all of Dorothy's ASL poems, this is the case. However, in *Total Communication* (p. 248) she uses the initialised sign with the 'I' handshape. This whole poem plays with the similarity of 'eye' and 'aye' and 'I' in English, so it makes sense to add an extra dimension of using the manual letter .I. in the sign meaning 'I'. It also fits much better into the formational pattern of the poem, which also uses a lot of 'Y' handshapes, having the marked arrangement of the little finger extended, as 'I' has. Again, we can see the poet breaking conventions for extra poetic meaning (Fig. 5.14).

Apart from fingerspelling, there are other influences of English that occur in Dorothy's poetry, especially the influence of English from the small 'grammar signs' that she uses in some of her poems. The poems containing the most English grammar signs are the 'blended poems', which were Dorothy's 'trademark' poems, working in two languages simultaneously. We will see more of the influence of English in Chapter 10, when we consider the language outcome of this type of blending of signed and spoken languages. For now, though, we will continue to explore the poetic effects created by visually motivated signs, as we consider the meaning that they produce.

6
Ambiguity

In everyday language, ambiguity is usually best avoided, but in poetry it allows poets to convey extra meaning without using any extra words. If a word or phrase could have more than one interpretation – and if each interpretation could possibly make sense within the context of the poem – ambiguity can be used to great effect. Although ambiguity in sign language poems can arise from established, frozen signs with more than one meaning (just as in spoken languages) productive signs are especially important for ambiguity because of the way that visual motivation is used as part of the sign-formation processes in sign languages.

Proforms are used in many highly visually motivated productive signs, and we have already seen (in Chapter 1) that proforms only take their full meaning from the context in which they are used. They are based on the shape of the referent, not on its size, and this can lead to ambiguity of scale unless the referent is clearly specified. For example, a loosely closed, circular handshape can represent an atom, a ball or a planet – anything spherical of any size. Individual fingers could refer to several people or several hairs – anything long and thin of any size. Perspective is an important feature of visual arts such as painting, and shifts in perspective and size can also be a notable feature of sign language poetry. The fluid relationship between the size of the hand and the size of the referent provides great potential for poetic manipulation of signs (Bauman, 2003). Under-specification, or lack of specification, is a deliberate device in sign language poetry, with widespread use. The motivating forces behind different types of visually motivated signs, and especially the under-specification of proforms, are exploited by sign poetry to produce ambiguities and shifts in perspective that create aesthetic images and add extra significance.

For our discussion of sign language poetry, we need to note that ambiguity in the same words rarely occurs in two languages. This is because the chance of two languages using the same word for the same two different, unrelated meanings is so small. English ambiguities and puns do not translate into BSL or ASL (any more than they might translate into French or German), and sign-language ambiguities and puns do not translate into English. The three words 'eye', 'aye' and 'I', which sound the same in English and which are used to poetic effect in *Total Communication*, are not formationally similar signs in either ASL or BSL. There is a greater chance that puns might make it across the boundaries between the two sign languages, because of their shared histories and because of similar origins in visual motivation but, even so, there can be no guarantee that they will work.

In *Our Dumb Friends* (p. 244) there is a pun between one of the lines in the English and ASL and BSL poems. The English line describing the short stumpy tail 'Thumb-thumb-thumpy' has a direct pun with the English word 'thumb' and the handshape that is used in the signed poems to represent that tail – an 'Å' handshape in which the thumb is extended. A similar pun occurs with the tail described in English as 'finger slender', which is indeed signed using a single finger – in the 'G' handshape. In these cases, the reader of the poem needs to know sign language in order to appreciate the pun in the English poem. *Our Dumb Friends* also contains a pun that works in two different sign languages, even though the signs carry different meanings (although the pun does not work in English). In describing the sizes and shapes of the different dogs' tails, one part runs (in English):

> Finger slender
> (seems to say 'Where,
> where's the excitement?
> Let me share.')

We can imagine a dog wagging his tail, wanting to get in on the excitement, but that is as far as the English will take us. The ASL pun here lies in the fact that the 'finger slender' tail is made with the single finger 'G' handshape. As the tail wags in excitement, it wags side to side, and so the 'G' handshape wags side to side. This creates the ASL sign WHERE – an essentially arbitrary sign made with a 'G' handshape waving slightly side to side. The BSL translation of this ASL poem allows the visually motivated meaning of the 'finger slender' wagging tail to transfer from ASL with no problem. However, it loses the arbitrary ASL meaning WHERE so that pun is lost. Luckily, the same form in BSL means WHAT. This means that the dog's finger-slender tail is now asking 'What, what's the excitement?' and the pun continues to entertain a new audience (Fig. 6.1).

WAGGING-TAIL/
WHAT?/WHERE?

Fig. 6.1

GOD or TELEPHONE-
AERIAL

Fig. 6.2

'Hold a tree in the palm
of your hand'

Fig. 6.3

'Sail a boat on finger waves'

Fig. 6.4

SINGLE-PERSON   TWO-SINGLE-PEOPLE
or WHAT?   or WHAT?

Fig. 6.5

TWO-COUPLES
or LOOK-AROUND

Fig. 6.6

TEN-PEOPLE-RETREAT
or ONE-PERSON-RETREATS

Fig. 6.7

Another light-hearted pun occurs towards the end of *Unsound Views* (p. 250). The poem's theme is that hearing people will drop everything in order to answer the telephone. The penultimate line in English runs: 'They live to serve their telephone God' and there is no obvious punning there. However, in BSL, it runs:

> THEY LIVE RESPECT THAT TELEPHONE
> HOLD-HANDSET
> THIN-AERIAL-ON-HANDSET AERIAL-MOVES-UP GOD
> TELEPHONE-AERIAL

Here, the aerial on the telephone handset is signed with the 'G' handshape that refers to long, thin objects. The BSL sign GOD is also made using a 'G' handshape, albeit in a different location, but when the aerial is moved up to the location where GOD is normally articulated, the pun elevates the telephone to the status of a god (Fig. 6.2).

On a few occasions, Dorothy managed to get puns to work simultaneously in English and sign language. In *Unsound Views* there is a 'double pun', which works with the idea of the telephone's bell creating a similar effect in hearing people as the bell for food did on Pavlov's dogs. In English, she uses the pun 'tele-bone', which might be an allusion to the rhyming-slang *dog and bone* for *telephone*, as she replaces *phone* with the very similar-sounding word *bone* to show the link between the telephone and the dogs. In the BSL poem, she also puns on the idea of treating a telephone like a bone, by making the sign visually ambiguous, so that it could be interpreted as meaning either a bone or a telephone. We will discuss this image in more detail in Chapter 8 when we consider similes, but here we can also appreciate that she manages to make puns in both languages.

Dorothy made great use of the ambiguity in signs to play with ideas of scale. Although many other poems use it as a device to add meaning to the sign, the best example of this changing scale occurs in *Language for the Eye* (p. 243). This poem begins with the injunction: 'Hold a tree in the palm of your hand'. In English, this might seem a tall order (unless the tree was very small indeed) but in ASL and BSL, it makes sense if we start to play with the scale of signs. The sign that ASL users and most BSL users today recognise as TREE uses the dominant hand upright with a '5' handshape and the elbow of the dominant arm resting on the back of the non-dominant 'B' hand. The dominant hand represents the tree and the non-dominant hand represents the ground in which the tree grows. To hold a tree in 'the palm of our hand', all we need to do is shift the referent represented by the non-dominant hand. When we turn the non-dominant hand over, it becomes a sign that directly refers to the palm of the hand. So in holding the sign TREE in the palm of our hand, we are also holding 'a tree' in the palm (Fig. 6.3).[1]

The third line plays a similar joke: 'Sail a boat on finger waves'. Here, we have to understand again that the audience is invited to look at the non-dominant hand in two different ways. At one level, they are asked to understand that the language is using the hands to represent objects of similar size in relation to each other: the dominant hand represents the boat and the non-dominant hand refers to the water it sails on. At another level, we are asked to acknowledge that the fingers that create the sign WAVES are just that – fingers. There are two meanings in the same one sign. Holding both in our minds at the same time gives another layer of significance to the poem (Fig. 6.4).

The second stanza plays the same ambiguity game again, this time with the handshape that is used to represent spherical objects of any size. In the English poem we are invited to 'Follow the sun from rise to set, / Or bounce it like a ball'. As with the invitation to hold a tree in the palm of the hand, bouncing the sun is not possible in English. However, the game in the sign language poem that allows us to impose the size of the referent on the proform handshape permits a quick mental flip so that the round handshape that was the sun becomes a ball. The flat handshape that was the horizon for the sun to rise and set behind now becomes the hand that bounces the ball and then becomes the ground over which the ball bounces.

This ambiguity of scale is a clever piece of fun in *Language for the Eye*. It is designed to show children one of the basic principles of sign formation in sign languages, and also to show them how signers can be creative with this. Ambiguity is seen in other poems, too, and for more complex poetic reasons. Ambiguous scale is used subtly in *The Staircase* (p. 246) where the poem is concerned with ideas of individuality and community. One individual helps others in the community to improve their lot so that, ultimately, the whole community benefits. This complex idea is shown partly by some ambiguous signs. The first lines of this BSL poem are translated into English prose as:

> A dark forest. A figure creeps forward, peering ahead,
> Then comes another and another.
> They draw together in uncertainty, then in a line,
> They advance

The signs in the BSL poem can be glossed as:

FOREST DARK
PEOPLE HAVE
ONE-PERSON-MOVES-FORWARD ONE-PERSON-MOVES-FORWARD
TWO-PEOPLE-MOVE-FORWARD TWO-PEOPLE-MOVE-FORWARD

In this section, the poet is clearly describing the actions of several individuals, using proforms to represent people. However, there are non-manual clues to an ambiguity which creates a more personal involvement in the poem, because the signs have a simultaneous alternative reading in which the narrator herself is a single character in the poem. The proform used to represent a single person in BSL uses a 'G' handshape, and the proform using a single hand to represent two people uses a 'V' handshape (this proform is usually used when the dominant and non-dominant hands are both active). The BSL sign WHAT? also uses a 'G' handshape with the same orientation and location as a single person proform. The sign WHAT? has a small side-to-side movement and the brows are slightly furrowed and the eyes slightly squinted. The sign produced in the poem could be read as a single person wandering and meandering, squinting in the darkness of the forest and wondering slightly. Alternatively it could be read as a single person thinking, 'What is this place?' or 'What is going on?' The fact that the sign is later made again with both hands is non-problematic for the poem. The use of a 'G' handshape proform on each hand simply represents a single person on each hand (and thus implies that there are two people), and in BSL it is possible to intensify the one-handed sign WHAT? by adding a second hand (Fig. 6.5).

The BSL sign LOOK-UP uses a 'V' handshape with the same orientation as a two-person proform with the 'V' handshape. The two-person proform is normally located at chest height and the location for LOOK-UP is usually near the eyes, but by shifting the hands to shoulder-height, there is just enough connection between the eyes and the location of the manual sign to allow an interpretation of 'look'. The connection is made stronger because the poet hunches her shoulders and looks around with her eyes. The wandering meandering movement of the hands to represent the movement of the people moving through the forest could also be interpreted as the wandering movement of the eyes as they look around. As with the sign WHAT? it is possible to duplicate the one-handed sign LOOK to use both hands. It does not mean 'two people looking' but rather 'one person looking around' (Fig. 6.6).

The number of people wandering through the forest increases until both hands use '5' handshapes, with all fingers open. When the 'ten' people (meaning 'many') reach a wall, they step back nervously. This is translated as: 'But they come to a wall. / They retreat'. The two '5' hands move back to represent the line of people retreating. However, the hands are not fully open. They are slightly relaxed so that the fingers, while not fully clawed to create a '5̈' handshape, are slightly rounded. The handshape, orientation, location and movement of the proforms in the sign meaning 'many people in a line retreat' are identical to those of a sign that means 'a person backs off'. In this case, the handshape is taken to refer to a single person's hands, not ten individuals. The non-manual features used with this sign in the poem consist of a backward movement of the head and body. This is appropriate for either interpretation of the manual components of the sign (Fig. 6.7).

We should note that the levels of ambiguity in this poem created by slight changes in the signs and the carefully ambiguous non-manual features are limited to the BSL poem. The English translation could not pick up the significance of the double meaning without becoming heavily wordy.

Exaltation (p. 242) is another poem that makes good use of ambiguity. Here it is not so much ambiguity of scale of proforms, but simply of identification of the referent. Towards the end of the poem, the trees have seemed to part the sky 'And let the peace of heaven shine softly through'. The signs in the ASL version may be glossed as ALLOW PEACE OF HEAVEN LIGHT-SHINES LIGHT/HAND-TOUCHES-HEAD. The ambiguity here arises because of the form of the sign LIGHT, which is made with a fully open '5' handshape. As this light shines softly on her head, we are also faced with the possibility that this open '5' handshape is not only a symbol for 'light' but really is a hand. If LIGHT-TOUCHES-HEAD is interpreted as HAND-TOUCHES-HEAD, the obvious question is 'Whose hand?' and the obvious answer is 'God's'. In many cultures, placing hands gently upon a person's head is taken as a blessing. The ambiguity of the sign here allows us to take the meaning that the light falling upon the poet's head was like the hand of God blessing her. This extra meaning is only available to us through the signed version of the poem, as the ambiguity is not there in the English words (Fig. 6.8).

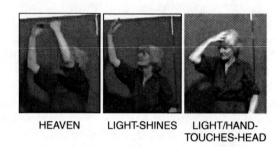

HEAVEN   LIGHT-SHINES   LIGHT/HAND-
TOUCHES-HEAD

Fig. 6.8

GOD   LOOK-IN-MIRROR

Fig. 6.9

PULL-SWORD-   HOLD-
FROM-STONE   CERTIFICATE

Fig. 6.10

Morphing

Another poetic device that relies on the formational similarity of two signs is the idea of 'morphing' or blending. Two signs that have very similar forms are used next to each other, so that they appear to blend. As the two signs blend, so the two meanings of the signs are brought closer together. Morphing is part of a particularly important device in sign language poems, namely the reduction of movements of transition between signs. Although minimal transitions between signs may be achieved with signs with varying degrees of formational similarity, morphing allows the minimum of transition between two signs because the two signs are so similar as to be almost identical.

In everyday signing, the end location and handshape of one sign are likely to be different from the start location and handshape of the next sign. Thus, in everyday signing, there is considerable change of handshape between the signs and considerable 'meaningless' transition movement between signs as the hands move to the next location. In signed poetry, cutting out this meaningless movement makes for a more fluid flow of signing and makes for a denser text. An equivalent to this reduction of transition in spoken language poems might be for each word to start with the same sound as the one at the end of the previous word.

We have already seen good examples of 'morphing' in Chapter 5 in the BSL version of *The Cat*, where the final handshapes of the letter -y- (from s-p-y) change gradually to become ears (see Fig. 5.13) and in the ASL poem where the final letter .Y. becomes the cat's head peering out from behind the wall (see Fig. 5.12). In the ambiguous signs where the shifting perception of scale of the signs causes us to change our understanding of the meaning, we are again seeing morphing in the signs.

The final two signs of *Exaltation* in ASL are signs that blend so perfectly that at one stage they are ambiguous. As so often occurs in Dorothy's signed poems, the last sign does not have an equivalent in the English *Exaltation*. The final line of the English poem is: 'I reached with them to touch the face of God.' The penultimate line of the ASL poem runs: I SAME REACH-HIGH TOUCH FACE OF GOD. Then, the final sign brings the sign GOD (which uses a 'B' handshape in ASL) down from its location above head-height (where the treetops are and where we might expect heaven and also God to be) so that the hand is closer to the face. The narrator of the poem then looks directly at the hand. By this stage, the sign has also become LOOK-IN-MIRROR (Fig. 6.9). Is she looking directly at the face of God? Or is she looking into a mirror? The Judeo-Christian tradition teaches that humans were made in the image of God, so by finding God in this moment with nature, perhaps she has found herself. These complex ideas and possibilities are, again, only possible through the morphing and ambiguity that occur in the ASL, not through the English.

A similar occurrence of morphing is used at the end of Dorothy's BSL poem *Sinai* (p. 245). In this poem, the poet is walking ahead of her friends, who are straggling behind her. In a similar dilemma to one that occurs in *The Staircase* (and *The Hang Glider*, which we will discuss in Chapter 11), she has to decide if she will walk on and risk possible failure, or turn back to the unchallenging safety of what is known. As in the other two poems, she decides to continue, and the last lines of the English poem are:

> Up this slope, perhaps
> Round this bend,
> Is the end
> Is the End.

We do not know of a record of a full performance of this poem in BSL, but part of it was filmed during the workshop session held in California in 1980, where Dorothy discussed it later with the audience as part of her 'work in progress'. She talked about the end of the poem, where the End of the trail is an impassable rock-face, signed with the 'B' handshape held close to her face. As the focus of her eyes changes, though, the hand is no longer something blocking her view that she looks *at*, but something that she looks *into* – a mirror. She has looked into something that appeared to be the End, and has seen herself. As with *Exaltation*, this MIRROR sign shows us that *Sinai* is a poem of self-discovery, and the key is the way that the sign ROCKFACE morphs imperceptibly into one that has the alternative reading of MIRROR. To use a capital letter for 'End' in the English poem indicates a second meaning of death. Although this second meaning is not indicated in the sign language poem, knowledge of both poems allows us to interpret this final sign END as also meaning that the poet has looked death in the face and seen herself.

Metaphors and similes (which we will consider in the next chapter) can also make use of morphing. In *The Staircase*, the characters gather around what they think is a sword embedded in a stone but when they attempt to draw it from the stone, it turns out to be the certificate awarded for completion of their university course. This apparently bizarre sequence of images is considerably less odd when we consider the BSL signs in the poem. The sign PULL-SWORD-FROM-A-STONE morphs to the sign HOLD-CERTIFICATE because the same 'grasping' or handling handshape is used for holding both a sword and a scrolled certificate, and only a slight change of palm orientation is needed to turn the first sign into the second one (Fig. 6.10). The morphing allows the metaphor here (comparing King Arthur's feat of pulling the sword from the stone with the people's feat of achieving their certificates) to come through clearly. Both feats confirm the fitness of the holder for their role in society.

Morphing occurs frequently in the ASL *Seasons* haiku quartet (p. 245). This should come as no great surprise because the style of the signed haiku requires signs to flow seamlessly into one another. In *Spring*, the sign SPRING morphs into the sign SUNSHINE, and with minimal transition becomes the sign CARRY-SUNSHINE. This sign moves across the signing space from right to left and morphs into the sign ON (which uses the same handshapes as CARRY-SUNSHINE) which in turn morphs into BREEZE. The sign BREEZE moves gently across signing space, slowly shifting orientation and movement until it has morphed into TREE that is caressed by the breeze (Fig. 6.11).

The BSL poem *Christmas List* (p. 240) also contains many morphed signs, especially in the productive signs that show the way the children played with their 'Useless Presents'. When they ask for candy cigarettes, the productive signs that follow may be glossed as CIGARETTE-FLOPPING-IN-MOUTH and EAT-CIGARETTE-AND-LICK-FINGER-WITH-SATISFACTION. In this second sign, the index finger represents the cigarette at first, as it goes into the mouth, but when it is drawn from the mouth it has morphed into the finger to be licked. They also ask for games like snakes and ladders and the productive signs that follow this may be glossed as:

SNAKE-FANGS
PLAYER-SLITHER-DOWN-SNAKE
SNAKE-JUMP-UP-AND-STARE-AT-FACE

All these signs have the same handshape and, again, the final location of each sign is the start location of the next sign (Fig. 6.12).

When they have received all their presents, the children argue over them: 'Then we squabbled over what was whose'. The BSL signs in this

98

SPRING SUNSHINE CARRY-SUNSHINE

ON BREEZE TREE

Fig. 6.11

SNAKE SNAKE-STARE-AT-FACE

Fig. 6.12

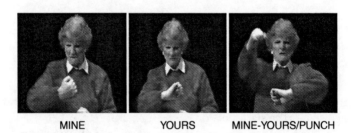

MINE YOURS MINE-YOURS/PUNCH

Fig. 6.13

section of the poem may be glossed as:

WE ARGUE MINE YOURS MINE YOURS MINE
OURS
OURS/YOURS/PUNCH-EACH-OTHER

The morphing that occurs here happens because the BSL possessive signs MINE, YOURS and OURS are made with the closed fist 'A' handshape. These signs are made with one hand when they are singular and use both hands when they are emphatic or plural. Adding the second hand and moving it randomly between the signer (OURS) and the location in front of the signer (YOURS) morphs the signs to become a random throwing of the fists until the signs degenerate into the traditional post-Christmas sibling fracas of flailing punches (Fig. 6.13).

Many other sign language poets use this morphing device. John Wilson's BSL poem *From the Depths* uses it to move between his two themes of the threat and suffering caused to whales through whaling and the threat to sign language and suffering to Deaf people caused by oral education. One of the many examples of morphing seen in this poem comes when the whale is finally harpooned and the 'G' handshape strikes the chest to show the harpoon striking the whale. However, the facial expression changes from one of pain to one of questioning surprise as the scene shifts to the school and the sign has morphed to become the sign ME as the Deaf child caught signing is asking, 'Do you mean me?'

Wim Emmerik's Sign Language of the Netherlands (SLN) poem *Tuin van Eden* (*Garden of Eden*) makes great use of morphing. At first, the forearms, each with a '5' handshape, sweep horizontally across signing space to sign GROUND or EARTH before one of the forearms gently moves upright to become the sign TREE with the same handshape. Later, the apple from the tree is lying on the ground and the snake crawls across to it and burrows inside. The snake's movement is made by the index finger of the 'G' handshape flexing and straightening at the three knuckles. Once the snake is inside the apple, however, (as the 'G' hand is held by the closed fingers of the other hand) the orientation of the finger changes so that the sign morphs to become a finger beckoning Adam to temptation. Then the finger is sharply drawn out from the other enclosing hand. This could be interpreted as a productive sign meaning that the snake quickly leaves the apple (rapidly leaving the scene of the crime) but it is also the SLN sign meaning YOU-LOSER! At the end of the poem, Adam bites into the apple (signed with a '5' handshape) and holds it away from his mouth in disgust as he realises what the worm has done. The end of this sign has now turned into the SLN sign (also with a '5' handshape) that is perhaps best glossed as the expletive YOU-STUPID-BASTARD!

Ambiguity peppers good poetry in any sign language, and we have seen that it has many functions. We have briefly mentioned that it is used in metaphors and similes in the poems, and it is to these areas of poetry – increasingly concerned with the meaning of the poem rather than the form of the poem – that we now turn.

7
Themes in Sign Poetry

A major contribution of sign poetry to the empowerment of the Deaf community is the way that the poems can portray the day-to-day experience of Deaf people. Some poems are explicitly on subjects that are relevant to Deaf people, being directly related to the Deaf experience, especially the celebration of sign language and the visual world and the relationships between Deaf and hearing people, but at other times 'Deafness' is woven deep into the fabric of the poem. Other themes, of course, such as nature, love, and life and death, are properly explored in sign language poetry, but as the poems are composed with the perspective of a Deaf poet, even these apparently general themes are used to create 'Deaf' images. In order to explore the themes of Deaf poems in more detail, we will again focus on Dorothy Miles' work, but a study of the compositions of any sign poet will show how the themes of sign language poetry reflect the poet's identity as a Deaf person.

Dorothy Miles created three main types of poetry – written English poetry, sign language poetry blended with spoken language poetry (which Heidi Rose (1992) has suggested may be termed 'signed poetry' to reflect its relationship with English), and sign language poetry composed with no reference to a spoken language. We may expect the sign language poems to have strong Deaf themes containing powerful visual images, and we will see that this is the case. Animal themes, especially, provided plenty of scope to show visual description of the animals in her poems, as she characterised birds, cats and dogs in poems such as *The Ugly Duckling*, *The Cat* and *Our Dumb Friends*. Dorothy's poems frequently sparkled with the sheer pleasure of sign language. She considered wit and entertainment to be very important elements in sign language poetry and many of her poems provide tremendous visual fun. In her volume of poetry *Gestures* she wrote, about *The Cat*, 'Many animal characteristics are easy to imitate and fun to watch, so animal stories are good for showing sign language.' The poems do more than merely show sign language, however: they also show it off. Part of Dorothy's aim in her earlier compositions was to prove that sign language was capable of complexity and thus a worthy medium of creative composition. Even Dorothy's English language poetry reveals her Deaf perspective on life and her 'visual' perspective of the world. Despite the fact that several of the poems contained in *Gestures* were composed in English, in 1980 Dorothy said, 'apparently I have a visual writing skill'. This visual writing skill later allowed her to create translations in ASL that contained many features of sign language poetry, as we have already seen in our references to *Exaltation*. Her visual approach to written poetry, however, is also seen in her poems influenced by 'concrete poetry'. This style of poetry was composed especially during the 1950s to 1970s and explored the relationship between the written form of words and their layout on a page to their meaning. Draper (1999) sums up concrete poetry, saying:

> [T]he distinctive quality of 'concrete' is that it uses the visual as a structural principle based on spatial rather than temporal relationships. In its purest forms it is generated from vertical and horizontal placings that must be *seen* to be perceived. ... [It] develops and enhances the incipiently visual element inherent in many rhetorical devices. (pp. 221–2)

In a concrete poem by Emmett Williams, *Like Attracts Like*, the idea of 'like attracting like' is shown physically in the layout of the words in the poem. There are 13 lines in the poem, and the words are always the same ('like attracts like') but as the poem progresses, the words get closer to each other and finally start to overlap in order to show what happens when like attracts like. The first line starts:

Like   attracts   like
like   attracts   like
like   attracts   like
like   attracts like
like attracts like
likeattractslike
likattractlike
likttaclike
liktalik
litalik
ltali
lal
a

Dorothy's diary from 1977 contains the jottings of several small concrete poems. They are not specifically Deaf poems but they experiment with visual themes in poetry. One, carrying her theme of flight, runs simply:

First came birds
Later airplanes
e
r   f
e   o
h   r
T   e
The Sparrow is the jumbo jet's
Big Brother

Some of the visual poems that Dorothy wrote in English did have specific Deaf interpretations, however. In August 1974 Dorothy wrote 'Thoughts on learning the name of a young deaf woman whose mother is a leading advocate of Oralism' (unpublished). The poem is concerned with the plant *Parthenocissus quinquifolia*, the Virginia creeper (we can assume that the young Deaf woman's name was Virginia), and the latter part of the poem runs:

When grown on walls and fences, it needs
ATTENTION!
To keep the growth
Within
)limits(
but
it is seen at its best when unpruned and
u n h a m p e r e d
it climbs
to
the
tops
of
lofty
trees
Virginia creeper, trained to arrange yourself
Trimly along the fence, about the wall,
Are you content?
Or would you rather clamber free and tall?

Although this is ostensibly a poem about a plant, it is an attack on the educational and language philosophy of Oralism, which advocates the
promotion of speech for Deaf people and the rejection of sign language
and Deaf culture. The feelings of Deaf signers towards Oralism are very
powerful and frequently negative, as many Deaf people view oral
communication as unnatural, undignified and repressive, and it is often a
symbol of the oppression of Deaf people by hearing people. The poem here
draws parallels with the abundant growth that comes from the freedom of
signing and the restrictive 'tidiness' of Oralism. Oppression of the natural
sign language of Deaf people is shown through the oppression of nature
by training and pruning the creeper. Even when it is written in English,
this poem uses visual elements. The word 'unhampered' is allowed to
spread unhampered across the page by using extra spacing between its
letters, and the reversed parentheses bind the word 'limits' tightly. The
single-word lines show how far the creeper can reach when it is unpruned.

Another unpublished poem in Dorothy's papers (untitled and
undated) runs:

> Me Hippopotamus
> GAPE
> Grey all over, tough of hide
> GAPE
> People frequently discuss
> Gape Gape Gape
> Why I open wide.
>
> Am I tired am I bored
> Y A W N
> Am I just about to sneeze
> AA A A A -CHOO
> Am I startled
> G A P E
> Am I oral trying to please?
>
> I'm a HIPPOPOTAMUS
> G A P E
> Tough of hide since I was born
> GAPE
> Why I gape, I don't know
> G A P E

Although this is also an English poem, the scope for visual games when it is performed in sign language gapes as wide as the hippo. Even in the English poem, there is an increased visual element in the increased spacing between the letters in the words GAPE, YAWN and AA-CHOO. The poem follows traditional English patterns of rhyme and meter (although the punctuation is unconventional) but there is no doubt that this is a 'Deaf' poem because it also addresses the issue of Oralism. The placid hippo appears to be cheerful enough, but is bemused by its own behaviour – just as Deaf people are often obliged by hearing people to try to make sense of a bemusing world. The first line deviates from the normal rules of English grammar – 'Me hippopotamus' – and appears to be broken English (calling to mind Tarzan's broken English, 'Me Tarzan'). However, it can also be read as a rough attempt to show a translation from sign languages into English. BSL does not use distinct subject and object pronouns, so that the first person pronoun is the same for both, and it does not use the verb 'to be'. (BSL is like many other sign languages in this respect, and there are also many spoken languages that do not show subject–object distinction in pronouns, and many spoken languages that do not use the verb 'to be'.)

Thus, through the choice of English grammar, we are told that the hippo is Deaf. It is also tough of hide – just as Deaf people have to become if they are to survive in a hearing world. Use of the word 'discuss' implies that people frequently talk *about* this hippo, but they do not talk *to* the hippo. This, again, is a common experience for Deaf people as they find that hearing people talk about them and form opinions of Deafness rather than engage directly with Deaf people. The possible theories to explain the hippo's gape (being tired, about to sneeze or startled) all at least have some natural explanation, but the final suggestion that it is just oral and trying to please, again shows the attitude towards Oralism. A Deaf person may collude with Oralism out of a wish to please others. The first line of the final verse repeats the same idea as that of the first verse, but now it uses English grammar, perhaps to emphasise the hippo's self-affirmation with the verb 'am'. However, the word HIPPOPOTAMUS is now in capital letters. This again can be read as an emphasis of the hippo's identity, implying that it gapes simply because it is a hippo, but the use of capitals has a further relevance to Deafness and sign language. When signs are written as English glosses, they are conventionally written in capitals (as they are in this book) so to use capitals is to reassert the importance of sign language. The BSL sign HIPPOPOTAMUS is visually motivated by representation of the gaping hippo mouth, so the hippo can conclude that it gapes because that is its name. It has been that way since it was born and doesn't know why it gapes, but it just accepts that it does. Hearing people are often interested in why a person is deaf, but many Deaf people consider the cause of their deafness irrelevant because they simply *are* Deaf. Although this poem contains many elements of fun, the complexity of the language and the political implications show that it is considerably more than just light entertainment.

Many of Dorothy's animal poems carried similar themes. *Stable Horse* and *Elephants Dancing* – written in English but also signed – were two of her earlier poems that drew parallels between humans subjugating animals and the oppression of Deaf people. In *Elephants Dancing* (p. 242), she observes that the elephants that dance for her pleasure and entertainment have been trained by chaining their legs. She told her audience, in a performance of this poem in 1990:

> I went to the zoo and I saw elephants 'dancing' with repetitive steps. I looked at them and thought about it and that's why I wrote this poem. The poem really thinks about Deaf people. Always being told 'do it like this, like this'. So the elephants' feet moving back and forth are like the *blah, blah, blah* of a Deaf person speaking obediently. (RSS translation)

Importantly, the poem ends on a positive note: 'I hope some day to see/ Elephants dancing free.'

One of Dorothy's favourite poems was *The Ugly Duckling* (p. 249), in which she uses the rejection of the young duckling from the Hans Christian Andersen story to symbolise the way that Deaf children are so often made to feel inferior and outcasts by hearing society. She developed the idea in prose and drama as well, but her BSL poem (which, incidentally, provides scope for showing the animal characteristics she loved to include in her poems) has been the most enduring. It is notable, too, for its happy ending.

Trees

Dorothy Miles loved trees, and trees occur in many of her happiest poems. As well as harmonising with her personal response to trees, they have two main areas of importance in her poems. Firstly, the connotations associated with trees – being solid, dependable parts of nature – allow her to develop such themes. The handshape and movement of the sign

TREE create an 'open' and uplifting sign. It has a fully open hand and all the fingers point upwards. Such a sign means that it is hard to treat trees negatively in a sign language poem. Secondly, the sign TREE is an excellent start for sign language creativity in poetry. The 'base' concept of the '5' handshape and movement of the one-handed sign gives considerable freedom to create rhymes and language patterns around the sign TREE.

Trees recur several times in the *Seasons* haiku quartet (p. 245). In *Spring*, the sunshine is 'borne on breeze, / among singing trees' and in *Winter* there is reference to 'bare trees'. In both instances, the opportunities for language play with the sign TREE are exploited to the full, as we saw in our discussion of neologisms in Chapter 5. Even in *Summer* and *Autumn*, where trees are not explicitly mentioned, their presence is implied through the use of 'green heights' in *Summer* and mention of 'Scattered leaves' in *Autumn*. *Exaltation* (p. 242) also uses trees to express ideas of happiness and freedom. The first sign used in the performance of this poem in ASL is one that refers to the welling-up of emotions (in this case, pleasant emotions) and the handshape and orientation are the same as those used for TREE. The trees in this poem provide a route to exaltation, with their ability to bring peace ('And let the peace of Heaven shine softly through') and bring humanity closer to God ('I reached with them to touch the face of God.') In *Christmas Magic* (p. 241), the tree is a focal point for the 'magic day / of love and glee' and, as in *Spring*, the sign TREE is involved in a wonderfully creative sign neologism as the fire's glow 'Touches the tree with a gentle gleaming'. In *Language for the Eye* (p. 243), the tree is a starting point for the language games that the poem plays with signs. The TREE is felled to become the sign BOAT in this light-hearted poem.

Flying and freedom

Flight and wings occur often in Dorothy's poetry, with implications of freedom and the positive implications of height that accompany flying, found particularly in *The Hang Glider* (p. 242), a 'blended' ASL-English poem, which we will discuss in depth in Chapter 12. The reverse side of this idea comes with ideas of falling, and those connotations are found in an untitled poem concerned with 'falling' in love, which appears in Dorothy's diary for 3 February 1977, a week before she was hospitalised for depressive illness. This untitled poem is composed in iambic pentameter and draws on Hamlet's famous soliloquy. It is a conventional English poem, in which there is nothing obvious to show that it was composed by a Deaf person. However, it demonstrates how much Dorothy's work was influenced by her reading of English literary texts, and also her preoccupation with moments just prior to attempting some huge undertaking:

> To fall or not to fall, that is the question
> As valid as any dealing with life and death;
> But, as a diver pauses on a cliff
> And stares with fascination at the sea –
> (sensing the bliss of plunging, but afraid
> of what may lie beneath – rocks, shallows, sharks
> or, that his skill will prove inadequate
> to that long plummet, and hurl him at the waves
> to the destruction of them both) so I
> peer into love, and wonder if the fall –
> exhilaration and abandonment –
> is worth the fear, the hurt, the pain, the loss.

Flight shown through the actions of a butterfly also occurs to allow creativity through sign language. Butterflies occur in *To a Deaf Child* and in *Language for the Eye*, where they rise high and lightly in moments of joy. In *To a Deaf Child* (p. 247), the sign BUTTERFLY already echoes the handshape in the signs LIGHT and LIFT (and in the BSL poem BUTTER-FLY is also very similar to the sign SIGN, although this is not the case in the ASL poem), occurring in the lines 'Your lightest word in hand / lifts like a butterfly' (Fig. 7.1). In both poems the butterflies also tumble, but at least in *To a Deaf Child* the tumbling is in a spirit of fun, as the lines continue 'or folds in liquid motion' where the sign morphs to become a waterfall. In *Language for the Eye* (p. 243) the suggestion in the English poem runs 'From your fingertips see a frog leap, / at a passing butterfly.' In the ASL and BSL versions, however, there is an extra image given when the butterfly has fluttered lightly upwards and then it falls tumbling from the leap of the frog (which is, admittedly perhaps, quite a bleak outcome for the butterfly).

Celebration of sign language and sight

Alec Ormsby (1995) has noted that themes of loss and compensation are common in many of the poems by Deaf writers, who apparently saw themselves as 'lacking'. He provides examples of such poetry, including

BUTTERFLY   LIGHT   LIFT   SIGN

Fig. 7.1

STILLNESS

Fig. 7.2

John Carlin's *The Mute's Lament*, written in 1847. The opening lines of this flowery Victorian poem run:

> I move, a silent exile on this earth;
> As in his dreary cell one doomed for life,
> My tongue is mute, and closed ear heedeth not;
> No gleam of hope this darkened mind assures
> That the blest power of speech shall e'er be known.
> Murmuring gayly o'er their pebbly beds
> The limpid streamlets, as they onward flow
> Through verdant meadows and responding woodlands,
> Vocal with many tones – I hear them not.
> The linnet's dulcet tone, the robin's strain,
> The whip-poor-will's, the lightsome mockbird's cry,
> When merrily from branch to branch they skip,
> Flap their blithe wings, and o'er the tranquil air
> Diffuse their melodies – I hear them not.

This poem was parodied in a 'song' signed by a group of Deaf Americans, filmed by Charles Kraeul in the 1950s and presented by Ted Supalla in a homage to Kraeul's work. The first few lines of the song (which continues in the same vein for several animals) are as follows:

> The birds sing, sing, sing, but I hear them not at all,
> Darn, darn, darn
> The cats meow, meow, meow but I hear them not at all,
> Darn, darn, darn

This widespread view of Deaf people as people lacking hearing was not the only view, however. Other poets recognised that a Deaf person's problems frequently arise not because they sign and do not hear but because hearing people hear and speak and do not sign. Many sign poems (including many of Dorothy's) have themes concerning some of the frustrations of Deaf people, but these are directed against a hearing world that seems intent on misunderstanding Deaf people (for example, *Walking Down the Street* and *Unsound Views*). They are not directed against deafness or Deaf people and give no suggestion that a Deaf person is lacking.

The sensory experience of Deaf people is a central feature of many sign language poems. Sound – and the lack of it – has very little place in this poetry. There are no longing laments for the loss of the mother's voice or a child's cry, and there is no sadness and yearning for birdsong and sweet voices in a choir. Sound and speech are simply irrelevant. Instead, ideas of sight are brought to the foreground, reaffirming the positive side of the Deaf experience of life. Time and again, the ideas of looking, seeing, of eyes and vision are woven apparently casually into sign poems. The references seem so unremarkable that it takes a moment of readjustment and consideration for readers (perhaps especially hearing readers) to recognise their significance.

This visual perspective on the world is seen clearly in Dorothy Miles' poems. Perhaps the clearest image of the importance of vision comes in *Language for the Eye* (p. 243), where she equates the eye with the heart. This poem has two stanzas. The final line of the first stanza runs: 'The word becomes the picture in this language for the eye.' The final line of the second stanza runs: 'The word becomes the action in this language of the heart.' By drawing on the analogy between eye and heart she invokes the associations with 'heart' common to all users of English and connects them to 'eye', thus asserting the importance of the eye to a language which relies upon being seen. This concern with vision occurs throughout her poetic work and, as the following examples show, they vary from pointed use of verbs of vision to everyday phrases which take on increased significance when placed in the context of her work as a whole. (To emphasise the references to vision, they have been set in bold type in these examples.) From *The Staircase* (p. 246):

> A **dark** forest. A figure creeps forward, **peering** ahead,
> ....
> ... they see a **light** that **glimmers, glimmers.**

In the 'Deaf' forest, the enticing image is light in darkness. For a society that values vision so highly, darkness is to be avoided and light is worth seeking. This makes the cat all the more strange, with its night vision. From *The Cat* (p. 240):

> in the **light**
> her **eyes** wink and blink,
> but at **night**
> they **open** as wide as the sky.

In some poems, looking and seeing are used to mean understanding (as in the English phrase 'Oh, I see!'). In *To a Deaf Child* (p. 247), Dorothy uses the idea of sight to make sense of the world in the line: 'that henceforth he who **sees** aright may **hear**'. This is signed in a BSL performance as: FROM-NOW-TO-FUTURE PEOPLE **SEE-ALL-AROUND** RIGHT CAN **HEAR UNDERSTAND**. In the English version, the link between hearing and understanding is implied. In the BSL version, it is stated explicitly with the two signs.

This idea that seeing is understanding occurs again in *Total Communication* (p. 248) with the lines 'I **look**, and **look** –/ and **see:**'. Seeing, in this poem, is directly connected to the eye, but it reaches further than this straightforward – although perhaps highly significant – use of the idea. In the English version, *Total Communication* makes a lot out of the pun of 'eye' and 'aye' and 'I' – three images that are self-affirming to a Deaf person:

> Must we forever;
> **eye** to **eye**;
> **stare** past
> to what we want to **see?**
> Or can our minds
> send messages,
> and your mind's **aye**
> meet my mind's **aye?**

Many hearing people believe that Deaf people inhabit a world of silence. This is an extremely powerful misunderstanding that is hard to overcome. Hearing people can only imagine what *their* world would be like if they became Deaf, and they imagine that they would experience the lack of sound as silence. For many Deaf people, who have little or no memory of sound, silence is not the lack of sound (how can people experience the lack of something they have never known?). Instead, silence is a visual experience of stillness and a lack of movement. The BSL sign that we would use to equate with the English word 'silence' has several English meanings – peace, quiet, silence and stillness (Fig. 7.2).

Dorothy makes use of the ambiguity covered by this sign in *Sinai* (p. 245), showing the visual side of silence:

> Around me
> **silence** infinite lingers;
> the wind
> has blown out, and the birds
> have flown from my listening **eye.**

Here the silence that lingers is not the silence that a hearing person would experience in the mountains and it is not the 'silence' that hearing people assume is experienced by a Deaf person who cannot hear sounds. Instead, the silence is the lack of movement in the mountains at the end of the day. The 'silence' is stillness when the wind has dropped and the birds have gone to roost. In the English poem, the word chosen is 'silence' but in the BSL poem the sign carries the meanings of peace and stillness as well.

In *Walking Down the Street* (p. 251), we see a different side to visual language. At first, we are introduced to the normal experience of walking down the street, and we are shown it immediately from the visual perspective:

> **See** me now, I'm walking down the street
> If you **watch** me bustling along
> Would you say that there was anything wrong?

However, the poem turns on the visual skill (and limitations) of lip-reading. What Deaf people see on the lips is not what hearing people think they see. In the build to the climax of this wickedly playful, angry poem, the hearing woman speaks to the Deaf character. Hearing people experience a chance request for directions as sound, but the poem shows this casual encounter as one of sight and of trying to recreate an English message based on lip-reading:

> So you come up to me (so many do) and say:
> 'Excuse me, wubble roh a bissel tiva meniday?'
> And I'll say:
> 'Would you say that again?'
> And your lips say:
> 'I jussápakka winter enzo rushy colla den'.

The poem is an angry reaction against Oralism and the expectation that Deaf people will lip-read easily. It is not primarily aimed at hearing people (despite the fact that it appears to address the hearing woman ('So **you** come up to me'). Instead, it is part of the shared Deaf experience and is really a poem for Deaf people to enjoy and to say, 'Yes, I've been there too, and it's OK to feel angry about it.'

The examples given here so far have been ones that occur in both the written (English) and the signed (BSL and ASL) versions of her poems. However, there are many more examples of occurrences of eyes and sight and vision in the signed versions, which do not occur in the English versions. All these occasions of 'looking' arise in the signed poems because of the importance of vision and sight to the Deaf poet and the Deaf audience. Placing these images in the sign language poem empowers poet and audience. In the BSL poem *Christmas List* (p. 240), for example, the snake in the game of snakes and ladders jumps up and looks the child straight in the eye. There are other times when the looking is done non-manually when the child looks on in satisfaction as the cannons shoot down the row of tin soldiers and later the child looks for help in playing the word-games. There is no mention of any of this in the English version of the poem. The first line of the English poem *Unsound Views* (p. 250) simply mentions that hearing people are odd ('Hearing people, I find them odd'). The BSL poem, though, uses the idea of vision: HEARING PEOPLE THERE / I **LOOK-AROUND-THERE** / STRANGE THERE. In the English poem, she remarks, 'The two of us, / we're face to face', but the BSL, again, explicitly mentions sight: WE-TWO SIT-OPPOSITE-EACH-OTHER **LOOK-AT-EACH-OTHER**. A similar construction occurs in *Our Dumb Friends* (p. 244), where the ASL version begins: DOG BEEN **SEE** DIFFERENT TRUE but the English first line runs, 'Dogs all over vary'. The English makes no reference to seeing the dogs.

Celebration of Deaf success and success of the Deaf community

Although many of Dorothy's poems are implicit celebrations of sign language and the Deaf community, her poems of 'Deaf Pride' clearly salute them. Several of Dorothy's poems are concerned with a familiar dilemma faced by Deaf people: do they stay safe within an undemanding but limiting life, or do they attempt to better their situation, risking the security of their unchallenging world? This theme occurs in such poems as *Sinai* and *The Staircase* (and *The Hang-Glider*, which we will discuss later in Chapter 11).

In *Sinai* (p. 245), the poet is alone, forging her path to the future, as her companions straggle far behind her. The path is lonely and frightening. There are precipices above and below ('To my left, steep rise; / to my right, steep fall') and she is aware of her vulnerability on this exposed trail ('I, puny plodder'). Despite the beauties of the path and the magnificent sunset, she is tempted to return to the safety of the group – the age-old dilemma for a member of the Deaf community. The thrust of this poem is that only by following the call within can the poet reach her destiny and truly know herself. We have already discussed the end of this poem in our consideration of ambiguity and morphing signs. The sign that represents the rockface that meets the puny plodder at 'the End' becomes the sign MIRROR, showing that only by continuing along the 'urgent trail' can the poet find herself.

The theme of *The Staircase* is one of Deaf people who are offered the challenge of climbing the staircase and winning great rewards. The challenge is not without risks and they need to decide whether or not to accept it. At first the imagined dangers of the journey are too much for them: fear of possible lions, swamps and giants puts them off their quest. However, one member of their group encourages them to take the risk and climb to success. The way that the group achieves success is shown in an especially 'Deaf' way in the poem. Firstly, the hero is not a typical hero in the 'Superhero' mould. He is described as being 'balding, spectacled and somewhat plump', yet he is the one who leads them to their triumph. The important message here is that anyone in the Deaf community can be a hero. Secondly, the hero leads the people up the stairs step by step. Often, the only way for Deaf people to 'succeed in life' was to leave the Deaf world and join the hearing world. Such an image might have been shown in *The Staircase* by the hero running to the top of the stairs and then beckoning to the others to follow him. The distance between the top and bottom of the staircase would be too great, however, and the others would not be able to make the journey alone. Instead, he climbs the first step, checks that everything is safe and helps people up. They, in turn, help other people onto that first step until they are all united in their small advance. Such an approach to success in the Deaf community comes from an especially Deaf perspective.

These themes that we have considered arose from a combination of Dorothy's own particular experiences and her experiences as a Deaf poet. These themes have dual importance for the empowerment of the Deaf community through the ideas expressed and the opportunities that these themes give to sign language for poetic creativity. Exploring the work of any sign language poet will reveal different themes, but they will all work in some way to empower Deaf people, and celebrate sign language.

8
Metaphor and Allusion

In the last chapter we considered the themes that occur in many sign language poems, using Dorothy Miles' compositions as examples. Frequently, the themes were used as metaphors and symbols for other ideas, and in this chapter we will now consider poetic metaphor in general. Earlier chapters have described several different ways in which poetic language becomes 'foregrounded' when it stands out as being different from normal, everyday language. Just as the *form* of language may stand out as being unusual in a poem, so may the *meaning* of the language be unusual, too. A key aim of poetry is to get the greatest significance into the fewest well-chosen words, and one way to do this is to create more than one layer of meaning in the poem. People usually do not expect hidden meaning in everyday language, but in poetry the audience can assume that there are hidden meanings to seek out behind the surface meaning that first presents itself. Metaphor allows poets to use one idea to express another, and this poetic device is as crucial to added significance in sign language poetry as it is in spoken language poetry.

Metaphor

Metaphors are found in everyday language, as well as in poetry. They are invaluable for our everyday thinking, allowing us to treat abstract things in a concrete way. We use spatial metaphors, for example, when we talk about the abstract idea of status. Powerful, important or respected people and institutions are – metaphorically – considered 'higher' than the less powerful or less important: we 'look up' to those we respect and 'look down' on those we don't. BSL also uses metaphors such as these, so that status and ideas of 'good' and 'bad' in BSL use similar spatial metaphors to English.

In poetry, though, metaphor allows the poet to bring together ideas that appear quite disparate and have perhaps not been connected before. It is helpful to think about metaphor using the terms 'tenor', 'vehicle' and 'ground': the tenor is what we are talking about; the vehicle is the image or analogue; and the ground is what we see as the link between the tenor and the vehicle. In some unpublished lecture notes, Dorothy Miles gave an example of metaphor in sign language play. She explained how 'a gull in flight will become an airplane dropping a bomb'. This uses the idea of the gull in flight as the tenor, but the idea of an aeroplane dropping a bomb is the vehicle. The ground is made by the formational similarities between the signs for the gull and the aeroplane, coupled with our knowledge from seaside holidays that many gulls have apparently finely honed 'target-servicing' skills.

Christmas List (p. 240) uses the metaphor of a seed planted in our head from which intelligence will grow. This is signed by taking a seed from the palm of the hand and placing it at the head, as though planting it there. The tenor is the idea that intelligence starts small but can grow. The vehicle is the idea that a seed can be planted in our head. The ground is that both seeds and intelligence can grow. Here we have to understand the idea that a seed of intelligence needs to be planted in the head because that is where we expect to find intelligence (and, importantly, that is where the sign INTELLIGENCE is located). Normally we expect the sign PLANT-SEED to move from the palm to an area of space in front of the signer used to refer to soil. The novelty of the new image stems from the fact that the metaphor in the poem uses a new end location of the head so that the seed appears to be literally planted in the head. The 'tenor' and 'vehicle' in a poem may be either concrete or abstract, but the poet's insight into an experience or situation links the two ideas through an original 'ground' or through the explicit and foregrounded use of a widely familiar concept. We are all familiar with the idea of 'planting an idea in someone's mind' but the poet's skill lies in presenting a visually literal interpretation of it. It is also quite common in poetry for the poet to present only the vehicle but not the tenor in the poem. In some way, we can say that the vehicle has been superimposed onto the tenor. Where this happens, the poet has achieved extra meaning without adding any extra words.

Extended metaphor and allegories

An entire poem can be a metaphor, in that it can be a vehicle for another idea. On the surface, a whole poem can appear to be 'about' one subject, when in fact it is 'about' another. In this case, only the vehicle is presented and it is the audience's task to identify the tenor and interpret the ground that links the two. Dorothy composed poems which were extended metaphors in themselves, and many of them concerned the experience of the Deaf community. Many of the 'nature' and animal-themed poems that we considered in the previous chapter were metaphorical. *Elephants Dancing* (p. 242) uses the idea of animals trained to serve humans at the cost of their own freedom, to parallel the idea of Deaf people being obliged to conform to the norms and expectations of hearing society. Nowhere in the poem is there any reference to Deaf people, but when we observe the poems in the light of the experience of Deaf people, we can look for this 'hidden' meaning. *The Ugly Duckling* (p. 249) also deals with the rejection of Deaf people as 'different'. Again, there is no explicit mention of deafness anywhere in the poem and the story is ostensibly simply a visually aesthetic signed performance of the well-known Hans Christian Andersen story, but we are expected to see the poem as a metaphor for the Deaf experience. The whole poem is a vehicle for a tale of a Deaf child who will initially feel rejected and different before meeting others like him and finding happiness.

The Staircase – An Allegory (p. 246) uses extended metaphor to tell a story of Deaf people being helped by other Deaf people to overcome their fears and achieve academic success. *The Staircase* is told as a story in which people are lost in a forest and come to a great staircase, which they fear to climb. One of their group leads them up the staircase, one step at a time, until they reach the top and are rewarded with certificates. The poem was composed to celebrate the graduation of the first Deaf students from the British Sign Language Training Agency at Durham University. When we know that this was the reason for the poem's creation, we know that it cannot simply be a poem about people lost in a forest who climb some stairs. The circumstances of a poem's composition and performance, then, also tell us to look for the extended meaning. However, if we were in any doubt that this poem was an extended metaphor, this time the words in the title '– An Allegory' tell us that it is, because an allegory is a particular type of extended metaphor that takes the form of a narrative, as this poem does.

There are many examples of these allegories in sign poems, particularly when the poet wants to show sign language or the experience of the Deaf community in the light of some other analogous situation. Ella Mae Lentz's ASL poem *The Treasure* concerns the discovery of a treasure chest and the reaction of different people to the discovery. She uses the vehicle of the precious and valuable treasure chest to draw parallels with the 'discovery' of sign language (so precious to Deaf people) and various reactions to this discovery (see Taub, 2001). Clayton Valli's *Pawns* (1995) is ostensibly about the fate of pawns in a chess game, but is actually about the AIDS epidemic in the American Deaf community, where Deaf people with AIDS are treated as perfunctorily as pawns in a chess game. John Wilson's BSL poem *From the Depths* uses the vehicle of the hunting and killing of a magnificent whale to describe the education system that destroyed a Deaf child's use of sign language.

Similes

In many metaphors, only the vehicle is expressed in the poem, and the audience is obliged to work out both what the tenor is behind the vehicle and what the ground is that links the tenor and vehicle (although not necessarily in that order). Similes, though, highlight both the tenor and vehicle and may also use words such as 'like' and 'as' to explicitly compare two ideas that have been brought together in some novel way. Even in similes, though, the ground is usually still left to the audience to identify. Similes also compare only one aspect of tenor with vehicle, so they do not require the imaginative engagement of more extensive metaphors.

Dorothy Miles understood that similes were a useful way of bringing imagery and metaphor into focus in her sign language poetry. She knew that the explicit marking of a comparison between two ideas helped audiences appreciate the imagery she was producing, especially when there was a pause or hold at the point where the comparison was introduced, giving the audience time to reflect. She wrote in her notes for a lecture in 1976:

> TAKE YOUR TIME. For both similes and metaphors, plenty of time should be given for the audience to follow the transformation from one image to another. For similes, pause after introducing the first image before signing the linking word ('like', 'looks like', etc.): for metaphor, pause and possibly freeze the sign after establishing the key image.

Her instruction that the poet could sign 'looks like' as a simile marker is especially important, and we will see that many of her simile images were based on some sort of visual similarity of signs as well as having a link through meaning. She used signs such as LIKE, MAYBE, SAME and WHAT-IS-IT in many of her poems to signal a simile clearly in her sign poetry. Again, we are invited to think why the two ideas are like each other. Particularly, in many of her uses of similes the two ideas are linked not only through their meanings, but also by the visual form of the signs that express the ideas.

Exaltation (p. 242) contains similes. The English lines run 'standing there, so high, / They seemed **like** fingers reaching for the sky'. In this obvious – and perhaps not very original – comparison of trees with fingers, we are clearly invited to consider the ways in which trees could be like fingers. The most immediate interpretation is that the branches of the trees have physical similarities to fingers. Thus far, the simile is not especially noteworthy. However, the simile in the ASL poem adds a new, visual and formational dimension to the linking of the two ideas. The ASL poem phrases the same lines as:

> STAND TREE-THERE SO HIGH
> TREE SEEM MAYBE FINGERS REACH-UP TOUCH SKY.

Here the signs SEEM MAYBE highlight the simile, but the crucial difference between the English simile and the ASL one is that the ASL simile links the tenor and vehicle through direct visual similarity in the signs. The ASL sign TREE is made with all the fingers of a '5' hand pointing upwards, and the simile relies on the way that these fingers change from being merely the abstract handshape of a sign to being real fingers. In the sign of the tenor, the fingers represent branches, and in the sign of the vehicle the fingers are really fingers.

Christmas Magic (p. 241) also contains similes relating to fingers. The English lines run 'And suddenly magic is all around me/ **Like** shivery fingers on my skin'. The signs in the BSL poem (some of which may be seen in Fig. 3.5) run:

> SUDDEN MAGIC
> MAGIC-EXPLODES-AND-CIRCLES-AROUND-HEAD
> LIKE FINGERS COLD
> FINGERS-TICKLE-UP-ARMS/MAGIC-TICKLES-UP-ARMS.

It is clear from the gloss how this simile works in the BSL poem. Firstly, as in the English poem, the simile is clearly laid out as MAGIC ... LIKE FINGERS but in the following sign the visual form and the meaning bring out several layers of poetic significance. To fully appreciate the way this works, we need to consider briefly the use of metaphor in the construction of certain visually motivated signs (Brennan, 1989, 1992). In some signs, individual fingers are used, in a literal manner, to represent things that are long and thin. This occurs in the BSL signs such as FRINGE, FENCE and GRASS; the fingers in FRINGE represent long thin hairs; in FENCE, long thin fence posts; and in GRASS, long thin blades of grass. We have already seen in Chapter 6 how a single finger can 'be' a dog's thin tail. However, the 'long thin' meaning of the individual fingers can also be used metaphorically for other signs, such as LIGHT and TELEPATHY. The fingers in LIGHT represent, metaphorically, the individual 'thin' rays of light. In TELEPATHY, they represent 'thought rays'.

Once we are aware of this aspect of metaphor and visually motivated signs, we can see that Dorothy's poem implies magic is in something like fingers in a deeper way than just the conventional gesture of casting a spell. In the BSL sign MAGIC, the hands open to give out metaphorical fingers of 'thin magic beams'. Beams of magic are logically expressed in BSL by individual fingers because the language uses individual fingers to represent any sort of emanation from a source. So, MAGIC is formationally like FINGERS, in BSL. Our arms are also covered in small hairs that stand on end when we are cold, frightened or excited. The hairs standing on end would also be signed using the individual fingers to represent the individual small hairs along the arm. Furthermore, fingers could lightly touch and tickle the arms. Formationally, then, fingers moving up someone's arms would look similar to a BSL sign showing the hairs standing up on someone's arms. Finally, the magic is also running along the poet's arms because it is all around her. We know that magic is going to be represented by the individual fingers because it is something 'emanating from a source'. So the magic rays covering the arms are formationally the same as the fingers touching the arms and the hairs standing up on the arms. At some level of meaning, these ideas are also conveyed in the English simile that likens magic to cold fingers because both would make the hairs stand up on our arms. In BSL, though, it is the visual similarity of the different interpretations that makes the simile work so well.

Unsound Views (p. 250), a polemic against hearing people's relationship to the telephone, also contains similes. Before text telephones were widespread, Deaf people objected strongly to the way that hearing people frequently treated the ringing telephone (which the Deaf person could not even hear) as a higher priority than the Deaf person who was present. The BSL poem uses similes, as we can see in the rough gloss given here. The comparisons are made using LIKE and WHAT:

HAVE ... WELL ... EXTRA LINE-FORWARD-FROM-NAVEL
LIKE BIRTH LINE-FORWARD-FROM-NAVEL
CONNECT THERE **WHAT** THERE
TELEPHONE
LIKE RUSSIAN HIS HAVE DOG

WHEN BELL-RING
DOG
EARS-PRICK-UP, LEGS-RUN
LIKE ... WELL ... REACH GRAB
HOLD-PHONE-TO-EAR
WHAT
TELEPHONE
BONE
TALK-INTO-PHONE/BARK-INTO-PHONE/CHEW-ON-BONE/
CHEW-ON-PHONE

Different ideas are brought together here in a novel way to highlight the relationship that hearing people have to telephones. The similes mock hearing people by comparing the telephone cord to an umbilical cord. The linking idea is that of a line or cord for both a telephone and the foetus. They are two 'lines' that people rarely connect together. The use of an umbilical cord in a simile places hearing people into the same category as helpless babies, tied to the telephone for all their 'nourishment' and unable to live independently. This little joke turns on its head the prevalent hearing view of Deaf people as somehow childlike and dependent.

The next dig at hearing people is to liken them to animals, unable to control their basest responses to a simple stimulus. The joke of the simile rests on the two bells – one rung for Pavlov's dogs and one ringing on a telephone. However, the comparison goes further in the BSL version of the poem, treating the dogs and humans as the same by showing a dog's ears pricking up but human legs running for the phone. The blending of the two identities is then taken a step further in the English poem by the play on words in 'tele-bone', blending 'bone' and 'telephone'. In the BSL poem, the pun occurs on the same signs (Fig. 8.1).

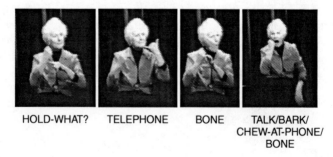

HOLD-WHAT?   TELEPHONE   BONE   TALK/BARK/
CHEW-AT-PHONE/
BONE

Fig. 8.1

The handshape used in a sign for handling a telephone and handling a bone is the same and the exact referent is only specified by the signing context. The joke works because the poet signs both TELEPHONE and BONE, so when she signs that the person picks up the object, it could be a bone or a telephone. This stanza of the English poem stops at this point but there is one more sign in the BSL poem: TALK-INTO-PHONE/BARK-INTO-PHONE/CHEW-ON-BONE/CHEW-ON-PHONE. Hearing people may like to believe that they give the impression of dignified sophistication when talking into the phone. For the disgruntled Deaf person, though, they look no more impressive than a dog gnawing on a bone or barking into the phone. The sign used in the final line of this section is beautifully ambiguous. The mouth opens and closes at the location of the dominant hand holding the telephone/bone. In everyday language, context would tell us whose mouth it is – a human's or an animal's – and why it is opening and closing – to talk, bark or eat. However, because we don't know if the dominant hand is signing telephone or bone, nor if the creature in question is a hearing person or a dog, we cannot clarify the meaning. Consequently, we can entertain all four possible interpretations at once, and laugh at the ludicrous images created by the simile.

Allusion

An allusion is an indirect reference to something else, such as a piece of art or literature or to another person or event, and is an important part of poetry. Poets are able to extend the significance of their work by planting allusions to other work. When a word or phrase in the poem brings to mind another poem or piece of work, the poet has managed to access a new source of meaning for the audience without using any extra words or signs. Allusion in poems may be to other poems by other poets, or perhaps to other great literary works such as the Bible or Shakespeare. They may also be phrases used by prominent members of a community, or may simply refer to other experiences and situations that a poet can expect the audience to share. Poets may even allude to some of their own poems.

Allusiveness can be subtle and the poet's intention for allusion is not always highlighted, so the audience might not recognise the allusion. However, so long as the poem does not entirely rely on the recognition of the allusion, this is no great loss. It is also possible for readers to find some resonance in a line that reminds them of another text, even when the poet did not intend it. In the end, it probably does not matter if the poet intended the allusion or not; if the audience finds an allusion and this provides a further element to the experience of the poem, then it is an important part of the appreciation of the poem.

Dorothy Miles could not make allusions to other sign poets in her own sign poetry because there were no other signed poems sufficiently well known at the time. However, after her death, one of her students, Barry Curtis, composed *Sweet Dreamer* containing allusions to her work. Two lines from *Sweet Dreamer* may be rendered in English as: 'Your hands and poems were like treetops blowing in the wind. / You were the pearl, freed from its shell.' In the BSL poem that these lines translate, there are many beautiful visual images in the signs used, and the English translation does not do justice to the poetic BSL, which is richly crafted. However, even from the English version we can see that Curtis deliberately alludes to several of Dorothy's poems. Through 'treetops blowing in the wind', he alludes to all the references to wind and trees that occur in Dorothy's work. These include *The Winds of Change* ('But I, uprooted, ask of the winds of change:'), *Cloud Magic* ('Upon a windy hill I lie') and *Exaltation* ('That sudden glimpse of trees against the sky'). This line also brings to mind the first stanza of *Trio* ('the wind dies / Stillness / See, in the pool / twin trees') and the haiku verse *Spring* ('Sunshine, borne on breeze, / among singing trees'). Through 'freed from its shell', he alludes to *The BDA is …* ('Deaf people everywhere are out of the shell').

It is important to note that we do not need knowledge of any of these poems by Dorothy to understand and appreciate Barry Curtis' poem, especially not his BSL poem. However, knowing the origin of his metaphors adds several new layers of meaning to it, because he has been able to refer to at least eight other poems without mentioning one of them directly. As the critic I.A. Richards put it (1929: p. 217), 'One familiar with [the allusion] will respond more fully and with a deeper sense of the situation; but a reader unfamiliar with it is not deprived of any major part of the poem.'

Although Dorothy was not able to refer to the sign poetry of others, there are allusions to other written poems and other literature in her work. She had a degree in English Literature from Gallaudet College and so knew how allusion could be used to show off the poet's knowledge of other literature, or to invite the audience to play games of one-upmanship when they spot a reference. Dorothy did not appear to indulge in such games herself but nevertheless did use allusion when it suited her. We know, from interviews with Dorothy recorded in the mid-1970s, that her fellow-Welshman Dylan Thomas was a great influence on her work and that she took part in a signed performance of his

A Child's Christmas in Wales. For this reason, when we see her Christmas poem *Christmas List* (p. 240) we should not be surprised to see allusions to *A Child's Christmas in Wales* in which Thomas describes the presents a small child could hope for, categorising them as 'Useful Presents' and 'Useless Presents'. Alluding to this famous piece of Welsh literature in *Christmas List*, Dorothy lists and describes the frivolous presents that she and the other children asked for, and the practical ones that the adults actually gave them. Thomas and Dorothy even refer to some of the same 'Useless Presents'. Thomas mentions (1952: pp. 307–8):

And a packet of cigarettes: you put one in your mouth and you stood at the corner of the street and you waited for hours in vain, for an old lady to scold you for smoking a cigarette, and then with a smirk you ate it.

And troops of bright tin soldiers who, if they could not fight, could always run. And Snakes-and-Families and Happy Ladders.

As we have seen, *Christmas List* also refers to candy cigarettes, tin soldiers and snakes and ladders. The two poets play different games with the language they use and the images they create with the toys. Nevertheless, Dorothy's choice of the same toys creates a strong link to Thomas so that we can add the images from his description of a child at Christmas in Wales to the one that she describes.

Other poems of Dorothy's contain allusions to other poems. In *Exaltation* (p. 242), the final lines are rendered in English as:

As if they sought to part the veil of blue
And let the peace of Heaven shine softly through.
Then for a moment from this lowly sod
I reached with them to touch the face of God.

John Magee, a young Canadian fighter pilot, wrote *High Flight* in 1941 after he had flown at high altitude to test the new Spitfire V. After describing the ecstasy of flying at such great altitude, the final line of his sonnet runs 'put out my hand and touched the face of God'.

Although Magee died shortly after he wrote the poem, it was widely circulated and became a part of several collections. As Dorothy wrote *Exaltation* in the 1950s, it is highly likely that she would have come across the poem. She uses a familiar phrase in a new situation, but in doing so calls to mind ideas of *High Flight*. In her poem, she touches the face of God from the ground, but with allusion to *High Flight* we can imagine another dimension of flight and freedom and all the elements of ecstasy described in that poem.

The Staircase – An Allegory (p. 246) carries a religious allusion to a Buddhist view of the path to Nirvana – a state of bliss or perfection. In *The Staircase*, people wandering through a dark forest are afraid to climb the steep staircase in case they should meet dangers, including a swamp. Nevertheless they do climb the precipitously steep staircase to reach their reward of the certificate. One Buddhist description of the 'Right Path' is that it starts in a thick forest and leads through swamps and precipices before reaching the flat land of Nirvana. The parallel between the two 'journeys' is striking. There is little lost from our enjoyment of *The Staircase* if we see the obstacles to the travellers in Dorothy's poem as merely a selection of possible dangers before they reach their longed-for goal of educational enlightenment. However, if we see them as equivalent stages on a quest to spiritual enlightenment, this adds an extra dimension to the poem. There is no need for Dorothy to make explicit mention of a spiritual element to *The Staircase* because the images she chooses can call to mind the spiritual path. A further trail of allusion begins in *The Staircase* with mention of the sword embedded in a stone. This is clearly a reference to the Arthurian legend and brings to mind another type of quest.

Although the allusions here are to myths or other works of literature, we should remember that allusion can be any invitation to a reader to share some experience with the poet. Allusions may be to events and people, as much as to literature and art. Thus, Dorothy's many allusions to the world in which Deaf people live are important elements in her poems. Her poem *Conversation*, in which she answers questions from ignorant hearing people (a sort of 'Frequently Asked Questions' list to Deaf people from hearing people), is an example of a situation so familiar to Deaf people that she does not need to fill in any of the background information. Many of the comments from the hearing person in the poem are simply inferred ('I lipread, yes … / Oh no! I don't read Braille … / Really not 'Wonderful! … '). There's no need to spell out to a Deaf audience what those questions are because they have all shared the experience and met such people, but hearing readers may find that they need to consider the questions asked.

There is also an allusion to the educational method of Total Communication in the poem *Total Communication* (p. 248). The philosophy of Total Communication was that any and all methods of communication should be used with Deaf children. It advocated the simultaneous use of spoken English on the mouth with signing on the hands, on the grounds that this would increase the children's access to the two languages. As we will see in our discussion of blended poems in a later chapter, it is physically impossible to speak grammatical English and sign grammatical BSL or ASL at the same time. The usual outcome is a garbled message. As a reaction against this unhelpful method of education, by the 1980s there were political button-badges in circulation that simply stated, 'Total Communication is neither'. Dorothy's poem *Total Communication* concerns the fact that although the two characters appear to be communicating clearly, they are not. Audiences who are aware of the problems with the educational method can enjoy the extra dimension of the irony that 'total communication is neither' in this poem from the allusion made in the title of the poem.

Although Dorothy Miles made considerable use of allusions and overt similes in her poems, these are less widespread in much contemporary sign language poetry. The general use of metaphor, however, and especially extended metaphor to describe the experiences of being a Deaf person, occurs extensively in the work of many sign poets.

9
The Poem and Performance

So far in our consideration of sign language poems, we have been treating them as though they have a recognisable, abstracted form of text, which contains the content of the poem. However, there are times when it is difficult to distinguish the 'text' of the poem from its 'performance'. Heidi Rose (1992) considers the performance of sign language poems, and having acknowledged that a 'text' may be defined as 'the original words of an author', goes on to the idea of a 'performed text', which 'would include all aspects of articulation, gesticulation and *mise-en-scène*' (p. 23). Geoffrey Leech (1969) notes in relation to English poetry that performance 'is clearly extraneous to the poem, for the poem is what is given on the printed page, in abstraction from any special inflections, modulations etc., which a performer might read into it, just as the play *Hamlet* exists independently of actual performances and actual theatrical productions' (p. 104). It is less easy to make this distinction in sign language poems, because the abstraction on the printed page is always a *translation* of the signed poem, and there is less justification for claiming that the sign language poems do exist independently of their performances. In this chapter we will consider the various elements of performance that form an essential part of sign language poetry, and see how signers use their performance of the poem to create an effect on the audience.

Whose poem is this?

A major distinction between 'oral' poetry and the poetry of literate communities is that literate communities recognise the idea of 'authorship' of a frozen, fixed poem text, whereas oral poetry is often unattributed to any author and it is shared by the community as a whole, with licence given to anyone to alter the text in the way that is appropriate for the moment. However this distinction is not always so clear, and oral communities do recognise some works as belonging to specific composers, just as literate communities do (Finnegan, 1977). Often in such circumstances, the composer of the work is the only person to perform it, and this has often been the case for sign language poets, too. In the absence of widely available video-recordings of poetry performances, other performers have not been able to study the work in sufficient depth to produce their own versions. This situation is changing, due in some part to the publication of video-recordings of poems. Heidi Rose (1992) describes a student performance at Arizona State University in 1991 of selected works composed by three ASL poets which had recently been published in the Poetry in Motion series of videotapes. She claims that:

> The performance was unique because it was the first time a collection of original ASL works were presented publicly, not by their creators, but by Deaf performers who interpreted them. Videotape made publication of these works possible; hence, the students could study and perform a text preserved on videotape the same way they could study a written text. (p. 62)

Increasingly, people other than the poet perform signed poetic works – especially the more popular ones, such as Dorothy's *Seasons* haikus or *Language for the Eye* or Clayton Valli's poems. On the commercial videotape of some of Valli's poems distributed by Dawn Sign Press, there are different performers for each poem. This has the effect of giving the Deaf community greater ownership of the poems there. Several performers are Deaf children, showing Deaf children that they can have a share in sign language poetry even when they have not composed it.

Cynthia Peters (2000) has observed that video-recorded performances of ASL literature have led to the increased acceptance of the idea that there is a definitive performance that is 'the' performance, and this may come to be regarded as 'the' text, so that other performers cannot alter it without it becoming a new, different work. How far another performer can acceptably alter the work of another poet in their own performance is still an open question. In some cases, performances of sign language poems may be the performer's own sign language translations of a written poem. For example, the actress Elizabeth Quinn has devised her own interpretation of several of Dorothy Miles' signed poems, based on the English text. Although other poets and performers have performed Dorothy Miles' signed poems (for example Jean St Clair's *Trio* and Ella Mae Lentz's *Total Communication*), there is still a general tendency for poets to perform their own sign language poems. This close relationship between poet, performer and performance has important implications for the 'ownership' of the content and emotions expressed in the poems.

In the usual, everyday use of language, 'I' is generally understood to be the person delivering the utterance and 'you' is understood to be the addressee, but in poetry this is not always the case. There is a general view among some poetic audiences that the world outside the poem is not relevant to the poem, and, instead, the situations made by the poem are the focus of interest. For this reason the 'I' and 'you' of a poem are often understood to mean the participants that the poem has decided should be called 'I' and 'you' (rather than the poet and the audience). The difference between the external, real-world 'I' and 'you' of poet and audience, and the poem's internal, created 'I' and 'you' can lead to different interpretations of the meaning of a poem, and we need to explore this further.

To know if the 'I' of the poem literally means the 'poet' or not we need to distinguish between the 'narrator' and the 'writer'. This idea is familiar to us in prose narratives where we frequently distinguish the narrator of the story from the person who put the words on the page. In *Jane Eyre* the narrator is Jane Eyre, even though the novel's author was Charlotte Brontë. When we read in the book, 'Reader, I married him,' we know that it was Jane Eyre, not Charlotte Brontë, who married Mr Rochester. Although we are usually content to separate narrator from author in prose, we might be more inclined to think that the 'I' in a poem should refer to both the narrator and the poet. Perhaps this is because we have an idea that the poem expresses something more personal than we might expect in a narrative. The tendency to equate the poet with 'I' might be thought to be the result of lack of education in the audience. An 'educated' audience for a poem might be more prepared to accept that there is a clear distinction between the poet and 'I', allowing wider interpretations of who that 'I' might be.

In fact, 'education' is not the key factor here. Rather, associating the performer or poet with responsibility for the utterance comes from the cultural heritage of the audience, most specifically if the audience is from a literate or a non-literate, oral culture. The right distinction here is between 'literate' and 'non-literate'[1] or 'oral' rather than between 'educated' and 'uneducated'. Sign language has a non-literate, oral culture (because sign languages are unwritten) and members of oral cultures have a greater tendency to adopt a subjective position about the ownership of an utterance (Ong, 1982; Branson and Miller, 1998). It is a natural part of an oral or non-literate culture to assume that the speaker is the person who 'owns' the utterance ('I') and that the audience is the addressee ('you') because communication always occurs face-to-face, and there is always a speaker and an addressee present for an utterance. It has only become possible to be more objective, and separate the speaker from the word, with the development of reading and writing (for which the writer or the addressee need not be present). As a culture becomes more literate, it may start to allow the suggestion that 'I' might be anyone other than the speaker and 'you' might be anyone other than the audience. The dissociation of 'I' and 'you' from the reality of the external world is a literate practice, not a non-literate one, so because of this (and because Deaf cultures are 'non-literate' cultures) we should expect a greater tendency to assume that the poet and performer 'own' their utterances in sign languages. Thus, oral audiences might expect a close link between the poet and the content of the poem (especially the emotional content), placing a certain trust in the 'sincerity' of the poem, and we must consider it here, because most Deaf audiences will be 'oral' in this respect.

Christmas List (p. 240) begins, 'When I was just a little girl,' and goes on to describe the experiences of a little girl's Christmas that we might want to trust were Dorothy Miles' experiences. We could accept that some things described in the poem are there for poetic effect rather than autobiographical accuracy but, taking the subjective, non-literate, oral approach to the idea of ownership of an utterance, we would expect the basic idea to be true. If we believe that the 'I' of the poem reflects the experiences of the poet, we would feel just a little let down if we discovered that her family never observed Christmas when she was a child. The poem would not be any less good, but we might feel differently about it. The factual content in poems does not need to be taken so literally, but we might still expect the poet's experience to be behind the emotions in them. Despite the fact that *The Hang Glider* (see Chapter 11) starts, 'Here are my wings', perhaps we would not feel any sense of betrayal if we learned that Dorothy never flew in a hang glider because we can recognise it as a metaphor. But we do want to believe that the emotions of fear, courage and exhilaration behind the encounter are genuine.

This idea that the poet should own the emotions in a poem can also be held by literate audiences. When we read highly moving, intensely emotional poems, we want to believe that we are seeing an expression of the poet's emotions. Many poems by Deaf poets are intensely emotional and have great emotional impact on a Deaf audience. If we cannot believe the sincerity of the poet, it can become harder for us to accept the emotions of the poem and the same emotions will not be re-created in us. On the other hand, many critics of poetry believe that knowledge of the poet and their ownership of the emotions can actually inhibit our appreciation of the emotion in the poem. If we do not consider the poet as part of the appreciation of the poem, and focus on only the text, it can free us to become more involved in the poem as readers or audience. We can place ourselves in the role of 'I', rather than merely being observers of the poet's experience and we can give the poet more credit for imagination. If poets can only write about their experiences, there is little scope for them to bring their imagination to poetic ideas, and there is less encouragement for us to use our imaginations to place ourselves in the poem. Although we can explore this idea here, we have to remember that ultimately this is not necessarily a non-literate, oral way of approaching poetry.

Knowing the poet's intentions can actually prevent us from exploring other ways of interpreting a certain poem. Biographical and autobiographical notes accompany Don Read's edited collection of Dorothy's poems, *Bright Memory*, and Dorothy provided comments on her poems in *Gestures* and at some of her performances. All these notes and comments can give us greater insight into some aspects of the poems. For example, it is useful to know that *The Hang Glider* was written when Dorothy felt anxious about her new life in California or that *To a Deaf Child* was composed as a result of a proposal to use sign language as a universal language to foster world peace. This information can help us understand the emotions behind the poems and will guide our reactions to them. However, if we only look at the poems from the perspective of the motivation behind their composition, we can miss out on other possible interpretations. Perhaps we could make other readings of some poems if we were not locked into the one interpretation that must be the 'true' one because it is based on the poet's experience.

The association of the poet with 'I' is especially strong when we consider poems performed by the poet (remembering that sign language poetry must be performed to exist). There is no problem in equating poet with performer when the poet *is* the performer because we can easily accept that, for example, the Dorothy signing *The Hang Glider* is the Dorothy who composed the poem, even if she never stood on that Californian cliff with her wings on her back. We can expect her to own the poem in different ways. However, when someone else performs the poem, we are faced with a dilemma: who owns the emotions and the experience now – the performer or the poet? It might be easiest to accept that while the poet and performer have some sort of legitimate responsibility for the poem, the emotions and experiences are most real in the *audience*, so that each person in the audience can feel that they are 'I'.[2]

On the whole, the non-literate audience might tend to expect the poet and the performer to stand by the ideas and sentiments expressed in the poems. When someone other than the poet performs the poem, there is a further understanding that the performer is bringing something else to the poem. Matterson and Jones (2000) use Robert Frost's poem *Stopping by Woods on a Snowy Evening* to illustrate this point. If we read it ourselves, or if we hear a man reading it aloud to us, we might automatically assume that the person stopping by the woods is a man, even though there is nothing in the text to signal this, simply because Robert Frost was a man. But when a woman performs the poem, we become open to the possibility that the person with the 'little horse' was a woman. The images created by the poem then shift into subtly different images.[3]

When poets perform their own work, we can understand it even more clearly, perhaps because we can see (and maybe hear) the link between the poet and the poem. Performance of any poetry composed today is often part of a poet's job (even when the poetry is also written) but signed poetry *must* be performed in order to exist and, as we saw above, it is usually performed by the poet. There is thus a direct relationship between the poem's 'I', the poet's 'I' and the performer's 'I' and this is in keeping with the oral or non-literate heritage of sign languages. Skilful poetry performances lead us to believe that the experiences and emotions in the poems are the emotions of the performer and the emotions of the poet expressed for us all to see, while at the same time asking us to share those experiences. Many signed poems also have a strong 'Deaf' element in their performance, especially those that have Deaf themes. A hearing person performing *To a Deaf Child* would create a different image in the minds of the audience, as the implication would be that a hearing person was giving the blessing to the Deaf child. Such an idea is not impossible, but the image created is very different from a Deaf person's blessing, such as we would expect if a Deaf person performed the poem.

Perhaps the wish to link the poem's sincerity to the credentials of the poet is particularly important for community poets. It is the job of a community poet to express the identity of the community and to represent community members in some way. We might claim that the automatic linking of the poet to 'I' is due to a lack of education, and that an ability and willingness to dissociate the poet from 'I' is more sophisticated. We might wish to argue that poetry should be about imaginative experience, so that it becomes a place where we can be other than we are. However, no matter how much we can claim that the ownership of a poem should not matter, it often *does* matter for members of minority communities using oral languages. Sign language poetry cannot be composed or performed by hearing people without a shift in the message. This is not a matter of sophistication, education, or otherwise – it is a cultural reality.

Performance and the audience

The importance of the audience cannot be underestimated when we consider a poem. The audience's enjoyment of the poem is perhaps the first issue, with their ability to understand it coming a close second. In some cases, their appreciation of the linguistic sophistication of the poem might also be relevant. Another vitally important consideration for a 'community poet' (as sign language poets might hope to be) is that the poems and their symbolism should have a resonance for the members of the community. For most sign language poets working today, the Deaf audience is the focus and the priority, but the term 'Deaf audience' covers many different people with different language skills. In a set of evaluation guidelines for assessing poetry composition and performance, Dorothy highlighted the importance of knowing the audience. She divided audiences for signed poems into several groups: Deaf adults with college education;[4] 'community' Deaf people (i.e. those with perhaps only the most basic education); Deaf children; hearing adults who know signs; hearing adults who do not know signs; and hearing children. She was aware that sign poems needed to be tailored to fit each of these groups.

The practical performance of a poem

Sign language poets and performers need to consider the audience when composing and performing their work. If the audience is to enjoy the poetry, the performer must have a good relationship with the audience. In one performance to a live audience made up primarily of members of the Deaf community, Dorothy Miles spent a short while in the introduction to *The Cat* discussing the different signs that audience members used to mean CAT and explaining which sign she was going to use. She also explained the background of the poems to her audience. These direct interactions with the audience helped her, as poet and performer, to bond with her audience.

Involving the audience in the poem is essential, but no amount of involvement will work if the audience does not understand the language in the poem, at least at some level. Dorothy's experience with the National Theatre for the Deaf (NTD) had taught her that Deaf audiences did not always understand the language used in the plays that the NTD performed. In notes from a poetry workshop in 1991, she gave the simple advice, 'Use language that can be understood.' The accuracy and completeness of signs is crucial for this and she cautioned would-be performers not to use 'slipshod' signs, warning, 'in signing "a grove of trees," where no base sign has been established, a careless movement of the hands to suggest trees may instead suggest the concept of "having a gay time".' (By 'base sign', she meant the frozen sign that is used to establish the identity of a referent.) In sign poetry, every sign should be as important as the next and clarity is essential for delivery. This is partly because poetry often brings together disparate images in new, pleasing ways, so context alone is not a guide for what a sign means because a poem could jump from one image to another without warning. For similar reasons, the positioning of signed images is also important in performance. Dorothy wrote, 'Place your images so that their relationship is clearly defined, and make sure that they do not "blur" or shatter each other.'

Even when the performer does not directly address the audience, the audience can still be drawn into the poetic experience through the performance. We know that it is not always possible to separate out which elements described here form 'part of the text' and which form 'part of the performance', but the key to appreciating the signed performance of a poem is to understand that they all work together to produce the final effect. Dorothy observed that the head, shoulders and torso should always be turned appropriately during the performance, and arms, elbows and wrists need to be controlled to increase poetic effect rather than interfere with it. Even the signer's legs and the stance and bending of the knees can be a significant factor in performance. Other elements of good sign performance were the 'visual qualities' of the signs. Performers should pay special attention to the size of the signs – were they large or small or varied? Dorothy also observed that signing could be 'jerky, bouncy, stiff, slushy or smooth' and while any of these movements in delivery might be used for poetic effect (see Blondel and Miller, 2001), where they were simply a part of the performer's poor diction they could seriously impair the poem. Performers also need to consider the energy or intensity behind the signs, making sure that delivery of the signs is neither too heavy nor too light. Speed and tempo will also impact on how well the language is understood. Again, these elements can be used carefully to poetic effect, but they can also simply be a part of the performer's natural signing style which could create the wrong effect on the audience. A delivery that is too fast will obviously impair enjoyment and understanding (on several occasions in her unpublished notes, and once in capital letters, Dorothy noted 'TAKE YOUR TIME'). However, a delivery that is too slow is not much better, and nor should the performer be hesitant or monotonous.

Gaze, an area where text and performance overlap, has many important roles in sign poetry, and one of the many uses of gaze is to draw the audience into the poem. In unpublished notes for a workshop in 1991, Dorothy advised poets and performers:

> Become involved with your images. Experience them while they are happening around you – look at them as you form them, and maintain eye contact as long as is necessary to keep your audience focussed in the right direction. At the same time, do not become so engrossed in your images that you ignore the audience. Glance at the audience from time to time to emphasize an image or event, to indicate a pause or change of image, and *especially* to convey an emotion or ask a question, or make a direct statement. (original emphasis)

The performer needs to consider other non-manual components too. Facial expression is extremely important (especially, as we will see in the discussion of personation below). The tradition in sign-mime such as was used by the NTD in the 1960s and 1970s was to produce signed poems (usually translations from English poems) in a style that used very few mouth movements and facial expressions that are important for understanding sign language. Facial expressions must be given their due importance, but can be communicated most powerfully when they are shown subtly. Dorothy wrote, in notes for a lecture in 1976: 'Try to convey your emotional response clearly, but honestly. It is not necessary to use exaggeration or sentimental expressions or movements. Emotions can be shown subtly through the eyes and posture, even at a distance.'

The use of the mouth is an element of signed performance that will vary depending on the style of the poem and its origins. It will also vary depending on the language of the poem. ASL generally uses relatively few mouth patterns derived from English, whereas BSL has a tradition of using many more (see Chapter 1). Even though BSL uses more English-derived mouth patterns, they need to be used carefully. Most importantly, the performer needs to make sure that the mouth patterns serve the signs in the poem and not the other way around. If English mouthings are allowed to dominate, they can begin to drive the structure of the poem, and its rhythm and tempo will become controlled by English (see Chapter 10).

Timing and speed of signing

The performance of a particular recitation of any poem – spoken or signed – is important for its rhythm. The timing and speed of the signs in performed poems have the potential to be varied according to the performance, and produce extra effect in the performance without any change to the grammatical or lexical content of the poem. In an interview for the BBC magazine programme *See Hear!* in 1983, Dorothy said:

> Hearing people use different ways to make you notice their meaning, like rhythm. If they want to make it exciting, they will have a fast rhythm. If they want it slow, boring, sleepy, they'll have a long rhythm ... Now, with sign language poetry, I try to use what sign language itself already has.

Almost any performance of her poems shows how important the rhythm and speed of her signing were. In the poems that were closest blends between English and sign language, the rhythm and speed were dictated by the rhythm of the English poems. This is especially clear in *The BDA is ...*, which is signed to the beat of the English rhythmic structure (see Chapter 10). However, for most poetry, the speed of the signing is dictated by the content of the poem and the mood that the poet wants the poem to create. We saw in Chapter 3 that patterns of speed and rhythm can be created from the movement and timing of signs in the text of the poem, but additional speed and rhythm can come from the performance of the poem.

In *Christmas Magic* (p. 241), timing, speed, and additional pauses are used to create the feeling of the excitement of the magic of Christmas. Importantly, these elements come from the performance and are imposed upon the timing and speed of the signs themselves, so there is no indication in the 'text' of the poem that they are part of the poem. The first section of the poem, which runs in English as 'I remember ... / In darkness, waking and wondering why / I feel excitement bubbling within' is signed with a slow, steady rhythm. The next line in English runs, 'And suddenly magic is all around me.' At this point the signs speed up, with the hold before the sharp release of signs such as SUDDEN and MAGIC, which reflect the bursts of excitement. There is a long pause before the repeat of 'I remember ...', as the poet takes the audience back to that time in childhood. The sharp, rapid movements of sitting up in bed and pushing back the bedclothes slow down and become much more relaxed with the description of the empty, limply hanging stocking. Contrasting speed again creates contrasting moods with the signs in the lines:

> Then out of bed and down the stairs,
> The magic still behind me streaming -
> Into the room where the fire's dim glow
> Touches the tree with a gentle gleaming

The first two lines here are signed rapidly, but at the reference to the fire the signs slow significantly to show the repeated glowing of the dim embers, allowing the soft, slow movements of the signs to reflect the ideas of 'dim' and 'gentle'. We should bear in mind that pauses are as important to the rhythm of poetry as the speed of movement of the signs, and there are many significant pauses in this poem, especially at the end of specific ideas, and at other division points in the poem. There is also a pause before the simile 'Like shivery fingers on my skin'. This pause is to highlight the visual similarity between the signs showing the idea of the magic feeling and the cold fingers, and is typical of the way that Dorothy used overt similes in her poems. Pauses also precede signs when they are creative neologisms, and additionally these signs are held or repeated for extra beats. We see this in the signs EXCITEMENT-BUBBLING-UP, MAGIC-EXPLODES, MAGIC-SHIVERS-UP-ARMS, FEEL-BUMPS-DOWN-STOCKING, FIRELIGHT-CARESSES-TREE, MAGIC-STREAMS-&-EXPLODES-ABOVE-HEAD. This use of timing and pauses in Dorothy's sign language poetry to highlight her creative neologisms is seen time and again. The poems slow for the neologism, which may be repeated several times (for example in many of the neologisms in *Christmas List*) or held for extra time (for example in *The Cat*).

The production of a poem

The visual nature of signed performances allows signers to experiment with styles of production that add extra visual impact to the poem. In some professional recordings of sign language poems there is scenery with props, but where poems are performed live, there are relatively few options for extra production, although lighting and some simple props such as a chair may be used. In most recordings of sign-poetry performances to live audiences, the poet simply stands in front of a plain backdrop.

The performance of sign language poetry also has unique features that arise from their visual nature. While the live performance of signed poetry may be no different from that of spoken poetry, filming techniques can also be used in conjunction with signed poems to draw attention to certain features of the poem. In signed poems, the camera can focus on a part of the signer such as the face or the hands or, even, a single hand. These articulatory body-parts are emphasised in order to highlight the sign being made. Focusing simply on the hands or the face at any particular time can add to the poetic significance of the performance. If the screen is filled by just the hands, it can serve to dissociate the signs from the signer. This can make the performer appear less salient and highlight the signs they are using. Humphrey-Dirksen Bauman (2003) has proposed that analysis of sign language poetry can borrow terms from cinematography, viewing ASL poems in terms of 'frames' and 'shots', be they close-ups, medium shots or long-shots, analogous to those used in films. When we consider that sign language poems today are increasingly presented in a film medium, we may expect a closer relationship between the poems and cinematographic techniques.

More than one performer

In most performances of sign poems, there is a single signer who is the central performer and takes on all the roles and characterisations in the poem, using role-shift and poetic personation (see below). Despite this, we should note that poetry does not need to be a solitary affair. In some poems, the performer can encourage the audience to get involved (as Dorothy Miles did at the BDA congress where she encouraged everyone to clap and stamp to her poem *The BDA is ...*). Signing choirs also have a long-established tradition within many Deaf communities, where choral works are almost always religious, and hymns are most commonly translated (or transliterated) into a sign language and signed as part of a communal act of worship in Deaf churches. Carol Padden and Tom Humphries have also described several communally produced, secular chants that were performed in ASL between the 1920s and 1960s and filmed by Charles Kraeul. Kraeul's films show several groups of Deaf people signing in unison, and also a 'duet' of two people standing facing each other and signing a chant. At a mass rally urging government recognition of BSL held in Trafalgar Square, London, by the Federation of Deaf People (FDP) in June 1999, the assembled crowd was encouraged to sign Dorothy's poem *The Hang Glider* in unison, led by the actress Elizabeth Quinn.

Original signed poetry composed for performance by more than one person is rare, but the Italian sign poets Rosaria and Giuseppe Giuranna have co-written – and co-perform – a poem *Grazie* (*Thanks*) in LIS (Italian Sign Language) as a duet. *Thanks*, according to Pizzuto and Russo (2000), 'describes deaf people's feelings and attitudes towards signed language, and how these can change with the growth of linguistic awareness'. There are many interesting features of this complex and visually stunning poem, but we will focus on the unusual performance element. The poem opens with the two performers facing each other, so that they appear side-on to the audience. The two characters in this poem hold opposing views on sign language, so the way they stand – in opposition – holds poetic and dramatic meaning.

One performer (Rosaria) expresses the view that sign language is the natural way for Deaf people to express themselves. The other performer (Giuseppe) claims that sign languages are limited forms of communication. In this section of the poem, the two performers take turns in signing. Although they take turns, they occasionally overlap and interrupt, so that the overall communication between them is unsettled and not smooth, reflecting their discordant views. In the next section, Rosaria presents a monologue outlining the reasons why she believes signed languages to be so important for communication and the Deaf identity. Giuseppe does not sign during her monologue but watches her. After this monologue, they revert to dialogue as she slowly convinces him of her view. At first they take turns in the dialogue, but as their opinions harmonise, so does their signing, so that he moves from saying the opposite of her and starts to repeat what she says. Gradually Giuseppe begins to sign with Rosaria. For a brief section, his signs echo hers, and then as he accepts her argument fully, their signs synchronise. Now that they share the same views, they are no longer in opposition but stand side-by-side in unity and co-operation. This is shown as they turn away from each other to stand side-by-side, and face the audience. They repeat Rosaria's original monologue but now as a duet – both signing the same thing in synchronous unison – showing that they are now of one mind. The rest of the poem is signed in unison. *Thanks* is a highly original poem that shows some of the potential for performance of signed poetry to add significance to the poetic meaning.

Enactment

Another important element of sign language poetry performance is the signer's ability to show the characteristics of a person or thing by taking that role and 'becoming' that person or thing, and showing this role-shift or characterisation through sign language. When the signer 'becomes' the person signed about, we use the term 'personation' (which we will consider in the next section) and when the signer 'becomes' the animal or thing signed about, we can term this 'enactment'.[5] Enactment is an important part of sign language literature generally and occurs in sign language narratives as well as poems. There are good examples of it in Dorothy's animal poems, and in her introduction to *The Cat* (in *Bright Memory*, 1998), she wrote: 'Using Ameslan [ASL], it's very easy to imitate animal characteristics and behaviour' (p. 26). She was perhaps being modest about her ability, and the ability of other signers when she said, 'it's very easy' because, although the language easily accommodates this imitation, it takes considerable skill and wit for a signer to do it well. The skill in sign language enactment is not to mimic an animal precisely but rather to blend the human and animal characteristics, using both manual and non-manual elements, while remaining within the acceptable parameters of the sign language. Although the gestures and facial expressions involved in enactment are not a central part of sign languages, their peripheral status is still controlled by the rules of acceptability for the language. Enactment is not *miming* the behaviour of an animal or thing, it is *signing* the behaviour of that animal or thing. The dividing line is not always easy for a non-signer to see but skilled poets or creative signers keep their signing within the boundaries of the language.

In *The Cat* (p. 240) there are manual signs that have been modified as a result of enactment. In reference to the fact that the cat can use her paws to softly powder her nose or put out her claws for a passing dog, the ASL poem may be glossed as:

WITH HER PAWS
PAWS-STAND
CAN SOFT
PAWS-STAND COVER-PAW-IN-POWDER PAW-POWDERS-NOSE
BUT
CLAWS
PUT-CLAWS-OUT
IF DOG
DOG-WALK-BY-UNCONCERNED
PUT-CLAWS-OUT

Although the gloss here does not show the non-manual elements of the poem, it does show how enactment is achieved manually. The sign PAW is introduced and then the poet shifts to 'become' the cat, standing alertly, with the two hands representing the cat's paws. They are not really communicating anything beyond signalling being a part of the cat. The posture of the body, the angle of the head, and the facial expression and movement of the eyes all work together to show the character of the cat but only the paws are shown manually. The poet then shifts back to the narrator's 'voice', signing CAN SOFT. Even here, though, she is able to retain some of the enactment, because the ASL sign CAN is made with an 'A' handshape. As this is the same handshape as the sign showing the PAWS, the idea of the cat is maintained (Fig. 9.1).

The performer then becomes the cat again, to show exactly how the cat uses her paw to tidy her face. Normally, if a human were to powder her nose, the handshape for the sign POWDER-NOSE would be a 'B̂', reflecting how we would hold a powder puff. The handshape used in the poem allows us to imagine that a cat would use her paw as a powder puff. It is not enough to enjoy the idea that instead of merely washing her face the cat is sophisticated enough to use a powder puff: the fun comes from seeing the way that a cat would do it.

The care and attention that the cat puts into her toilet is also seen in the face of the signer. English words cannot easily describe it, except to say that the poet performing the poem needs to have the facial expression of a contented cat. And yet, it is not of a contented cat, but of how the cat would look if she were a contented human or how a contented human would look if she were a cat. A similar shift occurs with the claws coming out when the dog passes. By the second signing of PUT-CLAWS-OUT, the narrator has shifted into the cat's character again, complete with hissing on the mouth, and the cat's eyes staring in fury at the nonchalant dog (Fig. 9.2).

These shifts are one type of enactment, in which the poet shifts from a role of narrator into the character of the animal. However it is also possible for the manual signs to narrate, while the non-manual elements show the characterisation. We see this in the lines that in English run as, 'in the light / her eyes wink and blink'.

These can be glossed as:

DURING LIGHT (and in BSL this sign can also mean DAY)
EYES
BLINK WINK

The manual signs glossed here are part of the standard sign language vocabulary delivered as narration, but while they are being signed, the eyes are showing the character of the cat, as she winks and blinks (Fig. 9.3).

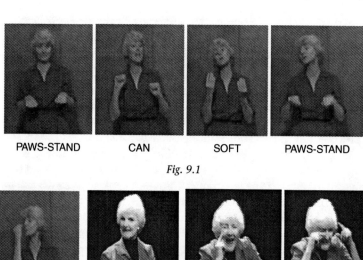

PAWS-STAND   CAN   SOFT   PAWS-STAND

Fig. 9.1

POWDER-NOSE   CLAWS-OUT   EYES   WINK-AND-BLINK

Fig. 9.1 (cont.)   *Fig. 9.2*   *Fig. 9.3*   *Fig. 9.3* (cont.)

MOTHER-DUCK-ASHAMED   PADDLE-PROUDLY   PADDLE-WORRIED

Fig. 9.4

Stance of hearing character   Stance of deaf character

Fig. 9.5

This simultaneous use of enactment and direct narration also happens in the last line of the ASL poem, which follows the last line in the English version 'Would make a perfect spy.' In the ASL version, the sign continues after the sign SPY, to make a manual sign showing the cat peering out from behind a wall. Simultaneously, the non-manual elements of the sign have taken on the character of the cat, showing her head, body and eye movements as she peers furtively out, and her facial expression full of covert operations (see Fig. 5.12).

The Ugly Duckling (p. 249) takes the form of a narrative and so is more of an allegory than a simple lyric poem. It makes use of traditional sign language narrative techniques for enactment, to show the characteristics and behaviour of the duckling and the other farmyard animals. From the point of enactment, it is more complex than *The Cat*, because there are characteristics of several different animals to show, instead of just one. The Ugly Duckling himself appears through enactment, as well as textual description. The moment the shell cracks open (signed on the hands), we know that the duckling has the cheerful innocence of the neophyte from the cheerily goofy expression on the poet's face. As the duckling walks around the farmyard on his bandy legs (signed manually) we know about his interest in the world and his unassuming confidence from the facial expression and eye-movements of the enactment.

The poor duckling is rejected by his mother and laughed at by the lambs, the cows and the hens. Each time, the poem introduces the character through direct narration (MOTHER DUCK .../ SHEEP ... ./ COW .../ BIRD [hens]) and then we see more about their movement, actions, behaviour and reactions through non-manual actions. The hens are shown with their hands over their mouths in shock at the sight of the duckling and then they snigger. This is done as they hide behind their wings – a raised arm indicating a raised wing – and the non-manual elements remind us constantly that animals, not humans, are signing.

The idea of hens sniggering shows a crossover between the idea of enactment (where the signer takes on the character of the animals) and anthropomorphisation. Anthropomorphisation (literally, 'taking the form of a human') is a device in which inanimate objects, such as a chair or tree, or non-human creatures, such as a cat or a bird, are given the characteristics of humans. This device is an important part of sign languages, even in non-poetic, everyday use, especially for humour. Dorothy gave the example 'a person will describe driving a car on a busy street and make the car elbow the other cars out of the way'. In

The Ugly Duckling, human actions such as teasing and blaming, and human characteristics such as glee, shame and spite are given to the duckling, the mother duck and the other animals. Again, these are given especially non-manually, as the facial expressions given to the animal characters are those for humans. The mother duck looks at her ugly duckling and signs 'AWFUL!' with a look of horror on her face. The duckling paddles happily in the pond, and the facial expression is one of a happy person but when he has seen his reflection, the paddling is with a worried facial expression. Clearly, hens cannot snigger and a duck's facial expression will not show happiness or worry, as these are all human characteristics. But this anthropomorphisation is shown by the facial expression in the enactment of the performance (Fig. 9.4).

Anthropomorphisation is not only shown by facial expression, however, but also in signs. *Autumn*, in the *Seasons* quartet (p. 245), shows anthropomorphisation of leaves, in both the English and the ASL versions. The haiku suggests that the scattered leaves turn to watch people hurry by. We know that leaves cannot watch people, but we are encouraged to imagine that it might look as though they do when they whirl to face the direction of the hurrying passers-by. The ASL haiku shows us the way that leaves would look up at the people. This is done simply by moving the sign WATCH from the normal eye level to waist-level – the height that represents the ground on which the leaves are whirling – and angling the sign upwards so that the leaves are looking up at people. The shifts in location and orientation allow the inanimate leaves to engage in a human activity.

Personation

In notes for a lecture in 1976, Dorothy explained what she meant by 'personation':

> Personation (a new term, not to be confused with Personification). I am using this term to indicate the sign-language technique in which the signer becomes the person or thing he is talking about when he is doing straight description or narrative and not metaphor. This technique has also been called the 'close-up'. Principles of personation include:
>
> i. The signer should have a clear idea of the location, size, height, etc. of other images in relation to himself, and be sure that this relationship does not change inappropriately.
> ii. The signer can convey two or more personations by slight shifts in

direction and posture, or by moving from one side to another. In both cases, action or conversation is directed towards the place where the other personation is supposed to be.

Even if the term 'personation' is unfamiliar to many people, the idea of it will be familiar to anyone with more than a passing knowledge of sign languages. It is often known as 'role shift' and is used in everyday signing as well as in poetry. A similar device, in which one person takes on the characteristics – especially the voice patterns – of another person, is also found in spoken English. Stand-up comedians may use personation as a way to identify and express the mannerisms of different people in a joke. The difference, though, lies in the way that the personation is shown, and the deliberate poetic effect that is created through it. For example, poetic effect is achieved by careful use of symmetry (as we saw in Chapter 4) so personation can allow a poem to show symmetry by placing the personations in specifically symmetrical locations. *Walking Down the Street* and *Total Communication* show personation especially clearly. In *Walking Down the Street* (p. 251) personation of the two characters creates a left–right symmetry, while in *Total Communication* (p. 248) there is more of a tendency towards a front–back symmetry.

Poetic personation can also break everyday rules of signing for poetic effect. The 'role shift' we see in everyday signing is limited to the 'slight shifts in direction and posture' that Dorothy mentions in point (ii) above. Everyday signing does not permit 'moving from one side to another'. In *Walking Down the Street*, though, the performer's whole body steps to the left and the right to show the separate personations. As with so much of the rule-breaking in sign language poems, the rules are not broken carelessly, but to make a point. A theme in this poem is that Deaf and hearing people are basically the same and should be treated the same. In this poem, a perfectly ordinary hearing person asks a perfectly ordinary-looking Deaf person for directions but then backs off nervously when the deafness becomes apparent. The similarity between these two 'perfectly ordinary' strangers is shown through the similarity of the body postures and resting hand positions in both personations. This alone would be a neat poetic device – all physical behaviours of the two characters are the same, and our only way of distinguishing between them is the 'slight shifts in direction and posture'. However, to emphasise that they are actually worlds apart, despite the superficial appearances, Dorothy uses the technique of 'moving from one side to another' – a large distance in signing space – to show a great social distance (Fig. 9.5).

The personation device in *Total Communication* also allows the poet to bend or break the rules of the language, again to create poetic meaning. In *Total Communication* the second character, addressed throughout the poem ('You') does not actively participate and the personation shift is not made as strongly as in *Walking Down the Street*. Instead, the location of this character is placed next to (and sometimes a little in front of) the central character ('I'). One theme of this poem is the failure to connect or make contact mentally and emotionally with the other person. This is brought out by the use of a personation, placing the other character in a separate space. Signs such as LIFE that normally require a body-contact for their location are made out in 'empty' space, where the other person ('You') has been located. There is no body-contact there, so the sign is technically ill-formed. The audience is obliged to imagine the second body that should provide the location for the sign, while at the same time accepting that the lack of the body implies the absence of the character.

The strongest impact of personation, however, lies in the emotion that the poet can convey by directly taking the role of the narrator or character, rather than describing it. It takes the emotions in the poem to a new level by obeying the old piece of advice given to all writers: 'Show, don't tell.' In *Walking Down the Street*, the text of the poem never explicitly mentions the exasperation and indignation felt by the Deaf character, nor the attitudes and unsettled behaviour of the hearing character. However, in the personation of the characters, the performer can show it to its fullest extent. The emotional impact arising from personation in the performance in *Hang Glider* is especially strong, and will be discussed in Chapter 11.

Many of the performance elements that we have described above arise out of the strongly visual nature of sign languages, and are frequently so closely bound with the sign 'text' that they are indistinguishable from it. In sign language poems that are more closely related to the spoken language, however, there is a clearer split between text and performance. The 'blended' poems that Dorothy Miles composed in her early work have a close relationship with English, and the text of these poems is more readily identifiable (although even here there are some highly effective poetic elements that come entirely from performance). We will now consider these blended poems, and the effect of influences from spoken language upon sign language poetry.

10
Blended Sign Language and Spoken Language Poetry

For most of our exploration of sign language poetry so far, we have paid little attention to the influence of spoken language on sign language, and the effect that this can have on sign poetry. While it is clear that sign languages are fully independent languages, and that their grammars and vocabularies are independent of spoken languages, it is possible for the grammar of spoken languages to influence a person's signing. As sign language poems are the highest art form of sign languages, they might be expected to be free from the influence of spoken language but this is not always the case, and certainly was not in the past. In fact, many of Dorothy Miles' earlier poems were strongly influenced by English, as she tried to create poems that worked simultaneously in both languages and it is these 'blended' poems that will be the focus of this chapter.

Where an utterance uses the grammar of English and the vocabulary of ASL or BSL, it is sometimes termed 'Signed English', to distinguish it from the sign languages that use visual-spatial grammar. However, the degree of influence from the spoken language can vary greatly, and there is no clear dividing line between Signed English and BSL (or ASL).[1] Spoken language grammar may be seen especially in the sign language of Deaf people who learned the spoken language before they learned to sign, but it also may occur where signers are working closely with written texts. As Dorothy Miles' mother-tongue was English, she composed poems in English throughout her life. Before she went to America to study English Literature at Gallaudet College she had some success in publishing short poems in newspapers (including *Exaltation*). While she was at Gallaudet, her tutors encouraged her English poetry skills, and she had some publishing success in her status as a 'Deaf poet'. In 1976, a selection of 15 of her poems written in English was published in *Gestures* (accompanied by a film of her performance of these poems in sign language). After her return to Britain in 1977 she continued to compose in English and her work became known and respected within the general disability movement as well as in the Deaf world. Some of her poetry was also published within the 'mainstream' poetic arena in London.

The English language poems that Dorothy wrote were firmly within the tradition of English poetry and would have been of little interest to – and perhaps inaccessible to – many signing members of the Deaf community. This was something that Dorothy wished to change. While she was acting with the National Theatre of the Deaf in the 1960s and 1970s, the group performed two items by Dylan Thomas – *Songs from Milk Wood* (an abbreviated version of *Under Milk Wood*), and *A Child's Christmas in Wales*. The performances were given in strongly artistic 'sign-mime', with a reader providing the English words of the text. Hearing audiences loved the production of *Songs from Milk Wood*. They could appreciate the combination of signs and words because their understanding came from the English, while the signs provided more of a visual embellishment to the spoken words. However, it was not a great success with Deaf audiences because they did not understand it. The 'sign-mime' that the actors used focused more on their form and less on their meaning and the Deaf people did not have access to the English words to clarify the meaning. This experience led Dorothy to create sign language poetry that both Deaf people and hearing people could appreciate, by composing poems in both English and ASL simultaneously. She wanted poetry that worked with English, but did not rely on English for its clarity of message. In this chapter we will consider some of the effects that this blending of the two languages had upon her poetry and upon the development of sign language poetry in general.

In the interview on *Deaf Perspectives* in 1976, she commented:

> [*The Cat* and *Hang Glider*] were written specifically for sign language. That is to say that they were written so that they could combine English language and sign language together. Because I grew up as a hearing person I remember English as my first language and a combination of the two I find is a very strong way of expressing myself.

She added, 'sign language combined with spoken English is my normal way of communicating so as an honest poet I feel more comfortable using both.' Heidi Rose (1992) has questioned whether we should call this sign language poetry 'ASL', claiming that the work in *Gestures* is 'more of a Pidgin Sign English rather than pure ASL' (p. 42). However, there is no doubt that these poems were original sign language compositions, and composed in a variant form of sign language that was recognised and used by well-educated American Deaf people at the time. After a live performance in California in 1980, in response to a question about her language of composition, Dorothy commented on the mixed heritage of some of her poems in *Gestures*:

> [T]here were a few poems that were written specifically to show sign language – *The Gesture* was written to show sign language to hearing people. Also, *Language for the Eye* was written to give sign language the chance to work. ... But a number of those poems were written interlinking the two languages. I thought of a way of signing it and then how to write it almost at the same time. I couldn't say which happened first ... They just fit together ... and it all dropped into place. There's no one way that things happen. Sometimes they happen one way and sometimes another.

Many of her poems written between 1967 and 1977 were composed to blend both English and ASL. In a television interview in 1976, she said, 'One of the things I am trying to do is write poetry that sounds fine in English but also at the same time it looks right and feels right as it is being signed in the same order as the words.' This radical shift in the approach to sign language poetry had great benefits. When a poem exists in two languages, the audience that knows and understands – and has access to – both languages can see extra meaning in each poem. The language used in one version of the poem informs the audience even while they experience the other language version of the poem. 'Tied images' are known to occur in written poetry when (usually, hearing) readers of a poem see the words while simultaneously 'hearing' the words inside their heads, and having a feeling of what it would be like to say those words. This increases the poetic experience for the reader because there are three simultaneous images occurring. Such tied images also occur when we know a poem in two languages. Hearing the English poem while knowing the sign language poem creates tied images, as does seeing the sign language poem while knowing the English text of the poem. Not all of Dorothy's poetry was designed to create tied images, but those poems that she composed with the intention of being seen as well as read do produce remarkably strong poetic images.

The poetic effects in the blended poems usually remain separate within the two language versions of the poems, and there are few instances where the same poetic effect is created in both languages simultaneously. Some of the blended poems work well in the two independent languages and the two poems complement each other. However, significantly, Dorothy remarked in her television interview with Greg Brooks in 1976, 'I really believe that sign language adds something to English and the combination is richer and more exciting than English alone.' We can see from this that she still saw English as the dominant language of the poems and we will see examples from her blended poetry where this dominance over sign language meant that the sign language potential of the signed poems was not always realised to the full.

Dual meaning and puns

One example of the separate effects of the two different languages is the use of puns in these 'blended' poems. There are many puns in the English versions of the poems that do not come out in the ASL or BSL versions. For example, several of the titles of her poems play on words. *Defiance* contains links to the words 'Deaf ' and 'I' in the title of a poem that comes from the personal viewpoint of a Deaf woman and is exceedingly defiant. In *Unsound Views*, the pun works with the idea that the philosophy in question is unacceptable, and also plays with the idea that this is the opinion (the 'view') of a Deaf person (who cannot hear sound). *Sinai*, is a pun on 'sign' and 'I' (and perhaps 'eye' too), as well as being the place where God spoke to Moses, for a poem about a type of divine revelation for a Deaf person. Although a signer with knowledge of English could appreciate these puns, they do not transfer into ASL or BSL. This is not a great problem for the poems, because the surface meaning of the title can still be interpreted without the pun.

Where the pun is a central part of the poem, it can sometimes work in both the English and the BSL versions of a poem. *To a Deaf Child* (p. 247) contains the line 'so giving / sign-ificance to Babel's tongues'. Here the neologism *sign-ificance* is made from *sig-nificance*, simply by separating the syllables at a different place, and it highlights the relationship between signs and meaning. The gloss of these lines from the BSL poem shows that the ambiguity of the sign MEANING and SIGN can carry a similar punning poetic effect to the English neologism (GIVE THROUGH SIGN/MEANING THAT GIVE UNDERSTAND DIFFERENT SPEAK). At other times, though, the puns do not translate. For example, the pun of 'sign-ificance' does not work in ASL because SIGN and MEANING have very different forms so there is no scope for the same shared ambiguity we see in English and BSL. *To a Deaf Child* also uses the word *lip-service* to dismiss lip-reading as the means of communication for Deaf people by using it with the word that claims to support something but gives no practical support. The English lines run, 'at frontiers where men of speech lend lip- / service to brotherhood'. The gloss of this section of the BSL poem, however, shows that the pun does not work in BSL (nor does it work in ASL), as the two signs together LIP and SERVICE do not form the compound *lip-service* with the idiomatic meaning that they hold in English:

BOUNDARY PEOPLE SPEECH GIVE LIP SERVICE -t-o- BROTHER^LINK
[brotherhood]
SPEAK-TO-EACH-OTHER

Although the puns usually remain unobtrusive in the sign language poems, there are other features of the English poems that can intrude upon the structure of the sign language poems.

Obtrusive use of mouth patterns

The use of mouth patterns in 'blended' poems is very different from the use of the mouth in the sign poems that are independent of English. We saw in Chapter 1 that mouth patterns in sign languages can be divided into mouthings (related to the spoken language word-shapes) and mouth gestures (unrelated to spoken language words). We also noted that mouthings occur much more frequently in BSL than they do in ASL. For this reason, our analysis of poetic use of mouthings will be drawn from BSL poems, although it should be noted that the relative lack of mouthings in ASL makes the simultaneous sign and speech in many of her early ASL poems very obtrusive.

Dorothy's aim to create blended poems that 'worked' in both English and sign simultaneously meant that mouthings were used very differently in her poems from the way they are used in everyday signing. Where the poems need to work in both English and a sign language, the structure and rhythm of the English words usually drive the structure and rhythm of the BSL signs, and mouthings become obtrusive. Where the poem was composed in BSL, and BSL forms drive the structure of signs, the mouthings are less obtrusive. We can see the way Dorothy's two composition styles affected mouthings, by comparing *The BDA is ...* and *The Staircase*, both composed at around the same time. *The BDA is ...* (p. 240) was originally composed (in 1990) in English and was intended to be used with English and BSL operating as simultaneously as possible, but *The Staircase* (p. 246) was composed in BSL (in 1988) without any intention to produce an English poem. The final verse and the chorus of *The BDA is* ... may be glossed as it was performed at the 1990 BDA Centenary rally as follows (mouthings that accompany a sign are given in brackets after the sign gloss):

> NINETEEN (nineteen) NINETY (ninety) WE INCREASE STRONG (strong)
> PRINCESS (princess) -d-i- (Di) TOP SHE (patron) CAN'T (can't) GO (go) WRONG (wrong)
> WE-ALL MOVE-FORWARD WORK (working) WILL (will) SEE (see) WELL-COMPLETED (well)
> ALL (every) DEAF (deaf) OUT-OF-SHELL (out of the shell)
> -b-d-a- (the BDA) WHO (who) YOU-ALL (you) ME (and me)
> TOGETHER (together) I (we'll) FIGHT (fight) ACHIEVE EQUALITY (equality)

This section in the BSL poem can be glossed with 30 signs. Accompanying these signs are mouthings of 29 identifiable English words including articles ('the'), pronouns ('you') and connectives ('and') that are not normally seen as mouthings in BSL. In some cases, the English words have driven the choice of signs in the poem. This may be seen in the line, 'we can't go wrong'. In the BSL poem here, there is no sign WE, but there is a sign that can be glossed as GO. The usual meaning of GO is one of moving (as in 'go to London'), but here it is part of a loan translation of the English verb phrase 'go wrong.' The poem needs the sign GO to keep the rhythmic structure of the BSL poem because the word 'go' in the English version of the poem is stressed. In the English poem, the word 'we' is unstressed, so the sign WE can be dropped without disrupting the rhythm of the poem.

Dorothy did not always sacrifice BSL grammar to meet the demands of the English poem and the mouthings, though. The skill in her poetry often lies in her feel for just how far she could bend the rules of the language (although there are times when the audience might prefer her to have sacrificed sign language grammar less than she did). Nevertheless, in the signed performance of *The BDA is* ... , she did forfeit some English mouthings to meet the needs of BSL grammar. In the lines 'we've grown so strong' and 'keep on working' exact translations of 'grow' and 'keep on' would give the wrong meaning. The BSL signs that she selected do not use English mouthings and instead Dorothy used mouth gestures appropriate for the signs meaning 'something increasing' ('grown') and 'moving forward' or 'persistence' ('keep on').

We saw in Chapter 1 that the meaning of the mouthing does not always match the meaning of the manual sign in everyday signing.

However, in *The BDA is ...*, Dorothy takes these mismatches considerably further for poetic effect when she blends the two languages in two poems. In this poem, the BSL signs are made to match the English rhythmic structure but the English mouthing does not necessarily match the BSL signs that are on the hand at the time. The effect allows the poet to do what is often claimed to be impossible – to produce grammatical BSL on the hands and grammatical English on the mouth. This is extremely irregular and is an achievement not unlike patting your head while rubbing your stomach.

In the line, 'Princess Di as patron' the stressed syllables in the English poem are the first syllable of 'Princess', 'Di', and the first syllable of 'patron'. The BSL sign PRINCESS only has one syllable compared to the two syllables in English. The sign for 'Di', however, is fingerspelled -d-i-, giving it two syllables in BSL, in contrast to the single English syllable. The unstressed English word 'as' is absent from the BSL poem. The sign used as PATRON also has one syllable, but Dorothy has made it into two syllables by adding a sign that means something like 'patron, her'. The result of the two different syllable structures of the two languages means that Dorothy has to work creatively to produce the lines in BSL where the rhythm matches the English poem:

Table 10.1

Prin	cess	Di	pa	tron
PRINCESS	-d-	-i-	TOP	HER

The final word of the English poem is 'equality' and – because the two poems are so close – the final sign of the BSL poem is also EQUALITY. The four-syllable English word *equality* needs to match with the two-syllable sign EQUALITY. Dorothy solves this problem by altering the movements within the sign EQUALITY to give it four parts. The poem slows down at this point so that each syllable of the word 'equality' is clearly articulated. The four movements in EQUALITY are made large and clear, and larger movements are made to match the heavier stressed syllables of the English word (Fig. 10.1).

In contrast to *The BDA is ...*, there are far fewer mouthings in *The Staircase*, a poem composed without reference to English. Fifty-nine signs can be glossed in the first section of the poem and, in this section, there are only 15 identifiable English-based mouthings. They accompany noun signs (such as 'forest', 'dark', 'wall', 'staircase', 'light', 'lion' and 'giant') and a few other signs (such as 'have') in a totally non-deviant,

155

EQUALITY (in four parts)

Fig. 10.1

BUTTERFLY-   LIQUID-FALLS
LIFTS

Fig. 10.2

WORD   WORD-IN-HAND

Fig. 10.3

DAY = SUNLIGHT   NIGHT = DARK

Fig. 10.4

WORD   WORD-LOCK

Fig. 10.5

HEAR   IGNORE   LIPS   SAY

Fig. 10.6

non-obtrusive way. (In this gloss the mouthings accompanying each
sign are in lower case letters in brackets after each sign.)

FOREST (forest) DARK (dark)
PEOPLE (people) HAVE
ONE-PERSON-MOVES-FORWARD ONE-PERSON-MOVES-FORWARD
TWO-PEOPLE-MOVE-FORWARD TWO-PEOPLE-MOVE-FORWARD
EIGHT-PEOPLE-MOVE-FORWARD
MANY-PEOPLE-MOVE-FORWARD
THERE-AHEAD BUMP-INTO-WALL
WHAT?
WALL (wall)
WHAT-IS-IT?
MANY-PEOPLE-MOVE-BACK
SHOCK
THERE STAIRCASE (staircase) HUGE-STEPS
FAR-AWAY-UP HAVE (have) LIGHTS (lights) LIGHTS-GLIMMERING
LOOK-UP-STAIRCASE
LOOK-AT-EACH-OTHER
WHO (who) CLIMB-UP WHO (who)?
LOOK-AT-EACH-OTHER
PERHAPS DON'T-KNOW CLIMB-UP THERE HAVE (have) THERE
LION (lion)
LION-STALK
LION'S-PAW-STRIKES
DON'T-KNOW OR PERHAPS (perhaps) WHO-KNOWS
CLIMB-UP SINK-INTO-GROUND GROUND-RISES-ABOVE-HEAD
PERHAPS DON'T-KNOW PERHAPS (perhaps)
CLIMB-UP THERE GIANT (giant)
GIANT-STRETCHES
DRAW-SWORD STRIKE-WITH-SWORD
HEAD (head) HEAD-OFF HEAD-HITS-GROUND HEAD-ROLLS-AWAY

The effects of blending English and sign language poetry

The earlier poems in Dorothy's signed repertoire – such as *The Cat* (1976)
or *Language for the Eye* (1975) – conform strongly to many of the poetic
traditions of English. Despite this, although they are not especially
grounded within the traditions of the Deaf community, they deliberately aim to draw attention to the beauty of the sign language in which
they were performed. Later poems – such as *The Staircase* (1988),

The Ugly Duckling (1988) and *Walking Down the Street* (1990) – were more 'community driven' and had more of a function of uplifting and empowering the community members. These later poems have lost some of the tightness of lyric construction and show fewer 'English poetry' features, but carry far more embodiment of personal and community feeling. There is a sense in which English poetry might 'show through telling', while sign language poetry can 'tell through showing'. There are times in Dorothy's earlier blended works when she sticks closer to English, perhaps at the expense of other sign language features. Often when role-shift or embodiment of character would have been enough to make the poem 'work', she still provided English-based expressions of the idea.

Most of Dorothy's ASL poems were either translations from her earlier English poems or were composed as these blends of two languages. In either case, they are examples of poems where the requirements of both languages and their poetic demands can work together for poetic effect or can create problems for one of the poems. We will focus on two 'blended' poems here, *To a Deaf Child* (which she performed in ASL and BSL, and where English has a strong influence on the sign poem) and the *Seasons* haiku quartet (where English is far less obtrusive in the ASL poem).

To a Deaf Child is a celebration of sign language for Deaf people. Hearing people have often insisted that signing cuts a Deaf person off from society but that using speech allows that person to join society. This poem turns that idea on its head, showing how speech cuts hearing people off from the 'universal brotherhood of man' but signing allows Deaf people a direct access to universal understanding. A note in *Bright Memory* (1998: p. 76) explains the origin of the poem. 'In 1973, speaking before an audience at Gallaudet College, the anthropologist Margaret Mead suggested that sign language might be adapted and adopted as the language of universal diplomacy to bring understanding and peace to men who were separated by the "Language barrier." '

To a Deaf Child (p. 247) has elements in it that make it worthy of study in BSL and ASL as well as in English, but, although the poem has a very positive attitude towards sign language, there is no doubt that English grammar dominates the grammar in the sign language poems on many occasions. Glossed examples from the BSL poem show this (bold type indicates especially strong influence from English):

-t-o- -a- DEAF CHILD
SKILL **IN** YOU SIGN
WHO IN WORD ALONE CAN SAY DAY SUNLIGHT NIGHT DARK

-o-r- SEE THAT SIGN -f-o-r- LIVE -o-r- INSPIRED EXCITED SEE
SIMILAR
EACH SIGN HOLD IDEA ACTION -o-r- SHAPE -o-r- REASONING
IN YOUR HAND MAYBE YOU HOLD CLEAR NEW
SEE-ALL-AROUND MAN THEIR PLAN -f-o-r- LIVING
BOUNDARY PEOPLE SPEECH GIVE LIP SERVICE
-t-o- BROTHER^LINK [brotherhood]
NOT BOTHER -b-y- SOUNDS THAT DROWN MEANING
-o-r- -b-y- FEAR FOREIGN WORD WORD-CHAINS-WRIST IMPRISON
BETTER WORD WORD-IN-HAND HAND SIGN
THAN THOUSAND SAY WORDS-TUMBLE-FROM-MOUTH

The use of fingerspelling is particularly noticeable here. In BSL the fingerspelling -o-r- is accepted as an established loan sign from English
(although BSL does not need this grammar-word, and can show the
opposition implied by 'or' entirely spatially), but nevertheless, any use
of the manual alphabet is noticeably intrusive in sign language poetry.
The use of -t-o- is not commonly accepted as a part of BSL, so its occurrence in the constructions '-t-o- -a- DEAF CHILD' and 'GIVE LIP SERVICE
-t-o-' is a clear representation of English grammar brought about by the
scheme of the English poem. Although BSL can convey the idea
expressed by the passive voice in English, it is achieved through the use
of space and role-shift, not by a single word -b-y-, as in NOT BOTHER
-b-y- SOUNDS. The sign THAT is used in BSL as a demonstrative pronoun, but not as the pronoun for a relative clause in SOUNDS THAT
DROWN MEANING. BSL rarely uses spatial prepositions (as space is
shown by using space) and the repeated use of the sign IN is normally
inappropriate, especially when it is not used to describe relative locations (as in WHO IN WORD ALONE). The comparison using the signs
BETTER and THAN is also notably English in its construction. We have
already seen above that the pun on 'lip-service' using LIP SERVICE does
not make sense in BSL without knowledge of the original English
phrase. In other phrases such as with WHO IN WORD ALONE CAN SAY,
most of the signs are acceptable BSL signs but their order is obtrusively
English. In summary, then, this poem contains many elements of
English that intrude upon the normal form of BSL and, as such, there is
certainly no 'seamless blend' between the two languages.

However, there are also many parts of this poem that *do* work in BSL.
The celebratory theme of the joys of sign language in the poem is impor-
tant and the 'Deaf perspective' is once again conveyed through the sign
SEE and related signs. These occur in SEE-ALL-AROUND MAN THEIR

PLAN and PEOPLE SEE-ALL-AROUND RIGHT CAN HEAR UNDER-
STAND and also in INSPIRED EXCITED SEE SIMILAR where there is no
reference to 'seeing' in the English version.

Repeatedly in this poem the signs extend the meaning relationships
between ideas by showing the visual relationships of their signs. The
simile in 'Your lightest word in hand / lifts like a butterfly' uses the formational similarities of the signs LIFT and LIGHT (and the BSL sign
SIGN) and BUTTERFLY, which are all two-handed signs using the '5'
hand shape. Thus, in, this simile, the lifting of the light signs is like a
butterfly, both literally because of the shared formational parameters
and metaphorically in their beauty and carefree joy. In the lines, ('lifts like
a butterfly, or folds / in liquid motion') the sign BUTTERFLY rises, as a
butterfly would rise, to the point where the sign WATERFALL begins to
fall, as a waterfall would fall (Fig. 10.2). This may be glossed as:

YOUR LIGHT WORD WORD-IN-HAND HAND SIGN
LIFT LIKE BUTTERFLY [hand turns, descends, tumbling]
WATER-FALLS WATER-FLOWS

This blending of locations is just one example of the central idea in the
poem: in sign languages there is a strong relationship between the form
of signs and their meanings. The language in this poem uses the form
of the language to *talk about* language and also to *show* the language.
The central metaphor of the poem 'holding language in your hands' has
the idea of possessing the language but here the metaphor is made
literal. The sign WORD made by one hand is literally put into the other
hand (Fig. 10.3).

Time and again, the form of the language and the meaning overlap as
the poem shows the direct relationship between form and meaning. The
deliberate examples are highlighted in the poem, for example, DAY and
SUNLIGHT with NIGHT and DARK and the 'emotion' signs INSPIRE,
EXCITED and LIVE (Fig. 10.4). At the end of the second stanza, the sign
WORD morphs (by using the 'baby C' handshape of that sign) so that
the hand signing WORD locks against the other wrist, literally imprisoning it, while also meaning IMPRISON or LOCK. This shows the idea
that the word imprisons people but at the same time it shows the sign
WORD literally imprisoning the other hand (Fig. 10.5).

The repetitive use of handshapes is another way in which this poem
does work in BSL. Three handshapes dominate this poem: '5', 'B' and
'G'. Of the 153 handshapes used in the poem, 39 are the 'B' handshape,
34 are the '5' handshape and 40 are the 'G' handshape. This is over

two-thirds, and means that only 40 signs use some other handshape. However, we saw in Chapter 3 that the mere existence of so many signs using the same handshape is not necessarily evidence that there is any-thing poetic in the repetition. The extra significance comes when we look at the symbolism carried by the choice of handshapes in this poem. There is an underlying metaphor in this poem that the 'Hearing world' to a Deaf person is one-dimensional and somehow thin and lifeless (and speech, after all, is linear and one-dimensional). The 'G' handshape is a 'one-dimensional' handshape, with the index finger creating a line. The metaphor of a 'one-dimensional hearing world' is carried in many of the signs using the 'G' handshape that are related to the idea of hearing and speech: EAR, HEAR, IGNORE, LIP, SAY, SOUNDS, SPEECH and VOICE (Fig. 10.6). The metaphor of the 'Deaf world' is of something more solid and two- or three-dimensional (with sign language occurring in three dimensions) and the signs related to Deaf matters use signs that use the more solid and two- or three-dimensional 'B' and '5' handshapes: SIGN, HAND, OFFER, BUTTERFLY, CLEAR and MEANING (Fig. 10.7).

By keeping the same handshape or location for several signs Dorothy creates further poetic effect. There is a sign 'rhyme' between the second and third stanzas. The final sign of the second stanza IMPRISON differs only in small ways from the first sign of the next stanza BETTER. This device links the two stanzas together in form as well as meaning. The earlier stanza ends with a negative situation, but the subsequent stanza proposes a solution. It is interesting to note that the English version of the poem makes this same link using rhyming words – 'fetter' and 'better'. This is a good example of the two blended poems working closely together (Fig. 10.8).

Other repetition is at the word level, especially the phrase WORD WORD-IN-HAND HAND. This links the sections of the poem and brings a 'closure' that is important for the last line. It reinforces the important point that these signs are indeed 'words', rather than simple gestures. The repetition also highlights the central device of the poem – drawing attention to the form of the language as well as the content – in this case by physically putting the sign WORD into the hand to *mean* 'putting the word into the hand'.

The use of simultaneous signs in the poem also carries extra poetic meaning. There are three simultaneous signs (and the use of three is also a well-known poetic device, as we saw in our earlier discussion of repe-tition in Chapter 3) – at the beginning, the middle and the end of the poem. The first use of a simultaneous sign is to blur and merge the title with the main text of the poem. The final sign in the title -t-o- -a- DEAF

161

SIGN   HAND   OFFER   MEANING

Fig. 10.7

IMPRISON   BETTER
('fetter')

Fig. 10.8

d CHILD nd YOU

Fig. 10.9

HEAR   d HEAR—
              nd UNDERSTAND

Fig. 10.10

d EAR   d IGNORE
nd NONE   nd NONE—

Fig. 10.11

CHLD is maintained, while the other hand addresses the 'child' with the signs YOU HOLD (Fig. 10.9). This unusual form makes a very strong link between the title and the content of the poem and foregrounds the idea of the child as the addressee. The second simultaneous sign is used to make the point that hearing is only one way of understanding. The sign HEAR is held while UNDERSTAND is signed on the other hand (Fig. 10.10). The close symbolic link between these ideas and their complex inter-relationship comes from the fact that the signs are almost identical rhymes. They both have a final 'G' handshape and are both articulated at the side of the head, although UNDERSTAND is made at a higher level than HEAR. The final simultaneous sign occurs at the end of the whole poem, with EAR being maintained while signing NONE or EMPTY (given as '-less', as in 'hearless' in the English version of the poem). That sign is held while the other hand signs IGNORE (Fig. 10.11). The effect, again, is to make a strong link between ideas of hearing and the ear, and also ignoring and deliberately not hearing a message. Again, there are close formational similarities between EAR and IGNORE, with both having a 'G' handshape and being articulated at very similar locations. The movement for EAR is sharply inward to the ear location, while for IGNORE it moves sharply out from the cheek location.

The interaction between the English and BSL versions of the two poems adds meaning to them both. The interaction is seen in the phrase 'word in hand' which is very similar to the phrase 'bird in hand'. We know that 'a bird in the hand is worth two in the bush', and in the context of the poem, we can take this to mean that if you can sign, you should value the sign, rather than struggling to speak, which may be of limited use in the end anyway. This metaphor runs through the BSL version of the poem as well as the English version, but the proverb is strictly English.

To a Deaf Child is a blended poem, where English is obtrusive in the BSL. On the other hand, the *Seasons* haiku quartet, while being another example of blending between two languages, allows the two poems to complement each other and English is less dominant. The haiku form originated in Japan as a verse form of 17 syllables in three lines of five, seven and five syllables respectively. The poem expresses a single idea, image or feeling and the *Penguin Dictionary of Literary Terms* describes the haiku as being 'a kind of miniature "snap" in words'. Within some definitions, a haiku should refer to one of the seasons, and within other definitions, it should be concerned in some way with nature, yet it should also stir up feelings and emotions. The haiku's strong emphasis on creating a visual image makes sign language an ideal vehicle. In her introduction to the *Seasons* in *Gestures*, Dorothy explained how she had been impressed by the translations from Japanese haiku verses that she had seen performed by the NTD. She defined them as 'very short poems, each giving a simple, clear picture.' And of her poems, she wrote, 'I tried to do the same thing, and to choose signs that would flow smoothly together' (p. 19). It is these features that appear to have become the 'rules' for a signed haiku. Dorothy's four *Seasons* haiku verses – *Spring, Summer, Autumn* and *Winter* – have been performed in ASL by other performers and were analysed in depth by Ursula Bellugi and Ed Klima as part of their ground-breaking and highly influential linguistic description of ASL, *The Signs of Language* (1979). Their analysis of *Summer*, using their ideas of internal structure, external structure and superstructure is well worth reading.

The *Seasons* haiku quartet (p. 245) that Dorothy composed in English obeys the syllabic rules of a traditional haiku, following the pattern of five syllables in the first line, seven in the second line and five in the final third line. They have other 'poetic' features too, most particularly alliteration and consonance. In *Summer*, for example, there is alliterative repetition of the /k/ and /h/ sounds:

> Green depths and green heights,
> clouds, the hours quiet – – slow, hot,
> heavy on the hands.

In *Winter* we also see examples of consonance with the word-endings /t/, /d/ and /th/ and alliteration of /k/ and /b/ sounds:

> Contrast: black and white;
> Bare trees, covered ground; hard ice,
> Soft snow; birth in death.

However, while Dorothy's *Seasons* verses in English are enjoyable and well-crafted, it is her ASL poems that are of greater interest here, both for their similarities to the original haiku form and their differences. The subject matter of nature and the seasons, and the highly visual imagery, creating an emotional response in the audience are all retained – or even heightened – in the ASL haiku verses. On the other hand, they do not follow the strict syllabic structure of the spoken forms but instead show other highly disciplined features arising out of the formational rules of ASL. When Dorothy was composing her poetry there was very little formalised idea of what might constitute signed poetry discipline and even today there are no equivalent discipline norms such as iambic pentameters or sonnets with specific rhyme sequences. The one exception is now the signed haiku, which is sign language poetry at its most disciplined. It is perhaps one of the most important legacies of Dorothy's work, from the perspective of sign language poetic discipline, yet her original haiku poems were blended poems of English and ASL.

Although the *Seasons* are nominally four separate poems, they are all interconnected, not only by their themes but also by the patterns of signing that we see throughout them. Of the shared themes, *Spring* and *Winter* use a theme of trees, while wind is a feature of *Spring* and *Autumn*, and colour appears in both *Summer* and *Winter*. Of the patterns of signing, we may consider their use of signing space, the rhythm of the poems and the handshapes used in the signs.

Each of the four verses uses contrasting areas in the signing space. *Spring* and *Summer*, for example, start at the top right of the signer's signing space and finish at the lower left-hand side of space. The first sign in *Autumn* is made on the left and the final sign is made to the right. In *Winter* the contrast of heights of signs in the signing space is played out throughout the poem. Through the whole *Seasons* sequence, signs merge and blend into one another, so that there is rarely much (if any) transitional movement from one sign to the next. This is especially true in the three verses that start with the name of the season (only *Autumn* does not). The sign SPRING ends at the start location for the first sign of the poem SUNSHINE and both signs use the same handshape. The sign SUMMER ends where the first sign GREEN begins, and both signs use the same handshape. In *Winter*, the hands of the sign WINTER already oppose each other across the vertical axis, and they merely draw further apart and open from the fist 'A' handshape to the index finger 'G' handshape to create CONTRAST (Fig. 10.12).

The verses each have their own dominant movement and rhythm but sometimes the movement is shared with the preceding and succeeding verses. *Spring* has quick but increasingly relaxed fluttering movements, *Summer* uses slow, smooth movements, *Autumn* begins slowly but becomes much more staccato, and *Winter* begins with very sharp movements before shifting to gentler ones, even with some fluttering. The reintroduction of a fluttering movement in the final verse hints at the cyclical nature of the poems and the seasons – as the sharpness of winter ends, we come around again to fluttering and spring.

The choice of handshape used for the signs in the verses is very disciplined. *Spring* uses signs that are almost entirely '5' or 'B' handshapes, with only one 'V', an 'open 8' (which is very similar to '5') and one very

165

SPRING   SUNSHINE

SUMMER   GREEN

WINTER   CONTRAST

Fig. 10.12

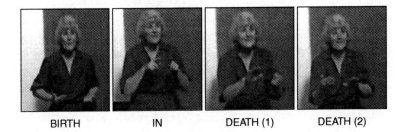

BIRTH   IN   DEATH (1)   DEATH (2)

Fig. 10.13

lax 'W' handshape (and this 'W' handshape so loose that it looks more like a '5'). *Summer* also uses a great many signs with '5' or 'B' handshapes, although the 'B̂' also occurs, and the 'G' handshape (which is a maximal contrast to the openness of the '5' and 'B') is a notable 'rhyme' in the signs SUMMER, GREEN and HOURS. In *Autumn*, the two handshapes of '5' and 'V' are the dominant ones, although 'F' occurs once, ('F' is an 'open' handshape, like '5'), and a 'K' handshape is used in PEOPLE (and the 'K' handshape is very similar to 'V'). The handshapes of the signs in *Winter* are more varied – as well as the '5' and 'B' handshapes that dominate the other three verses, there are also 'A', 'G', 'open 8', 'B̂', 'V̈' and '5̈' handshapes. This can be explained by the idea that *Winter* is the finale of the poem, using handshapes that have cropped up throughout the rest of the verses. This final verse is also one of contrasts, so it is appropriate to find such a range of contrasting handshapes throughout the poem. We should also note the use of the unusual 'open 8' handshape that is used in both *Spring* and *Winter*. This marked handshape has the same purpose as the fluttering movement we mentioned above – it links the two furthest poems in the quartet to close the circle of the cycle of seasons.

The majority of the signs in the *Seasons* sequence are made with two hands. Many of these signs have been chosen partly because they are two-handed signs, but where the signs are one-handed in their citation form they are articulated here with another one-handed sign on the other hand. In *Spring*, only the sign SUNSHINE is made with the non-dominant hand at rest. In *Summer*, only SUMMER, GREEN and HOT are made with the non-dominant hand inactive. All the signs in *Autumn* and *Winter* use both hands. Such a balanced use of both hands is noticeably different from everyday signing.

As with *To a Deaf Child* and many other of her ASL poems, the haiku verses also contain 'grammar-signs', such as ON and IN, which some people might consider have no place in the pure art form of the language. Yet, despite their 'alien' origin, they are worked into the scheme of the poem, so they are much less obtrusive than they are in *To a Deaf Child*. In *Winter*, the final signs BIRTH IN DEATH ('birth in death') include the English-derived sign IN, which has no legitimate place in ASL in such a context. In this case, though, it forms part of the poetic scheme in the haiku. This verse focuses on the idea of contrast, and the handshapes, locations and orientations of the signs are frequently used in contrast to each other. There is a pattern of wide, flat 'B' handshapes in the two signs BIRTH and DEATH and the contrasting narrow 'G' handshape in IN. Not only this, but the palm-orientation in the sign BIRTH is upward, the palm-orientation in IN is downward and in DEATH one palm changes from upward to downward, while the other changes from downward to upward. In both sets of contrast (of handshape and orientation) the 'alien' loan sign IN plays an essential role (Fig. 10.13).

The Italian Sign Language poet Rosaria Giuranna has created a poem simply entitled *Haiku*, which conforms to these patterns that we see in Dorothy's haiku verses. Pizzuto and Russo (2000) describe Giuranna's *Haiku* as a composition characterised by 'extreme concision and formal neatness. A short sequence of signs produced with continuous and fully symmetrical movements'. Such a definition is now fairly standard within signed poetry.

This review of some of the particular aspects of blended sign language and English poems concludes our description of the main features of sign language poetry for the purposes of analysis and appreciation. We are now ready to tackle a few poems in their entirety to show how awareness of all the features described so far will enrich our appreciation of the poems. The following chapters will consider four very different poems: *The Hang Glider*, *Trio*, *Five Senses* and *Three Queens*. The first two poems were composed by Dorothy Miles: *The Hang Glider* in 1975 as a blended poem using ASL and English, and *Trio* in the mid-1980s as a BSL poem without reference to English. The final two poems were composed in BSL by Paul Scott (*Five Senses* in 2002 and *Three Queens* in 2003) and have no reference to English in their composition.

11
The Hang Glider

The Hang Glider (p. 242) is a 'blended' poem, composed in 1975, and designed to work in both English and ASL. As such, it is particularly characteristic of Dorothy Miles' early work and is also an especially striking example of the power of blended poetry. In 1975, she left the National Theatre of the Deaf in New England and drove across the USA to California, where she was appointed to help set up a full programme in Sign Language and Deaf Theatre at the drama department of the California State University, Northridge. While she was there, she also met Ursula Bellugi and Edward Klima who were involved at that time in pioneering sign language research at the Salk Institute at La Jolla. They were especially interested in her poetry and invited her to perform some of her ASL poems for linguistic analysis. Their published results of this analysis were the first serious linguistic attempts at analysis of sign language poetry. For Dorothy, the experience was a huge boost to her confidence as she saw that people believed that her sign poetry was worthy of serious academic study.

However, on her arrival in California, she was very uncertain that she had made the right choice, and her poem *The Hang Glider* was inspired by her feelings at that time. In her introduction to the poem in *Gestures*, she wrote (1976: pp. 49–50) 'I saw for the first time a hang-glider – a man strapped to a huge wing, who stepped off a cliff and flew. This seemed so much like my own experience after leaving the NTD – stepping off into the unknown and hoping that I would keep on flying.'

One performance of the ASL poem, given in California in 1980, may be glossed as follows (entirely non-manual elements are shown in brackets and signs that may be considered neologisms are in bold type):

HERE MY WINGS
[look-at-wings]
[look-down]
THERE-BELOW **CLIFF-EDGE**
NOTHING THERE-BELOW
WAIT WIND
LIFT/CARRY MY WEIGHT
[look-down]
MY WINGS HUGE STRONG BUILT WITH MY LIFE MIND
WINGS WHAT? I BEEN MAKE OTHER WINGS BEFORE
TEST TRY WRONG BROKEN
THROW-OUT
I SEARCH-REPEATEDLY ASK SEE BUILD AGAIN
AND HERE I STAND WINGS
TAKE-UP COURAGE WITH PACK AND MOVE-FORWARD
NOTHING TURN-AROUND BACK
WINGS WON'T TURN-AROUND
WINGS **MOVE/JAM-WINGS** WINGS
[smile-confidently look-down look-worried]
CLIFF-EDGE
LONG-STEEP-DROP AND **SEA-FAR-BELOW**
I HATE DROWN
BUT PEOPLE THEM-OUT-THERE ALL-WATCH-ME
[flash-nervous-smile]
WINGS LOOK-AT-WINGS
BEEN SEE OTHERS PEOPLE DO THAT
WALK-UP-TO-CLIFF-EDGE-AND-JUMP-OFF
FLY
SO WHY CAN'T I
LOOK-AT-WINGS-WITH-LITTLE-ENTHUSIASM
RAISE-WINGS
SUPPOSE SUPPOSE WIND DIE-OUT
I **WALK-UP-TO-CLIFF-EDGE-AND-JUMP-OFF**
FALL-LONG-WAY-DOWN-CLIFF
FACE-ON-GROUND
SEA
[shake-head-determinedly]
WIND WON'T DIE-OUT
EXPERIENCE TELLS ME THAT

COURAGE AND FAITH IN MY EXPERIENCE
THAT ALL I NEED
HERE MY WINGS
FLY-ON-WINGS (x4)
WINGS
FLY-ON-WINGS
HERE MY WINGS (x4)

Repetition

The influence of English in this blended poem is very clearly seen in the patterns of repetition. In this ASL performance, there are no notable patterns of repeated handshape, location or movement, and, generally, the fairly extensive rhyming pattern in the English poem does not extend to the ASL poem. Instead, most of the signs selected for this ASL poem are constrained by the requirements of the English words, leaving little leeway for creating ASL rhymes in the signs. Perhaps paradoxically, the greatest repetition at the sub-sign level occurs when the influence of the English is most marked. The poem contains several 'English' grammar signs – or at least signs used in an English context – such as AND and WITH. In the lines TAKE-UP COURAGE WITH PACK (in English, 'Take up my courage/with my pack'), this use of WITH is only really demanded by the English equivalent (which creates the poetic device zeugma) but it does fit the rhyming scheme of the ASL poem. The sign TAKE-UP uses a '5̈' handshape closing to an 'A' handshape, and so does COURAGE. The next two signs WITH and PACK also use the 'A' handshape. Not only do they all use the same handshape, but they are also all two-handed signs, symmetrical across the vertical axis, so an overall poetic effect is achieved in both languages (Fig. 11.1).

Although there is little repetition of handshapes or other sign elements, there is a noticeable amount of repeated information or close variants of similar ideas. This is seen in the English lines 'I searched, and asked, and saw, / and built again,' and the ASL poem also conveys the parallel ideas expressed here. The same prolonged, sweeping movement of the hands provides the meaning of 'extensively' or 'all around' in three consecutive signs SEARCH ASK SEE, with each sign having a movement that swings from right to left across the signing space to mean SEARCH-ALL-AROUND ASK-ALL-AROUND SEE-ALL-AROUND (Fig. 11.2).

Repetition of individual signs is also used to considerable effect here. It is no particular challenge when blending two poems in two different

171

TAKE-UP (1) TAKE-UP (2) COURAGE (1) COURAGE (2)

WITH   PACK

Fig. 11.1

SEARCH   ASK   SEE

Fig. 11.2

LIFE   d MIND nd LIFE___

Fig. 11.3

languages to ensure that repetition of words in one language is mirrored by repetition in the other and we see such repetition at work in *The Hang Glider* where signs and English words are repeated with similar effect. This is especially seen at the end of the poem which twice repeats the opening words 'Here are my wings' and the corresponding signs HERE MY WINGS. In both poems, the repetition of the phrase emphasises the triumph and positive assertion that these wings are indeed there, hers and wings. In the ASL poem, however, there is not the simple repetition that occurs in the English version ('Here are my wings ... / Here are my wings!'). Instead, this final section may be glossed as:

HERE MY WINGS
FLY-ON-WINGS
WINGS
FLY-ON-WINGS (x4)
HERE MY WINGS (x4)

Here, the ASL poem shifts to show how the hang-glider felt as she stepped off and flew – using the important device of sign language in which the established, frozen sign WINGS is followed by a role-shift with neologism to show the way that the wings were used.

Repetition of signs and words is also used differently in the two poems when repetition occurs in the English poem but not in the ASL version. This is seen in the section that is written in English as:

Step off and dive

and dive

and dive ...

Here the simple repetition in English shows the great depths of the dive by taking a long time to express the idea through several extra words (and their layout on the page adds to this). However, in the ASL poem there is a single, long, complex neologism FALL which uses the dominant hand to show the person falling first sideways then twisting to fall head first and then feet first. At the same time, the non-dominant hand shows the cliff-edge slowly rising until it contacts the face to show the idea of being face-down against the ground. Both 'lines' need the same amount of time to express the length and terror of the fall, but the two poems use the two languages to show this idea in very different ways.

Throughout both the poems, the word 'wings' recurs frequently for good poetic reasons. Constant reference to the wings reminds us that they are the focus of the poem and underlines the message that the poet needs to come to terms with her conflicting emotions of fear, longing and exhilaration. In the ASL poem, WINGS is used at least 12 times, together with signs such as RAISE-WINGS and FLY-ON-WINGS, which is twice the number of times the word 'wings' is used in the English poem. The sign WINGS recurs at apparently haphazard moments in the poem – sometimes even as an aside or half-hearted sign – reinforcing the idea that the awareness of her wings, and the emotions that the wings instil in her, are ever present. Repetition of a sign can also increase poetic tension, sometimes by slowing the pace of the poem, and the repetition of the sign WINGS also controls the 'pace of the action' in the ASL poem, where pace of delivery is an important part of creating emotion in the audience.

Symmetry and balance

The Hang Glider makes careful use of symmetry and balance. The key sign in the poem WINGS is symmetrical, and, after all, successful flight relies on symmetrical use of wings (a single wing on just one side won't do). Of the 130 signs that may be glossed in the ASL poem, only 33 are one-handed. Twenty of those one-handed signs are 'grammar signs' such as I/ME, MY or AND which are unstressed. The effect is a poem where most of the 'content' signs are two-handed, creating noticeable balance.

However, some of the poem's one-handed signs are articulated on the dominant hand, while the non-dominant hand is still present, usually showing information from the previous two-handed sign. This device allows the poet to maintain the presence – and thus symmetry and balance – of both hands, even during one-handed signs. In the line that in English runs, 'built with my life in mind', the signs are BUILT WITH MY LIFE MIND. All these signs are two-handed and symmetrical, except for MIND. Although the two-handed sign LIFE is followed by the one-handed sign MIND, the non-dominant hand continues to hold the final element of LIFE while the dominant hand signs MIND (Fig. 11.3). Another example is:

d NOTHING THERE-BELOW WIND-AT-CLIFF

nd NOTHING_____ WIND-AT-CLIFF

('There, at the edge of nothing, / wait the winds')

Here, NOTHING is a two-handed sign and the non-dominant hand holds the final part of NOTHING while the dominant hand signs THERE-BELOW. Then both hands sign WIND-AT-CLIFF (Fig. 11.4).

174

NOTHING   d THERE-BELOW WIND-AT-CLIFF
              nd NOTHING___

Fig. 11.4

'The wings won't turn'   SEA-FAR-
                            BELOW

Fig. 11.5   *Fig. 11.6*

LOOK-AT-WINGS   LOOK-DOWN   LONG-WAY-
                                                DOWN

Fig. 11.7

In MAKE OTHER WINGS ('I have made other wings') the end part of the two-handed sign MAKE is held on the non-dominant hand while the dominant hand signs OTHER, before both hands sign WINGS. In TRY WRONG BROKEN ('Test-tried, wrong, broken'), the two-handed sign TRY is held by the non-dominant hand during WRONG before both hands sign BROKEN. These are just four examples from the poem, but the general practice of keeping the end form of the two-handed sign on the non-dominant hand while the dominant hand signs the new one-handed sign is used on nine occasions. The ultimate effect is that over 80 per cent of all signs in the poem are expressed as part of a balanced, two-handed utterance.

Neologism

Frozen, established signs account for nearly 90 per cent of all signs in this poem, leaving only 10 per cent of the signs as productively created neologisms. In comparison, the *Seasons* haiku (discussed in Chapter 10) uses nearly 40 per cent neologisms and the section describing the 'useless presents' in *Christmas List* (see Chapter 5) contains 34 per cent neologisms. The high proportion of frozen signs in *The Hang Glider* is related to the fact that this poem is tightly constrained by English, and there are no English neologisms in the poem. However, there is still scope for the production of ASL neologisms, which allow the creation of the powerful visual images that are so important for the emotion of the poem, particularly in reference to the cliff-edge and the height – and implications – of the possible fall.

We have already considered the most complex neologism of the poem, in which the poem describes the idea of falling from the cliff if the winds fail to hold the hang-glider. This neologism is the turning point of the poem and allows the poet to show the depth of her fears. The first neologism in the poem, however, occurs when the cliff-edge is introduced, with the non-dominant hand showing the extent of the flat land at the top of the cliff and the dominant hand showing the extent of the vertical drop. After this sign, however, there is a long stretch of frozen vocabulary, with no use of role-shift or other 'non-English' poetic devices, until the signs used at the English line 'the wings won't turn'. At this point, there is the sequential, dual expression of frozen signs and productive signs that we saw in other poems such as *The Ugly Duckling* and *Christmas List* (in Chapter 5) used to establish an idea and then portray it more visually. At this neologism, the emotions portrayed through the facial expression and body-movement begin to intensify. In this gloss, the neologism that shows a shift into the role of the hang-glider character is in bold type (Fig. 11.5):

WINGS WON'T TURN-AROUND
WINGS
MOVE/JAM-WINGS
WINGS

The following English lines, 'The cliff is high, / and far way down / the sea' are expressed with complex neologisms, using alterations to the frozen sign HIGH. In this case, the non-dominant hand in a 'B' handshape is held to mark the top of the cliff and the dominant hand, also in a 'B' handshape begins to sketch out the extent of the drop. At the lowest point of the drop, the handshape of the dominant hand changes to the 'H' handshape used for the sign HIGH and the hand rises to the level of the cliff-top again to show HIGH at the location of the cliff. The non-dominant hand then changes to an 'A' handshape, while the dominant hand, now in an 'Å' handshape moves down the 'cliff-face' again from the 'cliff-top', anticipating the handshape of the later sign DROWN. Partway down the 'cliff-face', the handshape of the dominant hand changes again to a 'G', pointing downward, and the hand continues to move down before finally opening to a '5' handshape to articulate the sign SEA as a neologism in a new location. Normally SEA is articulated no lower than hip-height but here it is located considerably lower to show how far down the sea is (Fig. 11.6).

Neologisms, at heart, break the rules of the language because they create signs that do not otherwise exist in the language. However, there are other 'rule-breaking' devices that occur in the creation of neologisms. In *The Hang Glider* signs are placed in locations outside the usually accepted signing space. Usual 'signing space' does not extend much below the hips, but in this poem, several of the neologisms are articulated well below this level, in order to show the distance to the sea below the cliff-edge and emphasise the fear and danger of any fall. Another 'broken' language rule in this poem occurs in the unusual use of gaze. Normally the signer looks at the audience while narrating, unless the eyes are directed to specific signs that are placed or moving in signing space, or even an area of signing space where some referent has already been identified. It is deviant to look at nothing at all, yet this is what happens in the opening section of the poem. The first lines in English are:

> Here are my wings;
> And there, at the edge of nothing,
> wait the winds

In ASL they are:

HERE MY WINGS
(look-at-wings)
(look-down)
THERE-BELOW CLIFF-EDGE
NOTHING THERE-BELOW
WAIT WIND

It is not deviant to look at the wings because they have already been mentioned. However, it is unusual to look down without first explaining why or at what. This deviant gaze to the depths causes the audience to notice the unusual signing and builds a greater tension than if we already knew that she was standing on a cliff-edge (Fig. 11.7).

A final example of deviance in neologisms occurs when the whole body moves forward when signing. It is generally accepted that movement below the hips is not a part of sign language. If the signer wishes to refer the forward movement of a person, it can be done using proforms and indeed this is done in the neologism WALK-UP-TO-CLIFF-EDGE-AND-JUMP-OFF (Fig. 11.8). However, when the hang-glider finally takes her step out into the unknown, it is shown through role-shift, as the performer takes a step forward to show the character stepping forward. Normally, this would be unacceptable (a proform would be used instead), but in the poem it adds to the idea of the great significance of stepping out.

Ambiguity and morphing

The Hang Glider starts with a small ambiguity, with the first line HERE MY WINGS. The ASL sign MY is usually one-handed and uses the 'B' handshape against the centre of the chest. However, one variant of this sign can be to use a closed fist 'A' handshape. To sign emphatically that something 'really is mine' this sign can become two-handed, with each hand contacting the chest. This sign, however, in a different context can mean BACKPACK, as it represents the hands grasping the straps of a backpack. In the context of the hang-glider, we not only see her claiming ownership of the wings but are also given a hint of a role shift into the character holding the straps that secure her wings to her (Fig. 11.9).

The most important use of ambiguity and morphing in this poem, however, occurs in the complex neologism used in place of the English lines 'Step off and dive /and dive /and dive ... .' In this neologism, the

WALK-UP-TO-CLIFF-
EDGE

MY/PACK

FALL-FROM-CLIFF

Fig. 11.8

Fig. 11.9

Fig. 11.10

LOOK-AT-WINGS

LOOK-AT-ONLOOKERS

Fig. 11.11

Quick nervous smile

Worried look

Fig. 11.12

Expression of fear and increasing
confidence in neologism after 'fall'

Expression of bliss during
final 'Here are my wings'

Fig. 11.13

Fig. 11.14

non-dominant hand, in a 'B' handshape is used to show the cliff-top, while the dominant hand in a 'V' handshape shows the hang-glider falling. As the hang-glider falls, the performer's head lowers, following the descent of the hand. However, at the moment that the face touches the non-dominant hand, the scale of the sign changes. What was simply the performer's head moving to follow the movement of a proform, now becomes the hang-glider's face. What was a large area of cliff-face now becomes the ground upon which the fallen hang-glider lies. Such a shift in scale brings the audience very close to the character in the poem, after the distance of being a mere observer of the movement of the proform (Fig. 11.10).

Themes and metaphors

The poem's theme is that of flying and the fear of falling. We have already seen that Dorothy wrote another untitled poem, in which there was no mention of hang-gliding but only of diving and falling from a cliff, to parallel the fear of 'falling' in love. Many of her poems used the idea of flight to symbolise freedom, and in both that untitled poem and *The Hang Glider*, flight is contrasted with the fear of failure and falling. While we would not want to suggest that this poem was a conscious reference on her part to any intention of suicide, nevertheless its theme and content now has great resonance to audiences who know that she did fall to her death in 1993.

The Hang Glider is clearly an extended metaphor. Although it apparently concerns the thoughts of a person trying to pluck up the courage to jump off a cliff-edge for a hang-gliding flight, we know – because she said so – that Dorothy composed it on seeing hang-gliders for the first time in California, when she was suffering a crisis of confidence. The poem's tenor is not hang-gliding but facing the fear of the unknown and having the confidence to leave a life of mundane security for the risky life of new opportunities. The theme allows allusions to the Greek myth of Icarus who flew too close to the sun on his home-made wings during his flight to freedom and fell to drown in the sea below. Although there is no reference to Icarus in the poem, the idea of wearing wings, taking flight to achieve some sort of freedom, and the fear of falling to a death by drowning have a powerful allusive effect.

Performance

In a television interview in 1976, Dorothy referred to some of her differences of opinion with the National Theatre of the Deaf.

She said:

> I sometimes felt that they made the signs just a demonstration –
> beautiful things but separate from personal feelings – and I believe
> that deaf people should be doing both of them together, feelings and
> signs. That's the idea behind my poem *The Hang Glider*, not to sepa-
> rate the signs and the feelings but put them together.

The emotion in *The Hang Glider* comes through remarkably powerfully in
the performance of the ASL poem, and it is perhaps the most notable
feature of the poem. The emotional expression is achieved especially
through the use of entirely non-manual signs and through the role of
personation, especially in the neologisms. The emotions are shown often
by the subtle use of eyes and posture. Although there are no signs or
words in the text of this poem that mention or even especially imply fear,
the personation of the central character shows her fear and the courage
in overcoming it, in a way that words or signs alone never could. The use
of the eyes is especially important here, as they portray uncertainty and
nervousness. We have seen that the opening lines in English run:

> Here are my wings;
> And there, at the edge of nothing,
> wait the winds

In English, these words are all we have, but in the signed performance,
the eyes add to the manual signs. They play an essential role as the
signer looks at her wings and then down over the cliff-edge, emphasising and increasing the element of danger in the choice to jump, making the following gloss (where entirely non-manual signs are shown in
brackets) more appropriate:

HERE MY WINGS
(look-at-wings)
(look-down)
THERE-BELOW CLIFF-EDGE
NOTHING THERE-BELOW
WAIT WIND

On several other occasions in this poem, the signed performance has the
eyes looking down over the cliffs or at the wings or around at the
supposed onlookers. The emotional impact of these glances is very

powerful. The emotion is not anywhere in the text but flows from taking on the persona of the person with the hang-glider (Fig. 11.11).

These uses of gaze sometimes accompany manual signs but also occur with no manual sign at all, causing the audience to focus entirely on the non-manual message and the emotions it carries. The quick, nervous smile that flashes after the signs BUT PEOPLE THEM-OUT-THERE ALL-WATCH-ME ME ('But they are watching me') is also not part of the written text. Nor is the confident smile that turns to worry after the line '(The wings won't turn.)'. These facial expressions come out of the personation of the character (Fig. 11.12).

As the hang-glider contemplates the disaster of falling ('Suppose ... / suppose the winds might die, / and I / step off and dive / and dive / and dive ...') in the signed performance, her head slowly lowers as her signs describe falling down the cliff into the sea. Her final brave decision to fly comes when she tells herself 'The winds won't die!' (WIND WON'T WIND-DIE). Between these lines, however, she has slowly raised her head and looked forward. She shakes her head twice, and then shakes it another three times with increasing confidence. The personation here shows the bravery and determination through the eyes, facial expression and head movement, without any manual signs, and perhaps words and signs could not express the emotions portrayed anyway. This complex, highly charged emotional section of the poem has no parallel in words in the English poem. In the written version, it is implied by the use of a line of asterisks. Asterisks are often used to imply what cannot be said directly, and here the readers are left to interpret them in their own way, and their use is an interesting solution to the problem of how to represent something so powerful that cannot be written (Fig. 11.13).

The expression of satisfaction and self-fulfilment at the end of this poem when she flies is also shown by facial expression, body-movement, head angle and closed eyes (also a deviant feature of signing, as signers are not expected to close their eyes for any length of time). Some of the satisfaction and triumph comes through the repetition of the English words, and the use of the '... ' and '!' in the final two lines, but it is considerably more powerful in the signed version (Fig. 11.14).

Our role as the audience is important here. The eye-contact with the audience, and the emotional facial expressions we see on the performer's face, draw us into the poem, making us spectators from close-quarters (and certainly much closer than we would normally be to a hang-glider). The end effect is to make us much more emotionally involved in the poem. We can feel more strongly for the hang-glider and, in feeling more strongly for her, we feel more strongly for ourselves in that situation.

The element of personation – not explicitly given in the text of the poem – means that another performance could give this poem a completely different emotional impact. A confident, outgoing Deaf person, who was facing just one more challenge and defying all that the world had ever thrown at her, might be the persona behind the performance. In that case, although the text of the poem would not change, the elements of fear and courage would be replaced by bravado and assurance, and the impact of the poem would be very different.

Despite the 'blended' composition of this poem, the poetry of the ASL composition comes across very clearly. The maintenance of balance and symmetry, the creation of complex, highly visual neologisms and the powerful emotions expressed through the personation in the performance all combine to produce a memorable work of art in ASL. However, blended poetry may be seen as an important historical and intellectual midway development in the evolution of 'pure' sign language poetry. We will now turn to a poem that was composed much later than *The Hang Glider* and has very little influence from English.

12
Trio

Unlike *The Hang Glider* discussed in the previous chapter, *Trio* (p. 249) is not a 'blended' poem and was composed without reference to English. The richness of language and its freedom from the constraints of English make it one of Dorothy Miles' finest sign language poems. Although *Trio* is not strictly a haiku (unlike her *Seasons* quartet), it shares many of the features that occur in the signed haiku discipline. It is made up of three very short poems, *Morning, Afternoon* and *Evening*. Each of these short poems contains rather more action than one might expect in a haiku, but the powerful visual images created and the 'nature' themes, coupled with the finely crafted language, make *Trio* the perfect example of the sign language haiku form that Dorothy pioneered.

The following five rough, unpublished glosses of several signed poems left in Dorothy's papers all have elements of the haiku about them. *Trio* clearly developed out of these poems. The superscript numbers here were Dorothy's way of showing how often the sign should be repeated, and the superscript letters show whether signs should be placed to the left or right.

RAIN[5]
PART-IT, GRASP
PULL CORD, SWISH
RAINBOW

MORNING
WIND BLOWN-OUT
THE POOL, SEE
TWIN TREES

AFTERNOON
^RBIRD BIG BELLY ^RPERCH
^LBIRD BIG BELLY ^LPERCH
ME BIG BELLY SIT
ALL SNORE

NIGHT (DARK)
CAT GO OUT
SLINK[3]
FUR COAT
DIAMOND-EYED

ENGLISH HILL
WALK UPWARDS
SUMMIT NEARS
STAND, LOOK AROUND
CHECKER BOARD

A gloss of *Trio* as Dorothy performed it on *See Hear!* in 1983 may be made as follows (signs that are considered to be neologisms are in bold type and entirely non-manual information is in square brackets):

[stand. deep inhalation. bright smile.]
MORNING
SUN **SUN-RISE.**
THERE RAIN **RAIN-FALLS-AND-DIES**
WIND **WIND-BLOWS-AND-DIES**
CALM/STILL-WATER
STILLNESS [I-see-stillness]
SEE THERE IN POOL
TWIN-TREES
[delighted smile.]

[sit. smile with closed mouth]
AFTERNOON
ME
I-EAT-A-LOT **I-SIT-BACK FULL-TUMMY** FULL
MY DOG ALSO
DOG-EATS-A-LOT DOG-SITS-BACK-FULL
BIRD **BIRD-FLY-DOWN**
BIRD-EATS-A-LOT BIRD-PERCHES

I-LOOK-AT-BIRD I-LOOK-AT-DOG
THREE-OF-US-DOZE
[peaceful small smile]

[stand. no smile]
EVENING EVENING[1]
SUN LIKE FLOWER SUNSET HOLD-SUN/HOLD-
FLOWER-FOLDED
DARKNESS
WINGED-CREATURE LIKE b-a-t
BAT-FLIES BAT-COVERS-FACE
DEAF BLIND ME
REACH-OUT REACH-OUT
[blink, blink.]

Repetition

Unlike the signed version of *The Hang Glider*, this poem has considerable repetition at the level of handshape, location and movement, and each stanza is dominated by a different set of handshapes carrying different symbolic connotations. The three stanzas, *Morning*, *Afternoon* and *Evening* are characterised by different themes – of freshness in the morning, contentment in the afternoon and fear in the evening – and the choice of handshapes reflects these themes. Ten signs in *Morning* use open '5' and 'B' handshapes because morning (and its metaphorical parallel, youth) is symbolically seen as a time for openness and positive feelings, when everything is fresh and new. The final sign TWIN-TREES uses two hands, each with a '5' handshape. *Afternoon*, however, only contains three signs using '5' or 'B' handshapes, and instead this stanza is dominated by 'Ĝ' and 'B̂' handshapes, which are neither fully open handshapes, nor fully closed, but a sort of 'medium', corresponding to the middle part of the day (and, metaphorically, to middle age in life). These handshapes occur in ten signs, including the final sign THREE-OF-US-DOZE. The 'H' handshape in AFTERNOON and DOG has a similar quality of being partway between open and closed. Extensive repetition of handshapes in *Evening* is less evident, but the 'V̈' and '5̈' handshapes do occur (the clawed aspect of these handshapes being associated with tension) as well as signs in which the handshape closes, such as changes from an open '5' to a closed B̂. These 'tense' signs and the closing handshapes help to emphasise the feelings of fear and withdrawal that can occur at night (or with coming old age). The main neologistic sign in this stanza DARKNESS/ BAT-COVER-FACE is made with the '5̈' handshape (Fig. 12.1).

186

TWIN-TREES   THREE-OF- DARKNESS/BAT-
US-DOZE COVERS-FACE

Fig. 12.1

EVENING   BLIND

Fig. 12.2

SUN   SUN-RISES

RAIN   RAIN-DIES   WIND   WIND-DIES

Fig. 12.3

Chiming occurs in the use of the 'V̈' handshape in this stanza. Chiming is a poetic device that uses the similar forms of two words or signs to make the audience look for a connection between them. The first line of the stanza is its title 'Evening' and is signed with two different signs, both of which mean EVENING. The second sign, made with a small downward movement of the 'V̈' handshape at the nose, is only one parameter different from the sign used at the climax of the poem BLIND. BLIND is made with the same 'V̈' handshape at the bridge of the nose but has a small side-to-side movement. Clearly, there is a connection between the form of the two signs and between the two meanings – especially in this poem (Fig. 12.2).

There is also a pattern of repeated locations and movement paths, where signs may be articulated on, near, or farther away from the body. This is in keeping with the symbolism in this poem that we considered in relation to the handshapes. Morning and youth are the time to be outward-looking, as the day and life are spread before us (out = forwards = good). Evening and old age are the time to be more inward-looking as our horizons appear to shrink (in = backwards = bad). *Morning* contains only two signs (MORNING and SEE) that contact the body (and SEE moves out, away from the body), and the rest of the signs do not contact the body, moving outward or being made further away from the signer. *Evening* has six signs that touch the body, two more that are articulated very close to the face, and two more that move toward the body. *Afternoon*, being the middle section between these two contrasting verses, does not show patterns of either forward or back, but the locations of signs are obtrusively to the left and right, and the movements are dominantly up and down.

Although we have seen that repetition can occur to create 'rhymes' at the sub-sign level, it also occurs at the higher, grammatical level. There is a repetition of three noun–verb pairs of a specific type in *Morning*. The three sign pairs:

SUN SUN-RISES
RAIN RAIN-FALLS-AND-DIES
WIND WIND-BLOWS-AND-DIES

are all similar in that the noun and the following verb differ only in their movement, and the handshape of the noun sign is included in the verb sign. This is not always the case for associated pairs of nouns and verbs because the noun may also be represented by a proform in the verb, using a different handshape (as we will see immediately below). The use of three of the noun-verb pairings in *Morning* creates a definite pattern that leads to the climax of the neologism TWIN-TREES (Fig. 12.3).

In *Afternoon*, there are again three noun–verb pairs (creating an effect of parallelism across the two stanzas). This time, though, the handshape of the verb is determined by the *class* of the noun and not by the noun, so that the noun and verb pairs are not visually similar. The signs I and (HUMAN)-EATS, DOG and DOG-EATS and BIRD and BIRD-EATS are paired in this way to create an effect of parallelism that leads to the final sign THREE-OF-US-DOZE (Fig. 12.4).

Grammatical information in sign languages is often shown by the movement and location imposed upon a sign. In *Trio*, there is grammatical information about the change in speed and duration of two different actions – the falling of the rain and the blowing of the wind. There is little clue to repeated grammatical patterns in the English translation, 'The rain stops – and the wind dies'. However, in BSL the signs RAIN-FALLS-AND-DIES and WIND-BLOWS-AND-DIES are made with the same movement that gives the same grammatical information and sets up a rhythmic pattern in the signing. In each one, the size and speed of the movement slowly lessens. In *Afternoon*, the movement of the signs describing how the poet, dog, and bird eat is repeated each time to show the same grammatical information of an action continuing for some time. Each character in the poem eats quickly for a certain period of time before slowing down and finally stopping and resting. This is shown by each of the three different signs (HUMAN)-EATS, DOG-EATS and BIRD-EATS using the same patterns of movement. For each sign there is then an upward and backward movement (of the body for the poet, and of the right hand for the dog and the left hand for the bird) before a hold, each time showing the grammatical ('temporal aspect') information that the action came to a gentle end.

Symmetry and balance

This poem uses symmetry extensively, with vertical symmetry most dominant, but there is also a fine example of the less common and more challenging horizontal symmetry. In *Afternoon*, vertical symmetry occurs through two-handed symmetrical signs close to the central vertical axis showing that she eats and sits replete. A gloss of the first part of the stanza shows this (two-handed symmetrical signs are highlighted):

I-EAT-LOTS I-SIT-BACK-FULL FULL **FULL-TUMMY**
MY **DOG** ALSO (Fig. 12.5)

189

Fig. 12.4

Fig. 12.5

Afternoon also creates symmetry by using two different one-handed signs simultaneously. During this stanza, the character in the poem is joined by her dog and a bird. Although the BSL sign DOG used in this poem is two-handed, the signs that follow to show the dog eating, resting and sleeping are one-handed (using a '$\hat{B}$' handshape), and these signs are placed to the right. The sign BIRD is one-handed, as are the signs that follow (using a '$\hat{G}$' handshape) to show the bird eating, resting and sleeping, and these signs are all placed to the left. The English lines of *Afternoon* run:

> I eat and sit, replete,
> My dog does too.
> A sparrow pecks and perches –
> The three of us doz-z-z-ze!

This may be glossed in BSL as follows (here the subscript letters refer to whether the sign is placed centrally, to the left or to the right):

I-EAT-LOTS$_C$ I-SIT-BACK-FULL$_C$ FULL$_C$ FULL-TUMMY$_C$
MY$_C$ DOG$_C$ ALSO$_C$
DOG-EATS-LOTS$_R$ DOG-SITS-BACK$_R$
BIRD$_C$
BIRD-FLY-DOWN$_L$
BIRD-EATS-LOTS$_L$ BIRD-PERCHES-BACK$_L$
I-LOOK-AT-BIRD(eyes$_L$) I-LOOK-AT-DOG(eyes$_R$)
THREE-OF-US-DOZE (Fig. 12.6)

We can see from this gloss that the signs relating to the dog are kept to the right-hand side of the central vertical axis while the poem refers to the dog eating and resting. The final sign is then held below shoulder height (appropriate for a sitting dog) while the bird is introduced on the left-hand side of the axis. The movements for the bird eating and resting are identical to those for the dog (although the handshape is different) and the final sign of this section is held above shoulder-height (appropriate for a perching bird). Apart from the height difference, these signs are mirror-images and we can say that they are symmetrical across a diagonal axis. In the following sign, THREE-OF-US-DOZE, the internal movements of the signs of the two manual signs are identical – showing that both the dog and the bird were snoring – making a symmetrical pattern from two separate signs. We should also add that the

191

LOOK-AT-BIRD LOOK-AT-DOG THREE-OF-US-DOZE

Fig. 12.6

DARKNESS or BAT?

Fig. 12.7

Looking at 'nothing'
before DARKNESS

Fig. 12.8

WIND-DIES

Fig. 12.9

'The sun, like a flower, folds'

Fig. 12.10

DARKNESS BAT-FLIES

Fig. 12.11

central vertical axis of symmetry in this stanza is marked by the human character.

The poem also provides a beautiful example of symmetry across the central horizontal axis in *Morning*, with the reflection of a tree in still waters. The English version of the relevant lines runs:

> See, in the pool,
> Twin Trees

The English gives no direct indication of the horizontal symmetry of the sign used to show the twin trees. The glorious neologism that Dorothy uses in the BSL poem has the elbow of the non-dominant hand joined to the elbow of the dominant hand. Using the elbows as the dividing line of symmetry, the sign becomes horizontally symmetrical with the non-dominant hand signing TREE but pointing down in a direct reflection of the dominant hand, which signs TREE while pointing up in the usual way. Aesthetically, it is a treat almost unparalleled in her poetry (see Fig. 12.1).

Neologism

Trio, free from the constraints of English, uses a high proportion of neologisms. Unlike the 10 per cent of neologisms that we saw in *The Hang Glider*, neologisms make up 40 per cent of *Trio*. The neologisms are used to build up an increasingly strong visual image of nature, animals and the emotions of the central human character in the poem, and they also allow the introduction of considerable humour in the earlier part of the poem. Some of these neologisms bend (or even break) language rules, as with the signs glossed as TWIN-TREES (in *Morning*), THREE-OF-US-DOZE (in *Afternoon*) and BAT/DARKNESS-COVER-FACE (in *Evening*) (see Fig. 12.1). The sign TWIN-TREES produces a strong visual image of the reflection of a tree in a still pool. It breaks the rules of ordinary BSL by having the two articulating hands in contact at the elbows. In BSL, the hands are allowed to contact each other at various points (such as the palm, the back of the hand or the fingertips) but not at the elbows. The sign THREE-OF-US-DOZE occurs when the poet, her dog and a bird have all eaten and then all take an afternoon nap. It uses three signs simultaneously and this is unusual in BSL. Articulating two signs simultaneously is reasonably common, but the articulation of three simultaneous separate pieces of information is stretching the rules. The image of DARKNESS/BAT-COVER-FACE uses a sign that covers the face entirely.

While the face is an important location for signs in BSL, there are no signs that cover the face entirely, so this sign also bends the rules of sign formation. In each of these three examples, the signs bend the rules of normal language to create extra poetic significance by foregrounding the aesthetic language.

In general, *Trio* is far removed from English influence (and this is reflected in the fact that only approximately half of the manual signs are accompanied by an English-derived mouthing) but there is one use of fingerspelling in the final stanza, *Evening*. The line from the English poem runs 'Darkness, like a bat, flies close'. In the BSL poem, this line may be glossed as DARKNESS LIKE b-a-t, followed by a 'non-sign' that is neither DARKNESS nor FLYING-BAT, but partway between the two. Many observers of the poem report that they do not like the finger-spelling of b-a-t, as it breaks the smooth flow of the rest of the signs. However, we saw in Chapters 8 and 9 that similes in sign poems are often highlighted, and using fingerspelling certainly draws our atten-tion to the fact that something unusual is happening, making us notice the simile.

Further 'rule-breaking' of the language for poetic effect occurs in *Morning*, when we see a deviant use of gaze during the sign TWIN-TREES. Normally, in the production of a sign that is part of narrative fact, the signer looks at the audience, not at the sign, but in TWIN-TREES this does not happen. Dorothy looks down at the sign she has made then she looks up at the audience before looking down at the sign again and finally back up at the audience. At one interpretation of this, the gaze might be that of someone looking delightedly at the reflection of the twin trees in the water, so perhaps it is not narrative fact at all but shows a role-shift into a character admiring the reflection. However, with a different reading of this sign, the poet (or performer) is inviting the audience to share in the enjoyment of the new sign. In *Evening*, there is another similar deviant use of gaze, when the eyes stare directly at the partially formed sign that is a combination of DARKNESS and BAT (Fig. 12.7). It is almost as though she is asking, 'What is this sign?' Clearly, such a question would rarely be asked in normal everyday signing because signers would expect to know what signs they were making.[2]

In another instance in *Evening*, the series of signs describing the sunset are articulated on the left-hand side of signing space and then, suddenly, the eyes are directed to the right. They appear to be looking at nothing at all and for no reason. Only after a pause, does the sign DARKNESS occur at this new right-hand-side location. The effect is to create con-siderable tension to show the fear of approaching night, and we saw a similar device to create tension in *The Hang Glider*, where the performer looks down at 'nothing' before saying what she is looking at. We saw in Chapter 6 that signed poems minimise transitional movements by blending signs, and *Trio* makes considerable use of this device, so, making a sharp shift from one side of signing space to the opposite side, *maximising* the transitional movement is very obtrusive. To highlight that the poem is breaking the poetic rules for a good reason, it breaks another language rule, this time of gaze (Fig. 12.8).

Morphing

The concise nature of this poem means that the potential for morphing and ambiguity in signs is carefully exploited to maximise the meaning in the small number of signs used. Morphing occurs as location and movement of signs are selected to reduce the transition movements between each one. In the first stanza, *Morning*, the wind dies and the pool becomes calm enough to show the reflection of the tree. The orientation of the sign WIND-DIES slowly changes so that the palms move from facing outward to facing downward, so that the sign morphs from WIND-DIES to show RIPPLES-ON-WATER and then, as the fingers cease to flutter, the sign morphs to CALM or STOP (Fig. 12.9).

In *Evening* there is a line that is translated as 'Like a flower the sun folds itself up.' In the BSL poem this is signed as:

SUN (left) LIKE (centre) FLOWER (left to right across the nose) SUN-SETS (right).

Here the sign FLOWER carries signs from left to right in the signing space, allowing the signs to move rightwards across the signing space with minimal 'wasted' transition movement. There are further uses of morphing and ambiguity to create signs used in similes, as we will see in the next section.

Themes and metaphor

Like *The Hang Glider*, *Trio* may be treated as an extended metaphor on another subject. Although it is ostensibly about three stages in the day – Morning, Afternoon and Evening – further study of the poem allows us to read it at another level with ideas of Youth, Middle Age and Old Age. The freshness of morning and youth give way to the contentment of middle age and the afternoon, before the fear and uncertainty of evening and old age. We have already seen how the poem uses many of its signs symbolically to imply this. The use of ambiguous signs also contributes to the construction of this metaphor. In *Evening*, the sign that can mean both EVENING and OLD is an important sign for the poem. We know that the poem is overtly concerned with the three stages of the day, and the other two stages have been introduced with the signs MORNING and AFTERNOON, so the primary meaning of this sign at the start of the third stanza is EVENING. However, it is possible to take the second meaning of that sign as OLD and use it to interpret the metaphorical meaning of that last stanza with reference to the closing stages of life.

As well as presenting us with an extended metaphor, the poem also uses two notable similes in the final stanza, translated in English as '**Like** a flower, the sun folds itself up' and 'Darkness, **like** a bat, flies close/ and closer – / deaf-blinds me!' We have been told clearly that the sun is like a flower but we have to understand why the sun is like a flower. From the comparison, we can say that some flowers close up when the sun goes down. We can also say that flowers are fragile so this simile makes the sun seem fragile and delicate when compared to the terrifying darkness that is approaching. We can also draw on the allusion to the psalmist's observation that the days of man are like the flowers of the field that fade as the sun sets (Psalm 103: 15–16). This might be especially useful, as we are already viewing the poem in terms of the passage of life described in the passage of a day. However, when we look at the signs SUN and CLOSING-FLOWER we also see that their forms are similar, and this is the key to understanding the simile in BSL.

The BSL sign SUN is visually motivated, with the idea that something is open and giving out rays of light. In fact, the manual component of the signs SUN and LIGHT can be almost identical, with an 'O' handshape opening to a '5' handshape. When a light is turned off, the sign LIGHT-OFF has a '5' handshape closing to an 'O' handshape. Given the relationship between the sun and light, we can understand that as the sun goes down, the light fades, so we should expect the handshape in SUN to close. This is also what would happen when the petals of a flower close. The parallel between the sun 'closing' and the flower closing is made so exact that the resulting sign is ambiguous, so that we could interpret it as either the sun setting or a flower closing (Fig. 12.10).

When we are told that darkness is like a bat, there are many ways that we can seek to interpret the ground of this metaphor. Bats come out at night – in the dark – and many people are afraid of both bats and the dark. Darkness can seem to wrap itself around a person, just as a bat might wrap its wings around a face. Darkness is also a time when sight is of no use, and bats do not rely on sight but sound (as in the common English phrase, 'blind as a bat'). Bats are therefore the complete hearing antithesis to Deaf people, who rely on sight. There is also a strong formational similarity between the BSL signs DARKNESS and BAT-FLIES. In DARKNESS, the two 'B' hands cross over in front of the face while, in BAT-FLIES, the two '5' hands cross over and link at the thumbs. In this way darkness is indeed like a bat because the signs are so similar. We should note that in both of these similes, Dorothy pauses in her performance to emphasise the relationship between the two ideas (Fig. 12.11).

Allusion is also relevant to this poem, as the final stanza calls to mind the poem *Do Not Go Gentle* by Dorothy's fellow-Welshman, hero and inspiration, Dylan Thomas. Here too, darkness is linked to the idea of death:

> Do not go gentle into that good night,
> Old age should burn and rave at close of day;
> Rage, rage against the dying of the light.

Trio makes use of two themes that are very common in sign language poetry generally, as well as in Dorothy Miles' compositions: trees and nature. These themes are also central to the haiku form, to which *Trio* is clearly related. However, the formational properties of the sign TREE, with its open, upward-pointing fingers, also allowed the development of powerful poetic effects that we have seen in our discussion of the repetition of elements and the neologisms. The introduction of animals – the dog, the bird and even the bat – allowed her to develop signs showing the actions of animals, especially in *Afternoon*.

Another theme in the poem that shows clearly that it is a poem from a Deaf perspective is the idea of silence equating with stillness (see Chapter 7). The English word 'Stillness' occurs in the third line, but the meanings of peace and silence wait behind the sign as alternative meanings in the BSL version:

> Sunrise
> The rain stops – and the wind dies
> **Stillness**

We saw in our discussion of themes in Chapter 7 that vision and sight are especially relevant to a Deaf poet. Although this poem is a general observation of the experiences of a life in a day (a common metaphor), it is told from a Deaf perspective, and the particular Deaf discomfort in darkness is also seen in *Evening*, where the ideas of night, darkness and being deaf-blind (with the accompanying associations of death) occur:

> **Darkness**, like a bat, flies close,
> and closer –
> **deaf-blinds** me!

Touch also becomes very important in *Evening*. When the sun sets, there is no suggestion of touch in the line of the English translation 'Like a flower, the sun folds itself up'. However, in the BSL poem, the sun becomes something that can be held once it has closed like a flower, as we can see in the gloss SUN LIKE FLOWER SUNSET HOLD-SUN/ HOLD-FLOWER-FOLDED. Similarly, when the darkness falls, the English translation simply says that darkness flies close and deaf-blinds the character but, in the BSL poem, the darkness (and/or the bat) physically wraps itself around her face so that contact is made and the darkness touches her. The final image that darkness 'deaf-blinds me' is one that only a Deaf person can truly understand from experience. When hearing people are in the dark, they can still make use of sounds around them. For a Deaf person in the dark, touch is the sense that is left. Although the English poem ends with the words 'deaf-blinds me', the BSL poem goes two lines further, with the reaching out of both hands to grope in the darkness and the eyes blinking desperately against the dark.

Performance

The performance of *Trio* recorded for *See Hear!* is made against a backdrop of a scene of an English garden, complete with a stone urn and a stone bench. The changing mood in the three stanzas that goes with the changing time of day is also marked by changes in the lighting. Clearly such production techniques are not essential to the interpretation of the text of the poem, but they do add to the audience's experience of the overall performance.

Personation is used to good effect in this poem. Although there is only one central character in the poem, in the middle stanza *Afternoon*, the poet is joined by a dog and a bird. The placement of the dog and bird is important for the poem. In the other two stanzas (*Morning* and *Evening*) she is alone (as we are at birth and death) but in the afternoon she is surrounded by companions (as we hope to be in the midst of life). For this reason, the dog needs to be placed on one side of her character, and the bird to be placed on the other side. The advice to other BSL poets that 'the signer should have a clear idea of the location, size, height, etc. of other images in relation to himself' (see Chapter 9) is followed carefully in this poem. The bird perches correctly at shoulder-height and the dog sits beside her, lower down. She looks at the correct height both at the bird and then the dog before they all sleep. Part of the enjoyment of the final line of *Afternoon*, ALL-THREE-SLEEP ('The three of us doz-z-z-ze!'), occurs because the personation is retained non-manually, while simultaneously showing the other two characters manually.

The emotions in *Trio* also come through powerfully as a result of personation, so that it is not clear what is part of the text of the poem and what is added through performance alone. The poem starts with a wide smile even before the first sign is made. Throughout *Morning* there are smiles. In the interlude between *Morning* and *Afternoon*, the smile is smaller and more peaceful. That smile occurs again at the end of *Afternoon* and then disappears as *Evening* starts. The end of *Evening* has wide eyes, staring fearfully into darkness and nothing.

This poem is probably one of the 'purer' BSL poems that Dorothy composed and performed. It was composed in the mid-1980s, when she had had the time to develop the idea of sign poetry without reference to English. The elements described here are created independently of English, so that the poetry comes from the sign language imagery and the patterns and symbolism produced by the signs. This form of sign language poetry, perhaps more than any other, has come to be a template for sign language poetry on both sides of the Atlantic. In the final chapter of this section, we will look at the poetry of a contemporary British Deaf poet, Paul Scott, who has used the poetic principles developed by Dorothy Miles and developed them to compose his own work – highly original and fully independent of English.

13
Five Senses and *Three Queens*

Five Senses

Paul Scott's BSL poem *Five Senses* (p. 252) personifies the senses in a celebration of all the senses from a Deaf perspective. As with any poem of empowerment for a minority group, this poem confounds the normal expectations of the majority culture. As Deaf people do not hear, surely one of the senses will be missing? This poem shows that nothing is missing. In the poem, the description of the first three senses (Touch, Taste and Smell) establishes common ground between Deaf and hearing people, as everyday experiences are presented imaginatively and humorously. These sections of the poem provide an opportunity to showcase the capabilities of BSL in the hands of a talented poet, but are not especially 'Deaf-themed'. The turning-point of the poem occurs when one of the hitherto obliging senses is unable to talk to the questioner. The first three senses have been able to explain what they do, but for the Deaf poet, the sense of Hearing cannot explain sound because it has no experience. At this point, we are explicitly presented with the Deaf perspective as Sight helps Hearing to do its job.

The poem may be glossed as follows (a translation is in the Appendix, on p. 252):

FIVE SENSES
RIGHT-HAND-CLOSES-LEFT-HAND
EXCUSE-ME (to thumb)
(thumb extends from fist) WAKE-UP
WHAT-DO-YOU-WANT?
YOU WHAT-ARE-YOU?
LET-ME-SHOW-YOU

SENSE-MOVES-FROM-HAND-TO-POSSESS-BODY
EMOTION-AND-FEELING
SHIVERS-RUN-UP-ARMS-TO-SHOULDERS
HUG-SELF
REACH-OUT-AND-TOUCH-WITH-RIGHT-HAND
HAND-IS-PULLED-BACK-BY-LEFT-HAND
RUB-HANDS-TOGETHER
REACH-OUT-TO-TOUCH-WITH-LEFT-HAND
SNATCH-BACK-LEFT-HAND-AND-SHAKE-IT-IN-PAIN
RIGHT-HAND-RUBS-LEFT-HAND WRING-HANDS
LICK-LEFT-HAND RIGHT-HAND-RUBS-LEFT-HAND WRING-HANDS
SENSE-LEAVES-POSSESSION-OF-THE-BODY-AND-RETURNS-TO-
    THE-LEFT-HAND
DO-YOU-UNDERSTAND-NOW?
OK OK-YES GOOD-FOR-YOU
EXCUSE-ME (to index finger)
(index finger extends from fist) WHAT-DO-YOU-WANT?
YOU WHAT-ARE-YOU?
LET-ME-SHOW-YOU
SENSE-MOVES-FROM-HAND-TO-POSSESS-THE-BODY
REACH-FOR-ICECREAM-AND-BRING-IT-TO-MOUTH
LICK-ICECREAM HOLD-ICECREAM LICK-ICECREAM DELICIOUS!
THERE SCOOP-FOOD-AND-TAKE-A-BITE HOLD-FOOD/SPOON
TAKE-FOOD-FROM-MOUTH-AND-THROW-IT-OUT
'DON'T-LIKE-THAT!'
SCOOP-FOOD-AND-TAKE-A-BITE HOLD-FOOD/SPOON THAT'S-NICE
SENSE-LEAVES-POSSESSION-OF-THE-BODY-AND-RETURNS-TO-
    THE-LEFT-HAND
(index finger extended from fist) THAT'S-ME
(to middle finger) EXCUSE-ME
(middle finger extends from fist)
YOU WHAT?
LET-ME-SHOW-YOU
SENSE-MOVES-FROM-HAND-TO-POSSESS-THE-BODY
SMELL FLOWER PICK-FLOWER-AND-SMELL-IT WONDERFUL
FRIDGE CHEESE IN-THERE BRING-CHEESE-TO-NOSE-AND-TAKE-IT-
    AWAY-AGAIN
FLAP-AWAY-HORRIBLE-SMELL
TAKE-SMALL-PIECE-OF-FOOD-AND-PUT-IT-IN-MOUTH
HOLD-SMALL-PIECE-OF-FOOD SNIFF-SMALL-PIECE-OF-FOOD-
APPRECIATIVELY

SENSE-LEAVES-POSSESSION-OF-THE-BODY-AND-RETURNS-TO-
THE-LEFT-HAND
(middle finger extended from fist) THAT'S-ME
(to ring finger) EXCUSE-ME
RING-FINGER-OPENS-FROM-FIST-THEN-CLOSES-INTO-FIST-AGAIN
EXCUSE-ME
RING-FINGER-OPENS-FROM-FIST-THEN-CLOSES-TO-FIST-AGAIN
(to little finger) EXCUSE-ME
LITTLE-FINGER-OPENS-FROM-FIST
YOU WHAT WRONG-WITH-RING-FINGER?
LET-ME-FIND-OUT
WE'RE-TOGETHER
YOU'RE-TOGETHER?
LITTLE-FINGER-AND-RING-FINGER-EXTENDED-FROM-FIST- 'NOD'
SENSE-MOVES-FROM-THE-HAND-TO-POSSESS-THE-BODY
EYES-OPEN-WIDE
TAKE-IN-INFORMATION-THROUGH-THE-EYES
INFORMATION ACTIVELY-LEARN COLOURS SEE-THINGS-MOVE-
AT-SPEED
PEOPLE-MOVE-FAST TAKE-IN-INFORMATION-THROUGH-THE-EYES
TAKE-IN-ALL-INFORMATION-THROUGH-THE-EYES-TO-BECOME-A-
PART-OF-THE-SELF
SENSE-LEAVES-POSSESSION-OF-THE-BODY-AND-RETURNS-TO-
THE-HAND
(index finger and ring finger) THAT'S-ME THE-TWO-OF-US
LITTLE-FINGER-AND-RING-FINGER-WAVE-GOODBYE
ALL-FINGERS-OPEN-AND-SPREAD-BUT-RING-AND-LITTLE-FINGER-
TOGETHER
THAT'S-ME

Repetition

Repetition is seen at several levels in the poem. The whole composition is clearly divided into stanzas, each identified by repetitive patterns and phrases, starting with the dominant hand tapping the non-dominant hand at the location of successive fingers from thumb to little finger. As we have seen, patterns of handshapes may be simple repetitive patterns in which the same handshape occurs again and again, or the patterns may be of changing handshapes. In this poem, the non-dominant hand starts open in a '5' handshape, and then closes to its polar opposite, the closed fist 'A' handshape. For the rest of the poem, there is a steady progression from this closed fist handshape to one with the thumb extended, then the index finger, then the middle finger (a highly marked, but legal, handshape in BSL), then the ring finger (an illegal handshape in BSL), then the little finger. From there, the extension of only the ring and little fingers creates another marked but legal BSL handshape. This pattern is enjoyable and predictable, and also satisfyingly symbolic because the one illegal and unsustainable hand-shape of the pattern is the one allocated to the unsustainable sense of hearing.

The finger representing each sense 'wakes up', extends and asks WHAT-DO-YOU-WANT? The questioner asks WHAT-ARE-YOU? And the finger replies AH-HOLD-ON, before the hand closes to the 'A' hand-shape and the dominant hand traces out the path of sensation from that fist to the chest as the sense appears to 'possess' the questioner and act through him. Examples of actions related to each sense are then per-formed, with attention paid to balanced locations in the signing space, before the sensation path is retraced, back to the closed fist. The finger for the relevant sense then extends again, confirms what it does and closes back to the fist. This pattern holds steady for the first three stan-zas, creating an expectation in the audience that the fourth stanza will follow the established pattern. This expectation is confounded when the finger for the fourth sense is unable to 'wake-up' fully and the pattern is only resumed when the final finger joins the fourth finger.

Apart from the changing patterns of signs, there are other rhymes created through repetition of handshape. Throughout the stanza for Touch, there are many signs made using the 'B' or open '5' handshapes; in the stanza for Taste, the dominant handshape is the 'A' or 'Â', while in the stanza for Smell, the 'F' handshape is noticeable (see Fig. 13.1).

Symmetry and balance

Two-handed symmetrical signs are not numerically dominant for most of *Five Senses*, because the poem uses an alternative device of keeping both hands in use, using different information on each hand. The non-dominant hand is permanently active, producing information that is perceived simultaneously with the information from the dominant hand. For much of the poem, the non-dominant hand holds the simple 'A' handshape representing the group of senses, or the handshape appro-priate to the particular sense – the 'Â' for Touch, the 'G' for Taste, the 'middle finger' handshape for Smell, the 'I' for Sight and 'BSL 7' for Sight and Hearing (Fig. 13.2). This maintenance of the non-dominant hand serves to maintain the focus on the sense under discussion, but it also

'B' and '5' handshapes in Touch

'A' and 'Å' handshapes
in Taste

'F' handshape
in Smell

Fig. 13.1

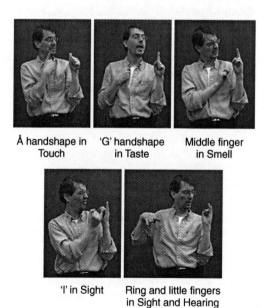

Å handshape in
Touch

'G' handshape
in Taste

Middle finger
in Smell

'I' in Sight

Ring and little fingers
in Sight and Hearing

Fig. 13.2

allows the creation of neologisms by providing unusual locations for the formation of signs.

Although infrequent, symmetry does occur in the poem. As we have seen, there are three main ways of creating symmetry in signed poems, and this poem shows examples of all three (sequential placement of one-handed or two-handed signs in opposing areas of space; use of symmetrical two-handed signs; simultaneous use of two one-handed signs that are opposed symmetrically). The use of symmetrical space in the poem has a pattern, so that for the first three senses, symmetry occurs predominantly through sequential location of signs in opposing areas of space. For instance, with Touch the right hand reaches out to the right to touch something cold and then withdraws before the left hand reaches out to the left to touch something hot. The use of space and hands thus reflects the opposing semantics of hot and cold. The same device of using spatial opposition for semantic opposition occurs with Taste. This time the actions are all performed by the right hand but it first holds and eats a delicious ice-cream on the right, then takes a scoop of something unpleasant-tasting from the left and finally takes a scoop of something more pleasant-tasting from the right. With Smell, the nice-scented flower is picked and smelled from the right, then the less-nice smelly cheese is taken from the fridge on the left, before the agreeable morsel (unspecified in the poem) that is eaten and then sniffed appreciatively comes from the right (Fig. 13.3). But in the fourth stanza, where Sight and Hearing work together, the sequential use of symmetrically balanced one-handed signs is replaced by two-handed symmetrical signs, as the senses of Sight and Hearing are themselves combined into one.

There are a few two-handed signs with symmetrical handshapes in *Touch*, and these are predominantly gestural neologisms such as RUB-HANDS or WRING-HANDS, although the neologism SHIVER-UP-ARMS and the sign HUG or CUDDLE are also symmetrical. These last two signs are especially notable because the hands cross the central vertical axis of symmetry (see the relevant picture in Fig. 13.1). There are no two-handed symmetrical signs at all in the stanzas for Taste or Smell. In the section for Sight and Hearing, however, the symmetry comes out especially strongly with the established two-handed symmetrical signs EYES-OPEN, INFORMATION-THROUGH-EYES (there is no ready English equivalent term for this idea of 'hearing through the eyes'), INFORMA-TION, SPEED, COLOURS, MOVEMENT, LEARN and finally TAKE-EVERYTHING-IN-THROUGH-EYES. The signs are all essentially sym-metrical across the vertical axis. The BSL sign COLOUR is not normally

Cold and Hot to right and left   Pleasant and Unpleasant to left and right
            in Touch   in Taste

Scented flower and smelly cheese to
right and left in Smell

Fig. 13.3

EYES-OPEN   INFORMATION-   SPEED   COLOURS
                       THROUGH-EYES

MOVEMENT   TAKE-EVERYTHING-
                          IN-THROUGH-EYES

Fig. 13.4

two-handed, but in this case the neologistic doubling with the second hand creates additional symmetry in this section of the poem. It is significant that these symmetrical signs come to prominence in this final section, as it is in this compound sense of Sight and Hearing that we see sign language coming to the fore, both as a topic and as a form of expression (Fig. 13.4).

The poem also creates symmetrical 'rhymes' of two one-handed signs articulated simultaneously, so that the dominant hand articulates signs with the same handshape as the current 'sense' handshape. Thus, at the end of the encounter with Touch (represented with the 'Å' handshape on the non-dominant hand), the dominant hand signs OK and GOOD, using the same 'Å' handshape. With Taste (represented by the 'G' handshape on the non-dominant hand), the beginning of the stanza allows rhymes as the dominant hand signs WHAT, YOU and AH-HANG-ON, all with a 'G' handshape. At the end of the description, this balancing, symmetrical handshape rhyme recurs with the dominant hand signing ME (using a 'G' handshape). For Sight (using the 'I' handshape on the non-dominant hand), the balancing rhyme sign on the dominant hand is WRONG (also using the 'I' handshape) (see the relevant pictures in Fig. 13.2).

We should also note here the shift in roles of dominant and non-dominant hands. In simultaneous signs produced as part of conversational BSL, it is expected that the non-dominant hand will be the less active hand and that the dominant hand will move. In this poem, however, the non-dominant hand is unusually active. In the stanza for Touch, the non-dominant hand is active to describe the reaction to heat (something we would expect normally to be done by the dominant hand) and throughout the poem the non-dominant hand moves independently of the dominant hand as it shows the actions of the senses represented by the individual fingers.

Neologism

Five Senses is full of neologism, so that approximately 80 per cent of the poem is made up of signs that might be termed 'productive' and only 20 per cent of the signs are best described as 'established' or frozen lexical items (a figure reflected in the fact that only 18 per cent of the signs in the poem are accompanied by an English-derived mouthing). In fact, glossing this poem is remarkably difficult because there are so few established signs, at least in the earlier sections. In the first three stanzas there are very few established signs at all – although WHAT occurs in each one. With Touch, we also see the strongly visual HUG and the emblematic OK and GOOD; with Taste, we also see ICE-CREAM and ME; and with Smell, there is FLOWER, FRIDGE, CHEESE and ME. Most of these established signs are strongly visually motivated. Only in the final stanza of Sight and Hearing, are there many more established signs: WRONG, TOGETHER, BOTH, EYES-OPEN, INFORMATION, MOVE-MENT, COLOURS, SPEED, LEARN and ME. As with the comments on symmetry above, we can see that this is fully in keeping with the theme of the poem – where the sense is Sight and Hearing, we can expect sign language to come to the fore as part of the celebration of the two senses working together.

Neologisms can use existing signs in a creative way with new meaning. This poem uses the very common sign language device of a 'listing buoy' (Liddell, 2003) in an unusual, poetic way. Most sign languages can use the fingers of the non-dominant hand as a buoy to allow the signer to list ideas in a cohesive way. For example, if the signer wishes to talk about five different countries, the fingers of the non-dominant hand are used successively as points of reference, so that the thumb is indicated by the dominant hand to mean 'firstly' and refer to the first country, the index finger means 'secondly' and refers to the second country and so on. (Speakers will also count things off on their fingers in a very similar way when they list things.) In normal signing, buoys do not carry any additional meaning. In *Five Senses*, the non-dominant hand is clearly operating as a 'listing buoy', as each finger serves as a cohesive device to link the five senses, but it is an unusual buoy because the fingers carry additional meaning. The fingers do indicate the first, second and third senses, and so on, and refer to each sense as would occur in a normal buoy but, additionally, they simultaneously have full identity as the characters of each sense and they converse and interact with the questioner, changing orientation to converse with the questioner and even nodding and waving.

Neologism also allows a poet to create signs using unusual, 'marked' elements in the language. The tongue is not a commonly used articulator of signs in everyday signing but in this poem it is a dominant part of two neologistic signs – once in Touch and once in Taste. In Touch, the tongue is an active articulator against the hand, as it licks the hand that has been burned. In Taste, it is the location for the articulating right hand as the hand removes the unpleasant food from the mouth. The tongue is also involved as a central articulator in signs such as LICK-ICE-CREAM, LICK-LIPS and SPIT-OUT-FOOD in the Taste stanza. Generally, this is a marked use of the tongue, as it is not so noticeable in BSL signs (Fig. 13.5).

208

Marked use of the tongue in Touch and Taste

Fig. 13.5

Illegal handshapes for Hearing and
the Poet's senses

Fig. 13.6

Childlike expressions in Taste and Hearing   Mature expression
of questioner

Fig. 13.7

WE'RE-   YOU'RE-
TOGETHER   TOGETHER?

Fig. 13.8

Of the marked handshapes in the poem, the 'middle finger' hand-shape in relation to Smell is very noticeable for its use at all. However, it is not involved in the production of any other signs. The marked handshape with the ring and little fingers extended (normally seen only in BSL in certain dialects for signs related to SEVEN) is used more pro-ductively with Sight and Hearing, when it is twice a location for a directed sign BOTH (in the question 'both of you together?') and when the extended fingers nod to answer 'yes' to the question. The repetitive flexing and bending of these two fingers in this handshape is extremely uncommon to the point of being on the limits of what is acceptable in the language, but in this poetic context it is perfectly acceptable.

The handshapes of two other neologisms break the rules of the language entirely. The fist closed with only the ring finger extended (the bewildered, uncooperative sense for hearing) does not occur in any signs in BSL and is physically very difficult to articulate, especially with the non-dominant hand. The final sign of the entire poem on the non-dominant hand uses all five fingers open and all spread, except for the little finger, which contacts the ring finger. This sign summarises the senses for the poet and is highly creative and so marked that it requires considerable skill on the part of the performer to articulate on the non-dominant hand (indeed, some people find it physically impossible to do) (Fig. 13.6).

Metaphor

Having each of the fingers extended as characterisation of the senses plays on the sign language practice of using fingers as proforms to represent people or other upright entities. Because the audience is used to interpreting digits as referring to both people or characters and mark-ers for enumeration on buoys, the audience for the poem can easily accept each finger as a sense that has been given a 'character' through anthropomorphisation (giving non-human entities the characteristics of humans). Neologisms also allow the signs to take additional mean-ing: most notably the anthropomorphised finger senses are made to nod using the finger joints. Usually manual signing of a nod is made at the wrist, but for Touch, the nod is made at the joints of the thumb and for Sight and Hearing, nodding occurs at the joints of the ring and little fin-gers. When each sense is addressed, it 'stands up' and in each case the raising finger carrles with it an anthropomorphised suggestion that the straightening finger is standing up or curling up again. For this reason, when the ring finger does not stand for any length of time, the curling at the joints is taken to mean the curling of the character.

Performance

So far we have commented directly on the elements of the text that signal that this is a poem in BSL. However, the performance of the poem is an integral part of the work, and the two cannot be separated as easily as they can be in written poems where the abstracted form on the page exists without any performance. Although we have already seen that the anthropomorphisation of the senses has created a situation in which they can be treated as characters, it is through personation in the performance that the poem can show the dialogue between the questioning character and the five senses. The personation in this poem is seen through the use of space and the non-manual features accompanying the signs. The facial expressions and body posture accompanying the senses convey a suggestion of childlike qualities. There is something endearingly naïve and obliging about them. When the questioner attempts to converse with Hearing, the non-manual features portray this character as sleepy and uncooperative, bewildered like a grumpy child who cannot be roused. The facial expression and body posture of the questioner show him as polite and attentive but definitely the more mature character in the poem. These non-manual characterisations are not central parts of the text but emerge in the performance (Fig. 13.7).

The location and direction of the performer's gaze to identify the characters is a crucial element of personation in the performance. When the senses are firmly located at the non-dominant hand, conversation between the questioner and each sense is conducted strictly left to right and right to left. The questioner always looks down and to the left (where the non-dominant hand is for this right-handed performer) to address the sense, and the sense always looks up and to the right to address the questioner. The feeling of scale, with the sense appearing small and the questioner appearing large is maintained throughout by the upward and downward direction of the gaze. When Sight informs the questioner that it works with the apparently recalcitrant Hearing, the dominant hand moves between left and right, between the locations that have been understood as belonging to the senses and the questioner (Fig. 13.8). At first, this may seem to imply that Sight and the Questioner are together, but we know from the facial expression and the direction of gaze that Sight is speaking and we are led to interpret the use of space as meaning that Sight and Hearing are together. Once the sense has possessed the questioner, however, the questioner looks forwards; yet there is still something about the body posture and other non-manual features that hint at the presence of a childlike sense in the mature body.

An important element of the poem is left to the coda which requires a shift of interpretation in the characterisation. Throughout the poem the characterisation has consisted of a single questioning character and the different senses, but in the coda, the poet/performer comes to the foreground of the performance and steps out of the expected role of narrator to say, 'This is me'. This is a strongly empowering moment, as the performer takes the boldly obtrusive step of explicitly 'owning' the content of the poem. Although any Deaf signer could perform the poem, if a hearing person were to perform it the meaning so powerfully conveyed by this act of identification would be radically changed – perhaps to the point of meaninglessness. In the light of this, we may say that the poem is an extraordinarily strong expression of self-identity by a Deaf person.

Three Queens

Three Queens (p. 253) is a celebration of the official recognition of BSL by the British Government in March 2003. It considers the changing fortunes of Deaf people under the reigns of three great English queens. The first detailed record of sign language use in Britain (in 1575, see Sutton-Spence and Woll, 1999) dates from the reign of Elizabeth I (1558–1603). Queen Victoria's family and descendants were often touched by deafness: her son, who later became Edward VII, married Princess Alexandra of Denmark, who was Deaf and they had a Deaf son, Prince Albert. Other descendants, as the poem shows, were also Deaf. The infamous Congress of Milan in 1880 (after which sign language was officially outlawed in many European and American schools) also took place during the reign of Queen Victoria (1837–1901). Official recognition of BSL as a minority British language came only in 2003, under the reign of the current queen, Elizabeth II (1952–).

This poem contains substantial narrative as well as description of appearance and actions, and it provides historical facts as well as visual entertainment. The poem combines general 'common-knowledge' history (such as the discovery of the potato and tobacco in Elizabeth I's reign) with less well-known facts (such as Philip, Duke of Edinburgh, being four generations descended from one of Queen Victoria's children). More crucially, it weaves Deaf history into the fabric of national history: it is perhaps not so well known that sign language was first documented in England during Elizabeth I's reign nor that deafness runs in the British Royal Family. The poem shows how the 'Deaf Nation' is a part of the British nation and the strands of Deaf history are integral to the national heritage, with everyone living under the same flag. Because the poem is composed and performed by a poet with a strong affinity to the Deaf community, it makes explicit use of Deaf methods of identifying Elizabeth I and Victoria, with emphasis on visual features familiar to anyone who has seen their portraits. The visual description of these two queens makes them immediately recognisable to the audience but also gives the poet the chance for creative sign language expression.

The poem may be roughly glossed as follows (a translation is in the Appendix on p. 253):

THREE QUEEN
RED TIGHT-CURLY-HAIR MANY-TIGHT-CURLS-ON-HEAD
HIGH-COLLAR HAIR-STIFF-UP-ON-HEAD
REACH-AND-PICK-UP-SOMETHING
SHELL SHELL-OPENS TAKE-SOMETHING-SMALL-FROM-SHELL-
    AND-HOLD-IT
p-e-a-r-l
FOUR-STRINGS-OF-PEARLS-ACROSS-CHEST-AND-BODY
HIGH-BACKED-COLLAR SINGLE-POINT-ON-TOP-OF-HEADDRESS
PUFFED-SLEEVES FULL-SKIRTS
WALK-PURPOSEFULLY
MAN TWO-PEOPLE-WALK-FORWARD-SIDE-BY-SIDE-BEHIND-ONE-
    PERSON
THERE
REACH-AND-TAKE-THEN-HOLD-AND-LOOK-AT-HAND-SIZED-
    SOLID-OBJECT
POTATO HOLD-POTATO THROW-POTATO-INTO-POT WATER-BOILS
PUT-SPOON-IN-POT-AND-EAT-FROM-SPOON
HOLD-PEN-READY WRITE
WALK-PURPOSEFULLY
THERE
SMOKE-CIGARETTE LOOK-AT-CIGARETTE
SMOKE-CIGARETTE WOOZY-HEAD
COUGH WOOZY-HEAD
HOLD-CIGARETTE
YOU WRITE
TWO-PEOPLE-WALK-FORWARD-SIDE-BY-SIDE-BEHIND-ONE-PERSON
THERE SIGNING RAPID-GESTURING

SUMMON MEET
YOU DEAF
COMMAND-SCRIBE WRITE
SIGNING IN AIR
TWO-PEOPLE-WALK-FORWARD-SIDE-BY-SIDE-BEHIND-ONE-PERSON
LOOK-UPWARDS
FLAG-FLIES
CROSS-OF-ST-ANDREW CROSS-OF-ST-GEORGE [i.e. 'Union Jack']
LONG-TIME-PASSES
BORN GROW-UP QUEEN
LONG-THIN-CURVED-NOSE MISERABLE-FACE LARGE-STOMACH
BORN ONE TWO THREE FOUR FIVE
NINE
THAT-ONE DEAF
GROW-UP SPEAK NO TEACH-ME NEED
HOW-INTERESTING IGNORE-REPEATEDLY
WELL
MEET MAN KING GREECE MOVE-WITH-OTHER-PERSON
BORN-FOR-FOUR-GENERATIONS
PRINCE p-h-i-l-i-p-o-f-e-d-h ['Philip of Edinburgh']
MEET
FLAG-FLIES
ONE-PERSON-WALKS-CLOSELY-BESIDE-ANOTHER-PERSON
MARRIED AEROPLANE-FLIES KENYA
WOMAN GO-UP-TREE
LOOK-THROUGH-BINOCULARS BEGINS-TO-SWAY
GO-UP-SHAKING-TREE   TAP-TO-GAIN-ATTENTION   ONE-PERSON-
   MOVE-DOWN-TREE
WHAT-IS-IT?
YOU QUEEN
ME?
AEROPLANE-FLIES ENGLAND
FLAG-FLIES
TIME-PASSES
DEAF ANGRY STRONGLY-OPPOSED
BSL MY LANGUAGE
CHILDREN HAVE-NOTHING-THERE-AT-ALL
MARCH-IN-PROCESSION
ACHIEVE-AT-LAST
RECOGNISE

FLAG-FLIES
THREE-PEOPLE/QUEENS-LOOK-UPWARD-FROM-THREE-
PLACES/TIMES
THREE QUEEN
THREE-QUEENS-IN-THREE-PLACES/TIMES

Repetition

The underlying motif throughout this poem is the number three. The poem begins with its title *Three Queens*, so that the first sign is THREE. This leads to a careful use of threefold repetition in many ways. At the largest level, there are three stanzas, each one dealing with one of the queens. However, the threefold repetition is seen at other levels, too. The description of Elizabeth I begins with three ways to describe her hair (red, tight curls and standing up) and the pearls she wears are placed at three locations at three different heights (around her neck, across her torso and in her head-dress). Repetition of the marked '4' handshape is also seen three times at different heights: first showing the hair piled up above the head, then to show the necklace at the neck, then to show it on the torso. As she makes her Royal Progress, the queen sees three new phenomena (potatoes, tobacco and sign language). In this first Elizabethan section, there are phrases and signs repeated three times, such as WALK-PURPOSEFULLY for the Queen, TWO-PERSONS-FOLLOW-ONE-PERSON as the scribes scuttle obediently behind her and WRITE-DILIGENTLY for her scribes. The sign FLAG-FLYING also occurs three times throughout the whole poem, linking the events described in the three stanzas. This sign is especially important for the morphing device that occurs at the climax to the poem (see below). The final signs in the coda of the poem create an image of all three queens (Elizabeth I, Victoria and Elizabeth II) simultaneously looking to the flag that has flown above them all, and the three queens and their three Deaf communities standing as part of the history of the nation.

The 'threefold' device also occurs at the sub-sign level. Repetition of movement within a sign is not uncommon in sign languages and threefold repetition of a sign is an unmarked – although none the less aesthetically appealing – indicator of plurality or duration (e.g. if an event happens many times or for a long time). However, in this poem that has such a strong 'threefold' theme, even the triple repetition within signs becomes a part of the poetic design. Signs in this poem such as IGNORE and WALK-PURPOSEFULLY have a threefold repetition within the single sign. A similar effect occurs when the scribe is ordered to record the potato and the tobacco. In conversational BSL we might expect the sign WRITE to be repeated three times, but here it is repeated first six (two times three) times, and on the second occasion nine (three times three) times. However, in Victoria's stanza, the poem confounds our expectations that repetitions will be threefold. When describing the birth of Victoria's many children, the poet might have signed BORN three times and then given the number NINE to show how many children were born. This would be normal in everyday conversational BSL. However, the sign is actually repeated seven times, increasingly quickly, making the repetition far more literal and obtrusively different from conversational BSL, and so lending poetic meaning to the text, delighting by surprising.

Apart from the threefold repetition that occurs in this poem, there are other general uses of repetition at the sub-lexical level to create poetic effects. In many cases, repetition of a handshape creates chiming effects through the poem. In Elizabeth I's stanza, the marked '4' handshape occurs unusually frequently in the description of the hair and pearls. In Victoria's stanza, the marked 'baby C' handshape used for tracing out the crosses on the Union Jack reappears a few signs later in the sign that traces out the monarch's long thin nose. The '5' handshape seen in QUEEN in the same section reappears in the sign MISERABLE. This same handshape from QUEEN also occurs in the final sign of the whole poem, placing the queens (and perhaps their communities of subjects) in space and time (Fig. 13.9).

Repeated patterns of locations are also shown in the description of Elizabeth I's garments. In the description of the necklaces, the collar and the head-dress, the signs move steadily and rhythmically upwards through signing space. Then they move steadily downwards for the description of the sleeves and skirts, before using the lower location for a smooth transition to the correct location for the first occurrence of the sign WALK-PURPOSEFULLY.

Repeated patterns of movement path also occur. Between the stanza about Elizabeth I and the one about Victoria, there is a description of the Union Jack. The hands (in a 'baby C' handshape) move in every direction in the vertical plane: diagonally right to left, and then left to right, before moving from top to bottom and then horizontally from left to right. The next sign TIME-PASSES moves forwards across the horizontal plane and, shortly after this, the same 'baby C' handshape is used to complete the movement patterns in the sign LONG-CURVED-NOSE (Queen Victoria). Here the sign moves with an arcing movement forwards and downwards.

'4' handshape for   'baby C' handshape for CROSSES-ON-FLAG and
PEARL-STRINGS   LONG-NOSE

'5̈' handshape for QUEEN and
THREE-QUEENS

Fig. 13.9

ONE-BORN   TWO-BORN   THREE-BORN   FOUR-BORN

FIVE-BORN   NINE   THIRD-OF-NINE   THAT-ONE-DEAF

Fig. 13.10

Symmetry and balance

The placement and location of articulation of signs in this poem allows the poet to produce symmetry and balance on many levels. In general, the non-dominant hand is more active than we would expect in conversational BSL. The description of the necklaces of pearls is made using both hands: the non-dominant hand shows the pearls at the neck, sweeping right to left and the end point of the movement is held while the dominant hand shows the pearls across the chest and stomach, sweeping right to left. As both hands use the same '4' handshape, this gives the pleasant aesthetic effect of contrasting vertical symmetries of left and right hands, and of leftward and rightward movements and contrasting horizontal symmetries of making these movements at two different heights (see the relevant picture in Fig. 13.9). This section is immediately followed by a two-handed vertically symmetrical sign HIGH-COLLAR and, once the pearl has been located on her head-dress, two more two-handed symmetrical signs for PUFFED-SLEEVES and FULL-SKIRTS. The overall impression from this section is thus one of balance in the signing space.

The potato and tobacco incidents show a balanced use of space with an alternating use of dominance of the hands to show opposition of the two ideas. The incident with the potato uses signs occurring to left and right but at first the potato is taken from the right-hand side of signing space, using the right hand. Her imperious command to the scribe is made leftward with the left hand. The potato is boiled and eaten on the left and the left hand is then used to order the scribe on the right-hand side to record it. To show the shift of role to the scribe, the scribe licks his pencil using the right hand. The incident with the tobacco shows a clear switch in dominance for the signer as the left hand indexes a location to the left and shows someone smoking a cigarette and holding it. The right hand takes the cigarette for the queen, but she continues to smoke it using the left hand. This is held while the right hand then signs coughing and feeling dizzy – again creating a balanced use of both hands.

The section moving between the stanzas of Elizabeth I and Victoria shows a noticeable use of one-handed signing. Just as extensive, uninterrupted two-handed signing is obtrusive, so is extensive, uninterrupted one-handed signing. From the first reference to the flag flying to the reference to Victoria's large stomach, the signs are entirely one-handed. In the context of so many poetically selected, balanced two-handed signs, this section of one-handed signing is refreshingly obtrusive and prepares the audience for the next, complex, use of both hands, where the birth of Victoria's children is shown using a marked use of the non-dominant hand. For each repetition of BORN, the non-dominant hand changes from 'Å' (a marked sign in BSL meaning ONE) to 'L' (a marked sign in BSL meaning TWO) to '3' (THREE), '4' (FOUR) and '5' (FIVE). In normal conversational simultaneous signing, the non-dominant hand would retain its handshape while the dominant hand would change (Fig. 13.10). Later description of the four generations that pass before Prince Philip, Duke of Edinburgh, is born shows another interesting use of the non-dominant hand. The '4' handshape representing the four indicators of four generations is used as the location for the sign BORN. Normally, BORN is a two-handed sign that is located at the signer's lower abdomen. Moving it to locate it at the non-dominant hand is a marked neologism and, while disturbing the natural balance of the symmetrical two-handed sign BORN, it produces a far more sophisticated use of the two hands (Fig. 13.11).

As with Paul Scott's other poem, *Five Senses*, *Three Queens* shifts in its final stanza to use far more two-handed signs (both symmetrical and non-symmetrical). While such signs are present in the first two stanzas, they dominate the final one, echoing the idea that everything is now 'coming together' as Deaf people finally campaign for recognition of their language and succeed. The two-handed symmetrical signs are all established vocabulary items, such as ANGRY, CHALLENGE, MARCH and SUCCEED-AT-LAST. The final sign of the entire poem is a neologism that produces additional symmetry by placing two signs (or classifier proforms) on opposing sides of signing space.

In a device similar to the one used by Dorothy Miles in her poem *Trio* with THREE-OF-US-DOZE, the poem ends using 'triple' simultaneity. We have already seen that creation of simultaneous signs showing separate information on both hands is an important part of poetic craft, but here the poem creates three signs simultaneously by using each hand to represent one character and the signer's body to represent the third. Thus, all three queens are able to look up at their flag simultaneously as the left hand and right hand both sign LOOK-UP-RIGHTWARD while the signer's head and eyes are also directed up and rightward. The final neologism in the poem of the three queens (and perhaps their communities of subjects, placed in space simultaneously by reference to their queen) also makes use of this triple simultaneity through use of the face, head and body. By retaining the regal facial expression and posture of the body and head following the sign QUEEN, it is clear that the body and head are being used to refer to one of the queens, while each of the

| THIRD-GENERATION-BORN | FOURTH-GENERATION-BORN | THE-FOURTH-ONE |

Fig. 13.11

(THREE-QUEENS-IN-TIME)-LOOK- AT-FLAG   THREE-QUEENS-IN-TIME

Fig. 13.12

RECOGNISE   FLAG-FLIES

Fig. 13.13

two hands (each with the '5̈' handshape that is used in the sign QUEEN) then can be understood to refer to the other two (Fig. 13.12).

Ambiguity and morphing

Within this poem, there are examples of unspecified signs, ambiguous signs and those that change almost imperceptibly from one sign to another or 'morph'. Clayton Valli observed in 1993, that in prose 'classifier predicates tend to be used after identifying arguments of the verb', while in poetry they are 'often used without identifying arguments explicitly.' (p. 126.) Examples here in *Three Queens* show this device. Elizabeth I takes something from a shell, holds it and looks at it, but only then are we told that it is a pearl. Later, the same pattern is repeated as she reaches for, holds and looks at something that we are then told is a potato. This guessing game played with the audience serves to focus attention on the form of the language used in the poem.

Signs that are not under-specified productive signs are also used to create ambiguities. During the Royal Progress of Elizabeth I, the proform sign TWO-PERSONS-WALK may also be taken to mean LOOK-AROUND, as both signs have the same handshape and the use of gaze allows either interpretation (an ambiguity we also explored in Dorothy Miles' poem, *The Staircase*, in Chapter 6). On an earlier occasion the sign LOOK-AROUND morphs to become TWO-PERSONS-WALK, inviting us to interpret this second instance of the same sign formation in both ways. This sort of ambiguity creates a richness that allows extra meaning to be taken from the poem, at the cost of no more signs.

Fine examples of morphing also occur in the poem, where one sign merges and blends almost seamlessly with the next. In the description of Queen Victoria's appearance, the hands that show the extent of her famous imperial stomach shift very slightly to become the sign BORN with minimal transition. Nine children are born and this is shown with the non-dominant hand showing FIVE and the dominant hand showing FOUR – to make single sign NINE. The dominant hand then becomes an index, counting along the fingers of the non-dominant hand until it reaches the middle finger to identify the deaf child. The handshape that was originally FIVE became a part of the sign NINE and now means FIVE-INDIVIDUALS (OF-NINE). It has not changed in any way, but the different meanings come from the context produced by the meaning of the dominant hand. Similarly, when one of Victoria's descendants meets the King of Greece, the sign MEET morphs into a simultaneous construction in which one hand becomes the proform sign ONE-PERSON and the other becomes an index to identify the proform. Likewise, when the second Elizabeth marries and then flies to Kenya, the signs MARRY and FLY blend seamlessly, as the non-dominant base hand for both signs remains the same and the 'F' handshape of the dominant hand in MARRY morphs into the 'Y' handshape for FLY.

Perhaps the best example of morphing comes towards the end of the poem, where the reason for the repetition of the flag motif between each queen becomes clear. The dominant hand used in the sign RECOG-NISE pulls back from the non-dominant hand and is raised – retaining the same handshape and orientation – to become the flag once more. This sign emphasises the importance for the whole nation of recognition of BSL as a national language (Fig. 13.13).

There is considerable ambiguity in the final sign of the poem, which shows all three queens. The handshape used for the signs QUEEN and CROWN, which also means 'person or group located there', is made by both dominant and non-dominant hands. This indicates that all three queens are part of the same heritage and also that the three groups of people in the poem (which by this stage may be understood to be Deaf people, especially) are at different historical stages of the same heritage.

Neologism

In comparison to *Five Senses*, the poem here contains a far greater proportion of established lexical items (and there is, correspondingly, a slightly higher proportion of mouthings than we saw in *Five Senses*, accompanying 25 per cent of the signs, although this figure is still very much lower than one would expect in everyday conversational BSL). This is partly because established lexical items are more commonly used for identification of facts, and this poem has a dual purpose of informing as well as describing and entertaining. The neologisms that do occur are used for descriptive elements in order to create strong visual images, but also have a further poetic effect, often creating repetitive patterns with the elements such as handshape or location in the signs. The description of Elizabeth I uses several neologisms to create powerful linguistic visual images that correlate strongly with the familiar visual images from the royal portraits. However, it also allows for the poem to create patterns using the marked, unusual 'X' and then the '4' handshape, with steadily ascending and descending locations and the balanced symmetrical movements. The repeated sign representing the two scribes following their queen allows morphing devices to shift between TWO-PEOPLE and LOOK-AROUND. Many of the more 'gestural' signs such as LICK-PENCIL or WOOZY-HEAD are used as part of the performance element of personation to create identifiable characterisations within the poem.

The neologisms in the stanza dealing with Victoria further allow repetitive poetic patterns, such as the description of the Union Jack with the movements in so many directions across a single plane of signing, to contrast with the movement in the sign showing the long curved nose. The neologisms may also break established rules for the location of signs, as we can see in the productive use of buoys, similar to what we observed in *Five Senses*. The citation form of the BSL sign BORN is located in front of the body at hip or waist height. In this stanza, BORN is made at a new location at the buoy showing four generations to give extra meaning. We know that buoys do not usually have any extra meaning, apart from their place in a list, but by articulating BORN at each finger of the non-dominant hand showing FOUR, the new sign meaning FOUR-GENERATIONS-BORN is created.

The description of Elizabeth II learning she is queen allows for further language play through neologism. The neologisms are primarily two-handed, creating balance within the poem, and they are carefully placed to minimise transition between signs. The neologism of the person swaying while looking through binoculars is followed by the sign showing the tree swaying, so that the marked swaying movement is echoed in both signs – once on the whole body and once on the hand. The final complex neologism of the poem is an opportunity for several poetic devices. It is highly deviant as, if the meaning of the sign is THREE-QUEENS-IN-DIFFERENT-TIMES, the sign QUEEN is being made at the wrong location. The correct location for the '5̈' handshape in QUEEN is at the head. The handshape cannot normally be moved in order to place the queen elsewhere in signing space – this is normally done using a pro-form sign with an upright 'G' handshape. To place the '5̈' handshape from the noun sign in space instead of the 'G' handshape proform representing the queen is technically 'incorrect'. However, here the poet has broken the rules of the language for poetic effect and the meaning is clear. This neologism also allows ambiguity, as it locates either the three queens or the three Deaf communities (which would be correctly shown by a '5̈' handshape) in space and time. It creates a 'triple' simultaneous sign, thereby not only creating an obtrusively noticeable sign but also finishing this poem of a 'threefold' theme with a 'threefold' sign.

We have seen that another way of using a 'new' sign in BSL is to use a loan from another language. Even though the word is not a neologism in the original language, it can stand out as unusual in the recipient host language. In this poem, there is noticeable use of fingerspelling of English words, which is obtrusive. Normally, fingerspelling is not expected in sign language poetry because we expect this highest sign language art form to be 'pure' and free from the influence of English. The fingerspelling of p-e-a-r-l and p-h-i-l-i-p-o-f-e-d-b-h ('Philip of Edinburgh') is highly deviant in poetry, and as such makes us notice the language used even more. In both cases, the fingerspellings serve to identify the unspecified signs. We know that something has been taken from the shell but not that it is a pearl and we know that someone has been born but we don't know who is born. The fingerspellings are used to clarify and establish facts again.

Performance

The performance elements of this poem include the role of the face and body to create meaning of personation and the use of gaze and body posture to indicate roles. There are several characters within this poem, as well as the narrator. In Elizabeth I there is the Queen herself, as well as the two scribes, the smoker and the signing Deaf person. The head posture and levels and direction of gaze also serve to create the clear character distinctions. The Queen always has a pompously regal facial expression and bearing and the scribes have subservient expressions and postures. In the stanza relating to Queen Victoria there is the humourless Queen and the Deaf person pleading for education. In the stanza concerning Elizabeth II, there is the Queen while she is on safari, the diplomat who breaks the news of her accession, and the angry Deaf person demanding rights. The facial expression here for the modern queen is far less haughty than either of the previous queens.

The personation indicating the three different Deaf people is shown through the performance alone. From the text, there is no suggestion that the Elizabethan Deaf person is simple and uneducated, but the facial expression shows it, as it also shows the pleading facial expression in the sign NEED during the reference to the Victorian Deaf person. In reference to the modern Deaf person, the facial expression shifts markedly. When the sign DEAF is made, it is accompanied by an angry facial expression, which continues through the description of demands for language recognition and only ends at the sign SUCCEED-AT-LAST.

As with *Five Senses*, this poem is an example of a sign language poem that celebrates the experience of being Deaf. In this poem, though, the poet weaves together the experience of being British, as well as being Deaf. The blending of the two identities is reflected in the blending of different types of language in the poem – frozen and productive signs, symmetry and marked asymmetry, non-derived signs and fingerspellings.

Artistic sign language brings a new dimension to British history and to Deaf history, making the poem an important expression of Deaf identity in early twenty-first-century Britain.

This is the final commentary on examples of sign language poems here. Throughout the book we have seen the richness and complexity of sign language poetry and have offered ways to direct audiences' thoughts about the poems to appreciate the skill of sign poets in creating this beautiful visual language art-form. Sign language poetry, while sharing many essential poetic elements with spoken language poetry, is also so different from it that understanding and appreciating its structure and poetic devices should inform and challenge current approaches to spoken language poetry. The value and importance of sign language poetry to literary studies must not be underestimated: the work of these Deaf artists can make – and should make – a major contribution to the wider hearing society. A greater knowledge and understanding of sign language poems should demonstrate to all audiences, Deaf and hearing, the potential of this art form. Serious analysis of the wealth of sign language poetry has barely begun, but we hope that this book will inspire readers to learn more, to study other sign language poems, perhaps to compose and perform their own poems, and to raise the profile of this extraordinarily beautiful cultural heritage of Deaf people.

Afterword: 'Here are my Wings' – Situating Dorothy Miles, Deaf Culture and Sign Poetry

Paddy Ladd

In this chapter I begin to sketch an outline of a full, formal framework within which sign poetry as a whole can be approached, and a proposal for the way we can measure Dorothy Miles' achievement and legacy. Attempting such a 'fullness' is necessary because there are a significant number of dimensions involved, and because several of these extend the boundaries of what we know about poetry and art. It is also necessary because many non-Deaf people still think of Deaf people in reductionist or diminutive terms, and may therefore fail to notice those dimensions which are features of Deaf community, culture and art which inform the works. Other crucial dimensions include the unique ways in which sign poetry straddles four other artistic 'concepts': the folk arts of Western and non-Western societies, performed song, song poetry, and Western poetry itself. For reasons of space these will only be mentioned at relevant points in the text, rather than elaborated on here. Once all of these dimensions are understood, future readers/viewers can then address Miles' work to evaluate the extent to which it manifests the features outlined, and how those features might be used to enhance the aesthetic appreciation of her work begun in this book.

Sign poets by definition have emerged from communities which are linguistic and cultural minorities. However, what is not generally recognised is that Deaf cultures are collectivist cultures (Mindess, 2000) and most do not recognise the conceptual category of literary artist. Even a sign poet is first and foremost a community member. Thus in examining Miles' work we are considering an artist for whom there was therefore no separation at all between her art, her community membership, her lifework, and her 40 years in paid occupations. Moreover this very absence of separation shaped her entire life's thoughts and actions so that once we have been given an opportunity to glimpse that total lifework, we will be able to begin to identify the deeper levels within her art. Before we begin to address the significance of this in Dorothy Miles' artistic communications, we first need to understand certain unique qualities of the Deaf collective experience – 'Deaf culture' and 'Deafhood' – and of sign languages themselves.

We must first set aside our Western cultural conditioning, and realise that the lives of communities of born-Deaf people are not centred upon lack of hearing, but upon the social and cultural constructions they create through the medium of sign languages. The first step is to remove the medical perspective and perceive them as they do themselves – as Sign Language peoples. To be a Deaf Sign-Language using person is a remarkable existentialist fate encompassing many dimensions, as will be seen.

For centuries, Deaf people have travelled, in order to gather together, to organise themselves, to construct national and international networks, sporting and artistic bodies, events and activities. In so doing they have travelled to seek Deaf partners for marriage. Five to ten per cent of these have then produced Deaf children, raised not just to take their place in Deaf communities, but to take responsibility for those communities, to lead them and to serve them. There are Deaf people alive today whose Deaf ancestry can be traced back at least nine generations. Indeed it is the sense of – and depth of – this history which marks one fundamental difference between Deaf people and people with disabilities. It is a history channelled through its language, so that a Deaf child today is communicating in signs which are known to stretch back to the time of Shakespeare and maybe even earlier.

This history of gathering together and communicating in a language quite unlike any which emerge from the tongue, has engendered a culture of collectivism; a 'togetherness' which binds, for example, the president of a Deaf university and a Deaf caretaker, so that both meet and talk as equals, knowing that they not only share many friends or acquaintances but also that they have their own responsibilities to the Deaf Nation, know that they have their own part to play in that greater whole, since that caretaker may even be the Chair of the local Deaf Association.

It is useful at this moment for the reader to recall that Western societies prior to the Industrial Revolution in many ways resembled or embodied collective cultures, and that although these have 'fragmented' into individualist cultures, remnants of these survive in folk traditions (Williams, 1958). But in Deaf cultures the words 'we' and 'Deaf' are inseparable. Speaking here as a Deaf writer, it is impossible to sign

'DEAF' and not to sense all of our peoples, our races, and all that it has meant to make that sign to other Deaf and non-Deaf people. For us there is an existential experiential reality – local, national and international – which we sign as 'FAMILY' or 'HOME'.

All of this, Dorothy Miles knew. All of this can be found at the heart of her work, referenced both overtly and more subtly. Her work was the expression of an individual, but one clearly rooted in the community. She saw her work as emerging from that community in its historical past, bringing light to the community in the present day. More than this, she hoped that the art form which she had devised and developed would bring to public attention the beauty and power of sign language itself, and would thereby help to raise the status of Sign Language peoples. In doing this, she hoped also to enable the world to learn about the 'century of darkness' during which those languages had been suppressed, thus helping to prevent such a tragedy from ever happening again. Thus, although Miles (rightly) hoped for recognition of her work as an individual, the forces and energies which drove her to create in all the genres she used, were collectivist ones. The platform which she sought for her work was one on which she intended that all Deaf peoples could stand and thus be seen.

Described in this way, then, it should not be surprising to find that Deaf peoples' cultures have significant aspects in common with other minority cultures and artists who seek to reassert the validity of their own art form in the period following their own initial liberation from colonialism (Pityana *et al.*, 1991). Like those, they may also be closer to manifesting their own folk traditions than the majority societies in which they are embedded. This being the case, it would not be surprising if Miles' achievement was in essence an example of an older kind of artist – a folkpoet.

Dorothy Miles' work asserted and demonstrated the importance of sign languages and their users, and their value to society as part of the richness of diversity, but she also took this vision to the next level – that sign languages could personally enrich the lives of non-Deaf individuals. In the 1970s sign languages began to achieve recognition from linguists of their status as bona fide languages, and Miles played a key role in this movement, both in the USA and the UK. However, she went further, insisting that sign languages should be regarded as fundamentally *different* from spoken languages, and that their own unique forms contained clues to a larger human-ness, which could be learned by non-Deaf people, enhancing their lives in the process.

The first aspect of this differentness is that, unlike all other races, Deaf people could not permanently 'switch languages': they could not take on the languages of the surrounding (hearing) majority as their own primary language. This has less to do with the inability to hear than the inability to speak in any way that could even begin to compete with the speed and fluency of visual languages. Thus there was no way that the languages could be abandoned, could die out, and quotations from earlier Deaf writers (over the last 200 years and of the 19th century particularly) illustrate this belief (Fischer and Lane, 1993). Miles pointed out that this inability to switch to spoken languages was not, as was asserted for so long, a disadvantage, but actually a strength of the languages themselves. It meant that, unlike many other minority languages, they would not disappear.

But what could happen was that a determined attempt to remove the languages might wreak damage on them by damaging their users. This did happen. Denying Deaf children Sign and Deaf teachers for over a century, physically and mentally punishing them for using the languages, is comparable to permanently stopping up the mouths and ears of non-Deaf, 'hearing' children and expecting them to function and grow up normally. It was a reign of psychic terror, a global outrage which has extended over an entire century into the present day (Lane, 1984).

Miles spent the majority of her childhood living under such a proscriptive regime. Having been born Hearing and become Deaf as a child, she had an advantage over most of her Deaf peers. She already knew English, and what it was to be a member of the majority society, and therefore knew what it was like to live as a person with 'normal' expectations. Thus, once removed to a place where communication was denied, and where those in charge of Deaf children and adults treated them as helpless infants, she was still able to remember what it meant to be treated as fully human, and she fought all her life to achieve Deaf people's right to this same experience.

To appreciate the extent to which such proscription affected Miles' experience, imagine that when alone, the aforesaid hearing children could surreptitiously remove their gags and snatch moments to communicate with each other, all the time at risk of being caught in the act and punished further. Imagine also that at the age of 18 they might be able to take off their gags and decide for themselves about their own future. Their languages might be covertly precious to them, but any sense of appreciation of them, any sense that they might be used creatively would be severely suppressed. Such languages would either regress to a functionalism, or in moments of their reaching into zones of creative pleasure might not be recognised or consciously valued for that creativity.[1] Indeed, broadly speaking, this is the history of the last century of sign languages all over the world, a world in which the only creative forms to maintain their existence – Deaf humour and Sign storytelling – have only recently begun to attain recognition, let alone formal awareness or pride. The beauty of Miles' achievement in fighting for the restoration of sign languages to Deaf education and to public respect was that it was embodied in her use of those sign languages themselves – their re-emergence and re-vivification would be exemplified precisely through the medium of those very languages. Enabling sign languages to reveal their true range and beauty, to both hearing and Deaf people, became her *raison d'être*. In her case, art was truly 'politics by other means'.

A century of diminished Deaf leadership has left a profound legacy of damage. However Miles also knew that the defiance of the human spirit existing within the generations of Deaf people enabled them to gather all that they thought, all that they knew, all that they thought they knew, and all that they had painstakingly gleaned from the world outside, and to pool that information in a living embodiment of the expression 'each one teach one'. By these means they began to let air into the vacuum imposed between themselves and the majority societies around them. Miles knew what it was like to share that defiance of terror, to find one's way to the open air outside, and to join the masses of Deaf people pushing on steadily, struggling step by step up a stairway towards the plateau of equality and cherishing each other every step of that way.

During the first decades of minority re-emergence, there was a concerted thrust towards establishing equality and equal human validity. Initially this was conducted with reference to concepts designed by majority society, but has latterly come to assert the validity of difference itself, positively valorising biological and other features of those minority groups. Miles perceived the Deaf experience in similar terms. The first steps in the Deaf liberation movement had been to refuse all biological examples, since they all constructed Deaf people negatively, as people lacking in a biological sense. This was reinforced by a construction of themselves as a linguistic people, and not as people with disabilities. Miles acknowledged this, but wished to draw attention to an even larger perspective, one which reclaimed those biological givens into a larger and more positive perception.

Deaf peoples' biological reality is uniquely interwoven with a linguistic interface. In the first place, to exist inside the Deaf-Mute experience is to construct a profoundly different sense of the world. This manifests itself on the visual plane, so that the world looks and behaves differently for those who use their eyes to observe and interpret it. It then manifests itself in the physical reality of Deaf bodies in respect of sign languages. Not only the hands, but the face, the eyes, eyebrows, cheeks, shoulders, fingers, arms and the upper torso, are all activated. Then there are the social roles of touch, vibration and rhythm, all of which coalesce to create communication.

Recently, people have begun to appreciate that sign languages across the world, as well as being uniquely expressive, are also uniquely physically constrained (Liddell, 2003). Unlike spoken-language grammars, which vary widely, sign-language grammars seem to be remarkably similar. In a very deep sense, their visual logic seems incapable of being adequately expressed except within certain parameters. Some might read this as limiting but Miles saw this as its opposite – an indication of a deeper 'existential' power. She saw how Deaf peoples could communicate across international borders, and indeed engaged in that process herself. In so doing, she gained a glimpse of something greater, which she brought back to us in her poetry: that Deaf peoples could serve as models of global communication and world citizenship, and thus of a step towards what she believed could bring world peace.

A necessary component of Miles' belief was that non-Deaf people could benefit from learning sign languages, as Sutton-Spence has indicated, so that they too could not only communicate with Deaf people in their native countries, but utilise these skills for international communication. Although Miles was a leading light in the sign linguistics movement, she also believed, as nineteenth-century Deaf writers constantly emphasised, that signing was as much an art as a science (Fischer and Lane, 1993). Somehow even the most mundane daily conversations were more vivid, more dynamic, more interesting, funnier, when rendered visually. Moreover, as she loved to point out, one could create new signs, whose forms had never been seen before, which would never be found in any dictionary, and yet everyone understood what they meant because of the power of visual logic combined with the rhetorical skill of the individual signer. These signs might last only for an instant, would not be remembered the next day, and yet somehow they spoke to the essential genius of visual languages.

At the time Miles was writing, Deaf histories had long been submerged under Oralism. However, in the decade since her death, more and more data has emerged from Deaf peoples' pre-Oralist writings and philosophies. The most powerful of these draw attention to precisely this more elevated view of Sign Language peoples – and what is more, there are numerous indications that hearing people were at one time able to grasp and accept such visions, as illustrated in the writings of Massieu, Clerc and de Ladebat (1815), Lane (1984) and Mirzoeff (1995). This affirms that Miles' vision sat squarely within Deaf pre-colonial traditions, so that her work was in a broad sense an attempt to reinstate those traditions in modern form.

Miles and literary arts in oral and folk-art cultures

What we have learned above about the negative effects of Oralism on Deaf cultures tells us that Deaf communities have been rendered non-literate in English for 100 years. This, taken together with the fact that sign languages cannot (yet) be 'written down' in the same way as spoken languages, indicates that we are dealing with communities whose linguistic reality parallels that of oral cultures. We might then expect to find within Deaf communities traces of very different ideas about what might constitute 'art'. They would be little more than traces, because of the overwhelming influence of majority societies on Deaf communities. Even without access to theatre or film, and with little access to literature, they would still be aware of these 'spaces' as art forms, and ones which carried social prestige.

But there were, and are, other cultural features which were not thought of as art, but which were intensely creative. These include sign-language games, ABC Stories (in the USA), and above all, storytelling in both individual and collective forms (all of which Miles used in her poetry). There are many videoed examples of individual storytelling, but since there are very few ethnographic descriptions of Deaf communities there is little recorded data on storytelling as a collective process. However, older records describe a group of Deaf people standing in a circle telling a story by taking it in turns to add to the improvised tale, whilst Ladd (2003: p. 364) gives similar examples centred around humour. These indicate that the aim of such informal events is to produce a group creation, one which serves to strengthen the collective culture.

We should note that sign languages contain several features which actually appear to predispose them towards storytelling. The first, role-shift, is discussed on pp. 32 and 140–7. This is such a fundamental syntactic device, that virtually any narrative sentence will display examples. This is augmented by the visual, linguistic necessity of placement in sign languages, and the emotive power this syntactic device contains. Something held above can be quite threatening, especially if we factor-in the simultaneous facial reaction of the signer to that sign and its placement. By contrast, a child placed below oneself can be the object of reactions of care and tenderness, and those emotions conveyed swiftly and intensely to the watcher. Facial expression (identified on pp. 5, 136 and 140–7) and the visual representation of size, substance and texture (pp. 7 and 75–84) are immediately absorbed by the senses when watching sign languages, and both these lend themselves to sign-language storytelling. The visual rendering of verbs in sign languages is often more emotionally vivid than speech, again due to a reduced use of onomatopoeia in the latter. A prime example is Miles' *Language for the Eye* (p. 243), a poem intended to draw positive and favourable attention to sign languages *per se*. The central motif of the poem is of word [Sign] become picture, which suggests stillness, movement captured and frozen. But her choice of images for each line of the poem actually illustrates the opposite – movement through a series of highly visual verbs – crash, splash, leap and so on.

These four linguistic features of sign languages are so central to its everyday syntax, that any discourse in Deaf communities, at clubs and events, at home or among friends, therefore utilises considerable story-telling. These cultural patterns are so entrenched that the community is often unconscious of them, and does not separate them from everyday life or designate them as art. A good storytelling leader might not even be recognised as such – people may simply gravitate to them because they find their conversation more 'interesting', as, indeed, was the case with Miles herself, as Dugdale (1993) so vividly recalls:

> Most evenings there would be a little crowd of girls entranced and oblivious of their bleak surroundings watching [Dorothy] 'tell a story' ... . She was the raging sea and the galleon ploughing the waves, the soaring eagle and the pilot of a damaged plane tumbling from the skies. She was as good as television ... . Awful as that school was, it was there that [she] began to be the BSL authority, the actor, the poet and writer ... .

Oralism and the devaluation of Deaf signing arts

The century of Oralism has no doubt contributed to the 'inability' to perceive signing skills and creativity as essentially 'artistic'. The profound stigmatisation of the languages meant that many of the 'best' signers are unable to appreciate the extent of their skills, the value of them over and above their everyday lives. In the USA, where Oralism did not attain a total grip on Deaf children, there is a much greater esteem of sign skills, giving us an idea of how much more they would have been consciously appreciated had Oralism never happened. Indeed, if we examine the evidence of Deaf writings prior to Oralism, we can find numerous references to the positive valuation of good Deaf signing and signers even within the UK (Dimmock, 1993). It is important to remember that it was from these roots that Miles' work grew. It was at school that she first displayed her signing talents, in surreptitious storytelling, continually at risk of punishment to herself.

In a sense then, many, if not most of her sign-poetic skills came from these storytelling roots, employing all of the principles above and more. Furthermore, using them in her work rendered them immediately recognisable to Deaf audiences, bringing both performer and audience very intimately together.

Thematic parallels

The prominence of animal themes and imagery in Miles' work is very striking, but the treatment of them, especially if the English text is given undue attention, can appear childlike, even twee. On the surface of it, these would not appear to be poems on any kind of cutting-edge. However, animals are central to folklore, and if Deaf cultures are comparable to oral cultures, we might expect to find an especial prominence given to animals in some cultural contexts. Indeed that is the case in many Deaf discourses, ranging from everyday conversation to storytelling, and to performed works on video. The sign dimension is also pertinent, since the languages' use of syntactic role-play is easily extended into role-play which involves the imitation of animals, since sign can do this much more easily then speech. Miles' commentary on sign language poetry described the manner in which signers can 'inhabit' animals, other features of nature and even inanimate objects. Once again, therefore, her work originates from the Deaf folk-soil. However, in doing so she situates her work distinctly within an art-frame, and in this respect is working closer to Western folk-art forms than other Deaf signers or oral cultures *per se*.

Another characteristic of these cultures can be located both in Deaf culture and Miles' work: attitudes to children, where there is concern to *consciously* pass onto them traditional wisdoms with the expectation that they will take part in a *collective, face-to-face culture*. Thus, some of Miles' work, especially her UK creations, is particularly concerned to address itself to children, whilst not 'talking down to' Deaf adults. Moreover, Miles executes them with a very clear awareness that in enabling Deaf children to access sign language in this way, she is setting them onto a path of appreciation of the power of their own language which will last their whole lives, and that in encouraging them to take these hitherto forbidden steps, she is also offering them a means to obtain a proper education in both scholastic and street-wise senses. Thus for her, as for so many Deaf adults, work with, or creations for, Deaf children, are charged with much more profound sets of resonances than for majority society children.

Miles, sign poetry, song performance and song poetry

In 'folk genres', ownership and authorship are not relevant concepts. Miles' work is, of course, very definitely self-authored and self-owned. This immediately requires us to find some other, additional means of evaluating her work, and for this we should turn to song poetry. All too often song poetry has suffered from what I term the 'literary fallacy', whereby far more attention is given to the lyrics than to the performance artistry itself (Bowden, 1982). When we first see the work of Miles or other sign poets, we are first of all aware of their ownership of their sign poem, but the more time we spend observing that work, the more it becomes clear that their performance of the work is inseparable from its content. Written poetry we might never hear recited; song poetry we might hear only on record and never see performed; but sign poetry is a 100 per cent visual experience, where content, form and performance are inseparable but profoundly related criteria for measuring one's aesthetic pleasure.

When we factor into this the linguistic features of sign language mentioned earlier, especially the tremendous range of possibilities contained within the medium of facial expression and other examples of 'affect', it quickly becomes apparent that sign poetry is song poetry taken to another level. In watching this kind of work, one can become acutely tuned into the slightest nuances which indicate that the performer is taking a different approach to a poem each time it is performed. These approaches may be conscious, may be based on the mood of the moment, or may simply be performative variations. All these factors can be clearly identified in Miles' work, as Sutton-Spence has shown on e.g. pp. 179–82, and it is interesting that the most profound examples of such variation lie in the secular poems such as *Total Communication*.

In sign poetry, there remains an irreducible sense in which the author is unmistakably and irrevocably present in his or her work, and that they are performed with the author's first-person perspective. Furthermore, the simple fact that sign poet and viewer must lock eye-to-eye for the work to have any meaning, automatically brings the viewer very close to the sign poet. *The Hang Glider* is an excellent example of a poem where performance is central to the poem. Those who know Miles' background will be aware that the poem's images of being close to a cliff edge and choosing whether or not to jump are an apposite summation of her life and work. Always pioneering, choosing to risk being misunderstood and become the object of derision or under-appreciation, not least because she was a woman in such times, there were many times in her life that she stood at that metaphorical edge. Indeed, knowing that in the end she fell to her death, we are also presented with one of those very rare poems which shows an artist contemplating her potential demise. One can compare two ASL 'versions' which exist in live performance. In the earlier version we have, performed not long after it was created, it is undeniably Miles herself on the cliff edge. The later version, whilst still impressive, is more of an 'enaction', Miles establishing a character through whom the poem is narrated.

At this point it is useful to reflect on one of the next steps in the development of sign poetry, one which pulls us towards the genre of song performance. As time has passed, more Deaf people are beginning to perform works by Miles and Valli, the two main examples. Thus one moves away from the relevance of authorship in evaluation and closer to evaluation of the power or otherwise of the performance itself. In my opinion, BSL performances of Miles' work tend to be of inferior 'quality' to her own performances. But making an informed sustained comparison of the two works would nevertheless be a very valuable exercise in evaluating what is Miles' genius, and what is sign poetry's own genius. One example of a performance that equals Miles in execution is Ella Mae Lentz's ASL version of *Total Communication*, although again Miles reveals a greater degree of vulnerability in her narrator, a quality which we might term 'soul'. Were we to study them both, we could begin to evaluate the medium and the performers, and from there could proceed to a deeper sense of the importance of authorship itself.

But if we are to grasp the full significance of sign poetry, we must appreciate that the heart of this embodiment lies in the earlier descriptions of Deaf community and culture – and its essentially collective nature. Miles' work is at times explicitly political, if one understands Deaf politics. *To a Deaf Child,* written at the height of Oralism, cannot be understood any other way. It is also, as we have seen earlier, implicitly political, simply because her intention in creating the sign-poetry medium was to gain respect and recognition for the peoples whose (oppressed) languages they were. Moreover, there is a profound sense of 'we the people', as it were, within her work and this is most visible in *The Staircase* and *The BDA is ...* , as earlier chapters have shown. This collectivism was also borne out in her lifework. Instead of remaining within an art-space as an 'artist' in the Western manner, she spent the last 15 years of her life back in her grass roots, teaching Deaf people the value of their everyday language, the word they held in hand, and training them to impart their language to others. It was an apparently mundane linguistic task, but one organically linking her life and art.

Another dimension of Miles' work which must be considered in any full evaluation is her biculturality. Most sign poets are essentially monocultural – they are not comfortable in English or with non-Deaf people – so what follows is more of a quality found in Miles' work alone. First of all, we need to refer back to one aspect of the existential Deaf concept. Most minority cultural membership is predicated on a certain immutability in respect of their own existential position, but a hearing person can become a Deaf person, if they are deafened at a young enough age to be socialised in the sign-language community. This was Miles' experience, and its effects on her work are also central to her whole artistic philosophy. Individualist societies' use of art forms and the concept of art-space itself was something which she brought across from such societies. We have to remember that in her time sign languages were still not considered to be powerful or prestigious languages, and the idea of writing 'poetry' completely in those languages was one which brought scorn and derision, even from Deaf people.

Miles therefore began by operating from a perspective that recognition of sign poetry could only begin to gain acceptance if it was in some way linked to English. A strong case can be made that in fact her work is a form of 'Signed English' rather than 'pure' ASL or BSL. However, Miles was aware of the difference between the two, and her goal, and, as Sutton-Spence has indicated throughout this book, her genius, lies partly in the way in which she brings ASL or BSL features to this situation, and partly in how she then uses the fact of working between two languages to enable them to play off each other and to shed new light on both.

Any evaluation of her work would therefore need to encompass examples where she has walked this tightrope both more and less successfully, such as is found on pp. 157–62. *To a Deaf Child* can be seen as an example of the latter. In particular, the English poetic style which is employed is especially 'literary' in its enunciation, and a native signer has to wait until the end of each line to try and 'back-translate', that is, to 'make sense' of the line, by which time the next line is being performed. I say that this is 'less successful', but those Deaf people who are most effectively bilingual can gain a greater benefit from such sign poems than a 'grassroots' person who might be comparatively monolingual. However, their appreciation would come not on the first performative 'reading' but from successive readings – once they have become aware of Miles' English text and can thence return to the performed version with a fuller knowledge of what the sign poem is emerging from.

Something of this re-experiencing process informs non-Deaf people's ability to access Miles' work. Those who know sign language can fall in love with it, as Sutton-Spence has so clearly manifested. But because of the existence of English text and translation, whether read from a page or TV caption, or heard in voice-over, a bridge exists so that those who know little sign language can begin to cross. One can be strongly moved by a song sung in an unknown language and this experience is heightened by having immediate access in one's own language to Miles' works, for here is a feature unique to sign poetry – one can watch it in one language and hear in another. It was also because of Miles' belief that non-Deaf people could and should learn sign languages, that she devoted the last 15 years of her life to devising teaching materials for them. Taking her cue from a meeting with the anthropologist Margaret Mead, and knowing such a unique feature existed, she consciously set out to entice them across the bridge, to fulfil their potential destiny as global citizens after the manner indicated in *To a Deaf Child*.

It is not a requirement of poets that they be visionaries, yet we would underestimate the achievements of Blake, Shelley and others were we to ignore that dimension of their work, and this is true too for Miles. To find the willpower and courage to step out and create the genre of sign-poetry in what was then a more hostile world, with the legacy of the proscription of signing in schools still all around her, required an underpinning of vision in the first instance. To grasp, as described above, a global sense of the importance of sign languages to non-Deaf people, also required vision, without which her work would not have existed. That she was also one of the first Deaf playwrights and television writers, stage director of the first known Deaf play of the twentieth century, was an actress and a puppeteer with her own puppets, would already mark her down as a significant artist. But without sign language, none of this work would have existed, and all that we would have would be a few minor English poems. In locating her Deafhood through these visions, she helped this writer and many others expand and envision their own.

There is also another dimension to the role of visions in her work. For at least 20 years Dorothy suffered from bi-polar disorders, a quality which has informed the work of many other artists, ranging from Spike Milligan to Vincent Van Gogh. Just as it is arguable that their work was 'transmitted' from a higher plane of vision that characterised their 'manic' phases, so we can find a similar experience underpinning her own work. Writing to the author after a spell in hospital, she noted on 15 August 1977:

> Yours was the only reaction that actually related to what was going on with me: Dionysian enthusiasm / mystical experience. All the others have fallen gladly on the medical diagnosis of 'lithium deficiency' – so now I'm taking drugs to cure what in other people is caused by taking drugs !

Subsequent conversations revealed that it was indeed from such mystical experiences that her vision of the role of sign poetry in 'helping to heal the world', as she put it, was triggered. One does not need to know this to gain limited appreciation of the work. But for fullest appreciation, awareness of this dimension is essential.

The chapter has taken us on a wide-ranging journey in order to lay the cornerstones for a literary appreciation of sign poetry and Miles' work. It will take time to analyse sign poetry and Miles' work, but it should be clear that in the journey towards that aim, not only will we learn much about Deaf people, but we will learn about the significance of visual languages. We will learn about the roles of arts in other cultures, about their roles in our own in earlier times. We will learn about other minorities' art forms. And in doing so, we will end up by shedding much light on the things we take for granted as members of Western majority societies – what we think of as culture, what we think of as 'true' Knowledge, and what basis we use for accumulating our own cultural capital.

What this book has created, then, is a powerful testimony to an artist, rooted in oral cultures and especially in a folk tradition, who has brought the strength of vision to be able to see beyond the boundaries imposed by colonialism to a newer, higher and better place, not just for Deaf peoples but for all humankind. And like several other visionaries, that pioneering came with a price, best summed up in the experience of Miles the hang-glider:

NO TURNING BACK !

(The wings won't turn).

Appendix: Texts of Poems

In this section we provide English texts of translations of the poems referred to in the previous chapters in the book. The poems are presented in alphabetical order, first those by Dorothy Miles, and then those by Paul Scott.

Poems by Dorothy Miles

(All English translations are by Dorothy Miles)

The BDA is ...

Now in 1990 we've grown so strong –
With Princess Di as patron we can't go wrong.
Let's keep on working and you'll see well:
Deaf people everywhere are out of the shell.

The BDA is you and me,
Together we'll fight for equality.

The Cat

The Cat!
With her long tail stuck in the air like *that*,
and waving as she walks by;
in the light
her eyes wink and blink,
but at night
they open as wide as the sky.
With her paws
she can softly powder her nose,
but claws
leap out when a dog comes by!
The cat,
with her whiskers ready at short-wave range, like *that*,
would make a perfect s-p-y.

Christmas List

When I was just a little girl with Christmas coming near,
Mother called us children to sit around the table,
And write a list of things we hoped to see on Christmas Day
For Santa Claus to bring if he were able.

The lists were done, we circled where the fire was burning bright,
And put them up the chimney to be sucked into the night.

But we of course were children, so we asked for funny pets,
All kinds of sweets and chocolates, and candy cigarettes
And cannon, and tin soldiers, and cut-out dolls, and swords.
And games like Snakes and Ladders, and games you play with words.
The adults gave us shoes and clothes – perhaps a golden chain.
Then we squabbled over what was whose – till Christmas came again.

I gave a lot of thought this year to my own Christmas list.
I think these should be given to all, and no-one should be missed;
The first and most important is that we should love to Love …
Ourselves – and then each other as we will in 'heaven above'.
And after that Intelligence, growing like a seed;
And then a little Discipline, a scolding when we need!
And last of all, when all these three are working as they should.
The right amount of Humour to make life good.

Christmas Magic

I remember …

In darkness, waking and wondering why
I feel excitement bubbling within,
And suddenly magic is all around me
Like shivery fingers on my skin
And I know at last it's Christmas Day!

I remember …

Sitting and pushing back the clothes
Groping to find the old black stocking
(Last night on its peg so limply hanging)
Now full of strange shapes from top to toe!
I've been good! And Santa has been this way.

Then out of bed and down the stairs,
The magic still behind me streaming –
Into the room where the fire's dim glow
Touches the tree with a gentle gleaming

There's a pile
of presents –
some for me!

For this magic day
of love and glee.

This Christmas Day, wherever you be,
I wish for you, and I hope for me,
A sprinkling of Christmas magic.

Elephants Dancing

Dum-de-dum,
Dum-de-dum,
There in the dust
You dance for me.

One step forward,
Pause, hold;
One step backward,
Pause, hold.
Back and forth
Again and again,
As if your legs
Were held by chains.

Chains!
Of course.
So that's how you learned
Your dancing laws.

One step forward,
Tug, stop;
One step backward,
Tug, stop;
And now that is
Your only dance,
You well-adjusted
Elephants.

I hope some day to see
Elephants dancing free.

Exaltation

I think I shall remember till I die
That sudden glimpse of trees against the sky.
All in a row they were, and newly dressed
In summer's green, and a light breeze caressed
Their topmost branches; standing there, so high,
They seemed like fingers reaching for the sky,
As if they sought to part the veil of blue
And let the peace of Heaven shine softly though.

Then, for a moment, from this lowly sod
I reached with them to touch the face of God.

The Hang Glider

Here are my wings;
And there, at the edge of nothing,
wait the winds

to bear my weight.
My wings,
so huge and strong,
built with my life in mind ...

I have made other wings before,
  test-tried,
    wrong-broken,
      cast aside –
I searched, and asked, and saw,
and built again ...
and here I stand.

Take up my courage
with my pack
and forward go –

No Turning Back!

(The wings won't turn).

** ** ** ** **

The cliff is high,
  and far way down
    the sea;
I'd hate to drown!

But they are watching me.

I have seen others do it –
step off and fly –
so why can't I?

Suppose ...
suppose the winds might die,
and I
Step off and dive
and dive
  and dive ...

** ** ** ** **

The winds won't die!
Experience tells me that
Courage
and faith in my experience,
that's all I need.

Here are my wings ...
Here are my wings!

Language for the Eye

Hold a tree in the palm of your hand,
or topple it with a crash.

Sail a boat on finger waves,
or sink it with a splash.
From your fingertips see a frog leap,
at a passing butterfly.
The word becomes the picture in this language for the eye.

Follow the sun from rise to set,
or bounce it like a ball.
Catch a fish in a fishing net,
or swallow it, bones and all.
Make traffic scurry, or airplanes fly,
and people meet and part.
The word becomes the action in this language of the heart.

Our Dumb Friends

Dogs, all over
vary   (true!)
almost as much as
people do:

size, shape, colour, weight,
smooth hair, rough hair,
curly, straight;
ears that point,
ears that droop,
floppy ears,
prickly ears,
ears like a scoop;
and tails
(wow!)
short and stumpy,
thumb-thumb-thumpy;
teeny-weeny-wiggle-waggle;
thick and bumpy;
long and hairy,
airy-fairy;
sweep-the-floor-brushy;
curved and bushy;
finger slender
(seems to say 'Where,
where's the excitement?
Let me share.')

Yes, dogs
vary
almost as much as

people –
yet
when dogs fight, it's
one to one;
dogs don't join
in groups
to shun
other groups
of different size
or colour – (oh, well),
dogs are dumb.

Or wise.
?

Seasons (*an exercise in Haiku*)

Spring

Sunshine, borne on breeze,
among singing trees, to dance
on rippled water.

Summer

Green depths and green heights,
clouds, the hours quiet – slow, hot,
heavy on the hands.

Autumn

Scattered leaves, a-whirl
in playful winds, turn to watch
people hurry by.

Winter

Contrast: black and white;
bare trees, covered ground; hard ice
soft snow; birth in death.

Sinai (The Leader)

To my left, steep rise;
to my right, steep fall;
through the valley a river fingers,
twin to this path
that crawls

at the edge of sky –
where I, puny plodder,
pass by.

Around me
silence infinite lingers;
the wind
has blown out, and the birds
have flown from my listening eye.
I feel the rock
of ages bearing me up,
bearing me down,
forcing me on ...
On the upward slope a bush
blazes!
My breath catches – no!
See there
from the opposite slope
the sinking sunfire's
reflecting glow.

Why do I go
lonely?
Behind me a group
straggles –
I could turn back, and blend
into the crowd.
But no!

Within me a call,
and I follow the urgent trail.
Up this slope, perhaps
round this bend,
is the end
is the End.

The Staircase – An Allegory

(prose translation from BSL)

A dark forest. A figure creeps forward, peering ahead,
Then comes another and another.
They draw together in uncertainty, then in a line,
They advance.
But they come to a wall.
They retreat, gazing upwards – what is it?
Ah, it's a huge staircase.

Suddenly at the tip they see a light that glimmers, glimmers.
They are drawn to it and look at each other – who will climb up first?

Perhaps the one who climbs will face a lion's claws.
Or sink into the ground.
Or meet a giant with a sword and lose his head.

They back away and turn to go.
Then one of them, balding, spectacled, somewhat plump – says No;
Goes forward, climbs, looks around, sees all is well;
Beckons them on and heaves up those on either side of him,
Who then heave others, until all are in line on the first step.
On his left is a woman, short-haired and spectacled too,
Eager to give support.
He moves on again, climbs up, beckons and hoists ...
Again the line is straight.
So up and up they go, stair after stair,
And see that the glimmering light now glows around
What looks like a sword embedded in a stone,
Such as a king once drew and held aloft.
They press forward and someone reaches to grasp the sword's hilt – Lo and behold,
it's a certificate!
One by one in a line they each get one.

But where's the man, balding, spectacled, somewhat plump?
He's sitting, looking on, applauding them, then rises and leaves.

And the woman – she takes up her certificate like a flag,
And leads the onward parade.

To a Deaf Child

You hold the word in hand;
And though your voice may speak, never
(though you might tutor it for ever)
can it achieve the hand-wrought eloquence
of this sign. Who in the word alone can say
that day is sunlight, night is dark!
Oh remark
The signs for living, for being
Inspired, excited – how similar they.

Your lightest word in hand
lifts like a butterfly, or folds
in liquid motion: each gesture holds
echoes of action or shape or reasoning.
Within your hands perhaps you form a clear
new vision – Man's design for living;
so giving
sign-ificance to Babel's tongues
that henceforth he who sees aright may hear.

You hold the word in hand
and offer the palm of friendship

at frontiers where men of speech lend lip–
service to brotherhood, you pass unhampered
by sounds that drown the meaning, or by fear
of the foreign-word-locked fetter,
Oh better
the word in hand than a thousand
spilled from the mouth upon the hearless ear

Total Communication

You and I,
can we see aye to aye?
or must your I, and I
lock horns and struggle till we die?
Your mind's
not mine,
and your experience, I
experience – not –
can never learn.
Reverse, the same:
my life transferred's
a blank.

We say 'communicate,'
smile, touch and kiss;
and I say
'This-is what I mean'.
You nod-at-me,
nod-nod-at-me
excitedly, and say
'That's – what we mean!'

Dismay!
Tight throat,
I look, and look –
and see:
that, on one hand,
that, on the other hand,
the same?
No, not for me.

Must we forever;
eye to eye;
stare past
to what we want to see?
Or can our minds
send messages,
and your mind's aye
meet my mind's aye?

Trio

MORNING

Sunrise
The rain stops – and the wind dies
Stillness
See, in the pool,
Twin trees

AFTERNOON

I eat and sit, replete,
My dog does too.
A sparrow pecks and perches –
The three of us doz-z-z-ze!

EVENING

Like a flower the sun folds itself up.
Darkness, like a bat, flies close,
And closer –
Deaf-blinds me!

The Ugly Duckling

Poor bird!
When first he thrusts and breaks the shell
And clambers out –
Pop-eyed, long-beaked, grey-furred and bandy-legged –
He doesn't know
Others will mock at him, retreat from him
His mother Duck, at first sight, will turn aside
Embarrassed and dismayed.

Poor bird!
When first he walks through the farmyard world,
Keeping in line
With mother and fluffy yellow brothers and sisters,
He doesn't know why
Lambs leap from him, cows low at him,
Hens, staring beady-eyed,
Snigger behind their wings.

The pond is reached:
He jumps for joy,

A splash! and a glide ...
But when he bows and sees himself –
He scuttles away to hide.

Poor bird!
When first he understands his difference
He is ashamed,
And blames himself, and shrinks from company.
He doesn't know
He will meet other birds who won't reject him,
He'll change, and be like them,
And bowing, see a swan.

Unsound views

Hearing people, I find them odd ...
they have
an extra umbilical cord
attached to
the telephone.
Like Pavlov's dogs,
at the ring of a bell
they cock their ears and run like ... well
to snatch
their tele-bone

The telephone is Robot Master
ignore it and
they face disaster.
How can I tell? ...
My friend is pondering her role
how to throw off the world's control
how to be strong and independent
and unrepentant.
Then – brrrr! The robot girl is back,
the phone has summoned, she's on its track.

Or talking business with the boss –
ten minutes, and
I must be off –
the two of us,
we're face to face,
upon the task united ...?
No!
A turn, a lift,
'Ba-ba-ba-ba-'.
I've disappeared without a trace.

I might be in a
close embrace

lips meeting lips, the world
well lost ...
Then the ear is caught
and the arm goes and, and
as for me
do I get tossed?

Nowadays there are
people who
walking, riding, driving too
commune all day with unseen beings
and never notice me and you.
They live to serve their telephone God,
Hearing people, I find them odd.

Walking Down the Street (*'I was all right until I met you'*)

See her now, she's walking down the street

See me now, I'm walking down the street
If you watch me bustling along
Would you say that there was anything wrong?

Oh, yes?
Hair's a mess!
Getting on a bit – a lot!
Somewhat plump
Looks like a frump
(Clothes from an Oxfam dump?)

Oh, yes!
But that's not what I mean.
If you'd been looking round for help and seen
Me bustling down the street
One head, two feet
Come on, what would you think?:
Looks kind,
And trustworthy
And intelligent, a little – a lot!
Seems to know
Where to go
And what's what.

So you come up to me (so many do) and say:
'Excuse me, wubble roh a bissel tiva meniday?'
And I'll say:
'Would you say that again?'
And your lips say:
'I jussa pakka winter enzo rushy colla den'

And I'll say:
'Sorry, I'm deaf!'

(And what do you do? You back away.
'Never mind' or 'That's all right', you say –
Whatcha mean 'All right?'
If you knew what I was thinking
You'd be shrinking!)

Poems by Paul Scott

(Translations by Rachel Sutton-Spence)

Five Senses

Excuse me, but who are you?
Who am I? Come with me and see.
Feel your arms tingle at my embrace.
Reach out – oh, that's cold!
Reach out – oh, that's hot!
So, now you know me.

Excuse me, but who are you?
Who am I? Come with me and see.
A lick of ice-cream – mmm
A scoop of that – yuck!
A scoop of this – yum!
So, now you know me.

Excuse me, but who are you?
Who am I? Come with me and see.
Pick a flower and sniff – lovely!
Take some cheese from the fridge – whiffy!
Pop this tasty morsel in your mouth,
Yes, and it smells good too.
So, now you know me.

Excuse me, but who are you?
Excuse me?

Excuse me, but what's wrong with him?
Oh, we're together.
Together?
Yes, come with us and see.
Eyes wide open, seeing and understanding.
Information and learning,
Colours, speed, action.
Learning and drinking in the world through the eyes.

So now you know us.

And now you know me.

Three Queens

(Prose translation from BSL)
Here is a queen with red curly hair that stands up on top of her head. She reaches down and picks up a shell, which she opens and takes out something. It is a pearl. She wears a pearl necklace and strings of pearls cross her chest. She wears a high collar, and a head-dress with a pearl at its peak. Her dress has puffed sleeves and full skirts. The queen walks purposefully, with her two courtier scribes behind her. She stops and reaches out for the object before her. It is a potato. She orders it to be boiled then she spoons some from a dish. She eats it, nods in approval and orders her scribe to record it. This he does, diligently. The queen walks on purposefully again. Someone is smoking a cigarette. She takes the cigarette and puffs on it. It makes her dizzy and makes her cough. She nods in approval and orders her other scribe to record it. This he does. She walks on, with the two scribes behind her. She sees people signing and gesturing, and she is puzzled so she summons them to her. They are deaf. She orders the scribe to record it. This he does, watching them carefully, thinking that their signing is like signing in the air. The two scribes follow their queen as she moves on. They look up and see the flag flying above them. The flag has crosses on the vertical and horizontal and on the diagonals.

Time passes and a queen is born and grows. She has a long, thin, curved nose and is humourless. From her large stomach, nine children are born. The third of them is deaf. The deaf person grows up without speech, needing and pleading for education but the pleas are ignored and dismissed. Then she meets the King of Greece and moves to live there.

Four generations are born and in that fourth generation is Prince Philip, Philip Duke of Edinburgh. Two people meet and the flag flies above them. They marry and fly to Kenya. A woman climbs a tree. She is looking through binoculars when she feels the tree shaking as someone climbs it. She comes down the tree, asks what they want and they tell her that she is now the Queen, so she flies to England, where the flag is flying above them. Time passes and deaf people are angry and ready to fight. They say, 'BSL is mine' and challenge the idea that it is not a language. They march together and finally succeed as BSL is recognised at last. And the flag flies above them. All three queens look up to the flag. Three queens from three times under one flag.

Notes

1 Some General Points about Sign Languages

1. Those readers who would like to know more about the linguistics of British Sign Language are directed to Rachel Sutton-Spence and Bencie Woll, *The Linguistics of British Sign Language* (Cambridge University Press, 1999). Those readers who would like to know more about the linguistics of American Sign Language are directed to Clayton Valli and Ceil Lucas, *Linguistics of American Sign Language* (Washington DC: Gallaudet University Press, 1992). Both are introductory texts to sign linguistics. Paddy Ladd's *Understanding Deaf Culture* (Clevedon: Multilingual Matters, 2003) is a good introduction to the social context in which sign languages are used.

2 What is Sign Language Poetry?

1. Readers unfamiliar with sign languages are reminded that British Sign Language and American Sign Language are two different, mutually unintelligible languages. Both are also entirely independent of – although to some extent influenced by – English. This very important point is made in more depth in Chapter 1, p. 1.
2. For example, many of the videotapes of Dorothy's works were lost shortly after her death. Fortunately a few people had records of some of her performances, and we have used some of these for our analyses in this book. There are doubtless more recordings of her work that we do not know about. Perhaps readers will have their own copies of poems that we have assumed are lost.
3. Clayton Valli (1993) suggested that original compositions of sign language poetry, within the definition we use today, did exist in the nineteenth century, especially in France, during the great heyday of sign language and the Deaf community before the damage caused to sign language and Deaf communities by Oralism. However, there is as yet no evidence either for or against his claim.
4. Ameslan was a name for the sign language of the American Deaf Community. The term was used quite widely in the 1970s. Most people now would refer to it as ASL.

3 Repetition in Sign Language Poetry

1. We should note, though, that the 'Å' handshape in BSL has the added connotation of 'good' due to the number of signs using this handshape which have positive meanings. Examples include GOOD, NICE, PROUD, HEALTHY and WISE.
2. The rhyme in the final two lines here, *swords* and *words* is sometimes termed an 'eye-rhyme' to distinguish it from a 'true rhyme', because although the two

word endings have similar spellings, they have different pronunciations. As a first-language English speaker, Dorothy would have been fully aware that the two words do not rhyme. However, as a deaf poet enjoying the visual attributes of language and poetry, perhaps she took particular pleasure in such visual rhymes.

3. We should note that orientation tends to vary depending on location and movement of the hand, but it can be included in the general scheme here.

4. Where all the sounds are identical in two English words, but the meaning is different, the poem contains a pun. Puns can be a poetic device, and were used extensively in eighteenth-century English satire and comic poetry. Puns in sign language can also be created when all parameters are shared between two signs with different meanings.

5. We have records of more than one performance of this poem. In one performance we see this pattern, but not in the other performance. This example shows that the performance can vary, weakening the idea of 'the text' of a sign language poem as a fixed entity.

6 Ambiguity

1. It is interesting to note that this poem originally worked much better in ASL than in BSL because the sign TREE most commonly used in BSL in the late 1970s was not the one described here. It involved sketching the outline of a generic deciduous tree. The poem could only be made to work in BSL when the 'sketched outline' sign was then replaced by the proform which was the same as the ASL TREE. Today, though, the same sign using the '5' handshape is used widely in BSL, as well as ASL.

9 The Poem and Performance

1. 'Non-literate' should be distinguished carefully from 'illiterate'. While 'illiterate' implies an inability to read in a society that uses writing regularly, to be non-literate means simply that the society or the language does not use writing to any great extent and has other methods for storing and remembering information. The term 'oral' here is completely unrelated to the educational philosophy of 'Oralism' that promoted speech over sign language.

2. We are faced with the same situation when we hear a love song. Do we believe the singer to own the feelings in it or the song-writer? We are usually content to accept that neither does. Indeed, perhaps some of the safety behind a love song comes from being able to sing it while claiming some sort of distance from the emotions in it, while trying to affect the emotions of the audience.

3. The same effect occurs, again, when a woman sings a song written for a male role, or vice versa.

4. This was possible in America where Gallaudet University created a body of college-educated Deaf signers. In Britain, where there is no equivalent institution, Deaf signers did not start attending universities in any appreciable numbers until the 1990s.

5. Other terms for this way of 'becoming' an animal as part of sign language could be 'mimicry', 'impersonation' or 'embodiment'.

10 Blended Sign Language and Spoken Language Poetry

1. The same situation occurs in other languages, so that for example there may be Signed Dutch in relation to Sign Language of the Netherlands (SLN or NGT), or signed French in relation to French Sign Language (LSF).

12 *Trio*

1. The two signs EVENING have two very different forms. They are dialect variants with the same meaning but the different forms have great significance in this poem.
2. The exception to this is when signers are aware that they have made a 'slip of the hand'. Then, they might look in confusion or even in mock indignation at their wayward hands. So, again, we have seen that the poet is using a device that we might occasionally see in the normal use of signing, but she is using it in a new context with a new meaning.

Afterword

1. Other forms of damage to sign-language users include literacy – school leavers having a reading age of 8½ (Conrad, 1979), a rate of *acquired* mental illness double the national average (Hindley and Kitson (eds) 2000), the virtual disappearance of Deaf visual arts (Mirzoeff, 1995) and much more.

Bibliography

Bauman, Humphrey-Dirksen (2003) 'Redesigning literature: the cinematic poetics of American Sign Language poetry', *Sign Language Studies*, 4, 34–47.

Blondel, Marion, and Miller, Christopher (2000) 'Rhythmic structures in French Sign Language (LSF) nursery rhymes', *Sign Language and Linguistics*, 3, 59–78.

Blondel, Marion, and Miller, Christopher (2001) 'Movement and rhythm in nursery rhymes in LSF', *Sign Language Studies*, 2, 24–61.

Bowden, B. (1982) *Performed Literature*. Bloomington, IN: Indiana University Press.

Boyes-Braem, Penny, and Sutton-Spence, Rachel (2001) *The Hands are the Head of the Mouth: The Mouth as Articulator in Sign Languages*. Hamburg: Signum Press.

Branson, Jan, and Miller, Don (1998) 'Nationalism and the linguistic rights of deaf communities: linguistic imperialism and the recognition and development of sign language', *Journal of Sociolinguistics*, 2, 3–34.

Brennan, Mary (1989) 'Productive morphology in British Sign Language: Focus on the role of metaphors', in S. Prillwitz and T. Vollhaber (eds) *Current Trends in European Sign Language Research* (International Studies on Sign Language and Communication of the Deaf 9). Hamburg: Signum Press, pp. 205–28.

Brennan, Mary (1992) 'The Visual World of BSL', in D. Brien (ed.) *Dictionary of British Sign Language/English*. London: Faber.

Brown, Brianne (2001) *Translucent Meanings: The Poetics of ASL poetry*. www.swarthmore.edu/SocSci/Linguistics/papers/2001/ brownthesis.pdf

Cohn, Jim (1986) 'The new deaf poetics: visible poetry', *Sign Language Studies*, 52, 262–77.

Coleman, L., and Jankowski, K. A. (1994) 'Empowering deaf people through folklore and storytelling', in C. J. Erting, R. C. Johnson, D. L. Smith and B. D. Snider (eds) *The Deaf Way: Perspectives from the International Conference on Deaf Culture*. Washington, DC: Gallaudet University Press, pp. 55–60.

Conrad, J. (1979) *The Deaf School Child: Language and Cognitive Function*. London: Harper & Row.

Cuddon, J. A. (1977) *The Penguin Dictionary of Literary Terms and Literary Theory*. (4th edn, 1998) London: Penguin.

De Ladebat, L. (1815) *A Collection of the Most Remarkable Definitions of Massieu and Clerc*. London: Cox & Baylis.

Dimmock, A. (1993) *Cruel Legacy*. Edinburgh: Scottish Workshop Publications.

Draper, Ronald (1999) *An Introduction to Twentieth Century Poetry in English*. Basingstoke: Macmillan.

Dugdale, P. (1993) 'Dorothy Squire Miles – my friend', *British Deaf News* (April).

Finnegan, Ruth. (1977) *Oral Poetry*. Cambridge University Press.

Fischer, Renate and Lane, Harlan (1993) *Looking Back*. Hamburg: Signum.

Freeman, Donald (1970) *Linguistics and Literary Style*. New York: Holt, Rinehart & Winston.

Hindley, P. and Kitson, N. (eds) (2000) *Mental Health and Deafness*. London: Whurr.

Humphries, Tom (2002) *Talking Culture and Culture Talking: Private to Public Expressions of Culture*. Paper presented to Deaf Studies Think Tank, Gallaudet University, Washington, DC. July 5–7, 2002

Klima, Edward, and Bellugi, Ursula (1979) *The Signs of Language*. Cambridge, MA: Harvard University Press.

Ladd, Paddy (2003) *Understanding Deaf Culture*. Clevedon: Multilingual Matters.

Lane, Harlan (1984) *When the Mind Hears*. New York: Random House.

Leech, Geoffrey (1969) *A Linguistic Guide to English Poetry*. London: Longman.

Liddell, Scott (2003) *Grammar, Gesture and Meaning in American Sign Language*. Cambridge University Press.

Mandel, Mark (1977) 'Iconic devices in ASL', in L. Friedman (ed.) *On the Other Hand*. New York: Academic Press.

Matterson, Stephen, and Jones, Darryl (2000) *Studying Poetry*. London: Arnold.

McManus, Chris (2002) *Right Hand, Left Hand: The Origins of Asymmetry in Brains, Bodies, Atoms and Cultures*. London: Weidenfeld & Nicolson.

Miles, Dorothy (1976) *Gestures: Poetry in Sign Language*. Northridge, CA: Joyce Motion Picture Co.

Miles, Dorothy (1998) *Bright Memory*. Feltham, Middlesex: British Deaf History Society.

Mindess, A. (2000) *Reading Between the Signs: Intercultural Communication for Sign Language Interpreters*. Yarmouth, ME: Intercultural Press.

Mirzoeff, N. (1995) *Silent Poetry: Deafness, Sign and Visual Culture in Modern France*. Princeton, NJ: Princeton University Press.

Ong, Walter (1982) *Orality and Literacy: Technologising the Word*. London: Routledge.

Ormsby, Alec (1995) 'The poetry and poetics of American Sign Language'. Unpublished PhD dissertation, Stanford University.

Padden, Carol, and Humphries, Tom (1988) *Deaf in America*. Cambridge, MA: Harvard University Press.

Peters, Cynthia L. (2000). *Deaf American Literature: From Carnival to the Canon*. Washington, DC: Gallaudet University Press.

Pityana, B., Ramphele, M., Mpumlwana, M., and Wilson, L. (eds) (1991) *Bounds of Possibility: The Legacy of Steve Biko and Black Consciousness*. Cape Town: David Philip.

Pizzuto, Elena, and Russo, Tommaso (2000) *Seven poems in Italian Sign Language (LIS)* (foreword to poems by Rosaria Giuranna and Giuseppe Giuranna). Rome: Graphic Service, Istituto di Psicologia, Consiglio Nazionale delle Ricerche.

Richards, I. A. (1929) *Principles of Literary Criticism*. New York: Harcourt, Brace & World.

Rose, Heidi (1992) 'A critical methodology for analyzing American Sign Language literature'. Unpublished PhD dissertation, Arizona State University.

Russo, Tommaso, Giuranna, Rosaria and Pizzuto, Elena (2001) 'Italian Sign Language (LIS) Poetry: Iconic Properties and Structural Regularities', *Sign Language Studies*, 2, 24–61.

Sternberg, Martin (1990) *American Sign Language Concise Dictionary*. New York: Harper & Row.

Stokoe, William (1960) *Sign Language Structure: An Outline of the Visual Communication System of the American Deaf*. Studies in Linguistics Occasional Papers, No. 8. Buffalo, NY: Department of Anthropology and Linguistics, University of Buffalo.

Sutton-Spence, Rachel (2001) 'British Sign Language Poetry: A linguistic analysis of the work of Dorothy Miles', in V. Direly, M. Metzger, and A. M. Baer (eds) *Signed Languages: Discoveries From International Research.* Washington, DC: Gallavdet University Press, pp. 231–42.

Sutton-Spence, Rachel (2001) Phonological 'deviance' in British Sign Language poetry. *Sign Language Studies,* 2(1) 62–83.

Sutton-Spence, Rachel (2002) Aspects of BSL poetry – An analysis of the poetry of Dorothy Miles. *Journal of Sign Language & Linguistics,* 3(2) 79–100.

Sutton-Spence, Rachel, and Woll, Bencie (1999) *The Linguistics of British Sign Language.* Cambridge University Press.

Taub, Sarah (2001) *Language from the Body: Iconicity and Metaphor in American Sign Language.* Cambridge University Press.

Taub, Sarah (2001) 'Complex superposition of metaphors in an ASL poem', in V. Dively, M. Metzger, S. Taub, and A. M. Baer (eds) *Signed Languages: Discoveries from International Research.* Washington, DC: Gallaudet University Press, pp. 197–230.

Thomas, Dylan (1952) 'A Child's Christmas in Wales'. Reproduced in Walford Davies (ed.) *Dylan Thomas: The Collected Stories.* London: Everyman, 1983.

Valli, Clayton, and Lucas, Ceil (1992) *Linguistics of American Sign Language.* Washington, DC: Gallaudet University Press.

Valli, Clayton (1993) '*Poetics of American Sign Language Poetry*'. Unpublished doctoral dissertation, Union Institute Graduate School.

Williams, R. (1958) *Culture and Society, 1780–1950.* London: Pelican.

Index of Poems and Anthologies

Index of Authors and Poets

General Index

Scale 79, 87, 90–3, 95, 179, 210
Sign chants 17, 22, 44–5, 54, 139,
Sign Language of the Netherlands
    (SLN) 11, 21, 99, 256
Signed English 3, 148, 236
Signed Hymns 22, 139
Sign-mime 136, 149
Similes 90, 96, 119–23, 138, 193,
    195–6
Simultaneity
    of signs 10, 144, 160–2, 206, 218
    of two languages 24, 90, 148–67
    signing and speaking 127, 152
    triple 192, 218
    in symmetry 59, 63, 64, 67–8,
        204–6
    of parameters 5, 42–3,
    reading of the same sign 91–5,
        207
Single-handshape games *see* ABC
    games
Stanza 53–4
Symbolism (*see also* Connotation)
    26, 48, 67, 134, 160, 185, 202
Symmetry
    general 55–68
    front-back 64–8
    horizontal (top–bottom) 63–4
    vertical (left–right) 59–63
Systematic variation 25, 34–6, 38

Text (contrasted to performance)
    128–47
Themes in sign poetry
    general 101–15
    animals 101–6, 118, 233–4
    celebration of deaf pride 20, 21,
        114–15, 229
    celebration of sign language and
        sight 19, 108–13, 229
    flight 107–8, 179
    trees and nature 106–7, 118
Tied images 150, 237
Transformation of images 119
Transitional movement 36, 45, 95,
    97, 164, 194, 215, 222
Translation of poetry 2, 17, 22–4,
    93, 102, 128, 129, 136, 157,
    163, 237

Under-specification of signs 87, 220
Unwritten languages *see* Oral
    languages
Unwritten poetry *see* Oral
    Languages

Video 17, 35, 129, 231, 233
Visual motivation 4, 6–7, 70, 84,
    87, 88, 105, 195, 207

Wit 101, 141

CPSIA information can be obtained
at www.ICGtesting.com
Printed in the USA
FSOW01n1156110417
32992FS